YO-BDX-709

Democratic Process and Administrative Law

Revised Edition

by Robert S. Lorch
University of Colorado at Colorado Springs

☆ ☆ ☆

Wayne State University Press, Detroit, 1980

Library of Congress Cataloging in Publication Data
Lorch, Robert Stuart, 1925–
    Democratic process and administrative law.

    (Waynebook; 39)
    Bibliography: p.
    Includes index.
    1. Administrative law—United States. I. Title.
KF5402.L6 1980   342.73'06   80-12461
ISBN 0-8143-1362-0
ISBN 0-8143-1513-5 (pbk.) ✓

Democratic Process and Administrative Law

for Barbara and John

Contents

Contents

8

Preface

This book is not written for attorneys. Yet for that reason it may appeal to them—a moment of escape from their world of somber legalese. Nor is this volume written for law students. Yet it may surreptitiously find its way to them—a moment of freedom from their world of ruthless texts.

Then for whom is this book written, and what is its purpose when great and authoritative studies of administrative law have been written by others? Unlike most books on administrative law, this one is for nonlawyers—for social science, political science, and public administration students, and for anyone else who wants a book that paints the subject in broad and lucid strokes.

Among the revolutions of our time is an administrative revolution. Administrators are no longer merely administrators in the old sense of the word. They are now heavily involved in doing what the Fathers of the Republic surely would have called legislative and judicial. Anyone who still believes that lawmaking is mostly done by legislatures, or that dispute settling is mostly done by courts, is far behind the times. Administrators do much of that now. They and their expert aides possess the technical knowledge required to make law and decide cases in a world which is growing so overwhelmingly technological and specialized. It takes experts to govern experts.

The study of administrative lawmaking and adjudication is an important part of general education, for it is central to an understanding of American government and the government of any other relatively developed country. Furthermore, the administrative revolution is something that should be closely watched by all who wish to preserve democratic institutions. It is creating a new system of government which vests much more power in administrators who, by their nature, are extremely difficult to control especially now that their work is almost impossible for the public or the public's representatives to understand.

This book is mainly a commentary on administrative exercise of legislative and judicial power, with special attention to administrative law and other devices for the control of that power. The first chapter attempts to explain why, of the three branches of government, the administrative branch grows more powerful today. A picture is drawn of rising executive power against a backdrop of declining legislative power and retreating judicial jurisdiction. Chapter 2 offers some reasons why the administrative process has not been a perfect cure for the shortcomings of courts and legislatures, and, therefore, why it is especially important that the holders of administrative power be controlled and the instruments of their power improved. The rest of the book offers comments, criticisms, explanations, and speculations about the more traditional areas of administrative law, and views that law as a means of controlling the burgeoning power of public executives in the interests of fairness and democracy.

Most of this volume was written during a sabbatical leave which was granted me by California State College at Long Beach. I was also helped by a faculty research grant from the Long Beach California State College Foundation, a recipient of National Science Foundation Funds.

R. S. L.

Chapter 1

Why Has Legislative and Judicial Power Passed to the Executive?

☆ ☆ ☆

THE EFFECT OF TECHNOLOGY UPON GOVERNMENT:

Can democracy, or anything like it, survive in a time of complexities so baffling that the public and the public's elected representatives can hardly understand the work of government? Is democracy archaic now?

Administrators already in one way or another enact much more law than legislatures and decide vastly more cases than courts. This within a nation of people historically suspicious of administrators, and historically wedded to representative government, to courts, to lawyers, to rule of law.

No country has changed more than ours in 200 years. The Constitution of 1787 was designed to serve a far different society than the one we know today. Then this was a nation of three million (now two hundred million); then the largest city was twenty-five thousand (now twelve million); then the population was 90 per cent rural (now 70 per cent urban); then the states were scattered and barely connected along a thousand miles of coast (now tightly bound together by a vast network of transportation and communication). The railroad was not yet invented nor the automobile. All sorts of new and complicated devices have come along since 1787 which go to the heart of the way we live and the way government must govern. The effect of the automobile alone upon society and government is astonishing. Consider the laws and governmental agencies it has given birth to. Planes, atom bombs, and the rest have had a profound effect upon government. In short, a technological society has required a technological government. To understand the administrative revolution it helps to fully realize the effects of technology upon government. The rise of the administrative process (meaning executive exercise of legislative and judicial as well as administrative power) is largely a product of modern technology which has negatively affected the ability of legislatures and courts to do their customary work.

CONGRESS VERSUS THE EXECUTIVE:

The American Revolution was in some ways a revolution against executive power and occurred after years of struggle by locally elected colonial legislatures against the king's governors. The Constitution-writers of 1787 designed a government that emphasized the role of Congress. (Article 1 dealing with Congress is by far the longest article in the Constitution.) In 1787 the presidency was viewed as something of a necessary evil and was backed off into a corner which was obscure compared to the center stage where Congress and state legislatures were to play their florescent roles. That situation now is almost totally reversed. Congress has become so ponderous that it can hardly act on significant legislation except under threat of calamity or force of overwhelming political pressure. Meanwhile, the executive branch has become almost the only force that can move Congress to legislate in large and significant matters. In fact, the president has become the chief legislator, and the executive branch overshadows Congress.

12

WHY THE ADMINISTRATIVE BRANCH
OVERSHADOWS CONGRESS:

Ability to Influence Public Opinion: Modern technology has blessed the executive branch at the expense of legislatures. Not in their wildest fantasies could the Fathers of the Republic have foreseen that the president would one day be able to personally buttonhole by radio and television every voter in the land in forty or eighty million living rooms. Today the president can reach and influence the public on a scale undreamed of at the Constitutional Convention, and through the people he can reach and influence every one of the 435 representatives and 100 senators. He can move the voters who can move the Congress. He can reach a congressman's district better than the congressman himself.

Predominance in Foreign Affairs: For many reasons (including our technological and industrial development) the United States has become the leading political power on earth; foreign relations have become the leading preoccupation of the nation. More than 30 per cent of the federal budget goes to war and diplomacy: past, present, and future. Technology has not only made us powerful, it has also shrunk the world and made presidential powers in foreign affairs all the more critical to our survival, prosperity, and tranquility. Foreign relations, of course, have always been the primary responsibility of the president. The Constitution gives him sole authority to communicate with foreign powers officially which he does through his ambassadors, consuls, and other representatives. The Constitution also makes him commander-in-chief of the armed forces and he can and does commit those forces to battle without the consent of Congress. Because the central role in foreign affairs belongs to the president and not to Congress, and because Congress seldom feels competent, willing, or effectively able to challenge his judgment in foreign relations, the Congress has become a kind of vassal to the president in the biggest undertaking of the federal government.

Executive's Image as "The Great Provider" in the Service State:
Whatever Congress may do by way of passing legislation, the public seems to give most of the credit for it to the president and the
executive branch. Not only is the president ordinarily the most visible public champion of significant legislation, but also he and the
executive branch are the ones who distribute the benefits of that
legislation once passed. The help, relief, and benefits enacted by
Congress in recent decades in response to public demands has not
made Congress more popular or influential. Rather, it has established the executive branch in the hearts of millions of people as
the great provider—the executive branch has reaped the rewards of
popularity and influence. This has depressed still further the ability of Congress to resist the power of the executive. Often the public's conception of the role of Congress is shaped more by the loud
minority that opposes service state legislation than by the majority
that pass it. In summation, the growth of technology has created
social interdependence; this has given rise to demands for governmental help, service, and benefits; this has established the executive's image as a great provider when those demands have been
met by the federal government; and this has made the executive
branch still more powerful and influential with Congress.

Discretionary Power: Because the United States is so large and so
complex, Congress could not possibly avoid giving vast discretionary power to the various executive agencies and to the chief executive to carry out the purposes of legislation. Therefore, Congress
has empowered executive agencies to grant subsidies, approve corporate mergers, raise and lower tariffs, let contracts, condemn land,
regulate credit, and do many other things of vast economic importance. These powers endow the president and his agencies with
immense power to reward, punish, and affect the welfare of whole
industries, great corporations, and entire regions of the country.
For example, Des Moines and Omaha may be equally good sites for
a new regional headquarters which is to be opened by a government agency. Wherever it is opened, the headquarters will bring
large payrolls and will significantly bolster the prosperity of the
community. Decisions of this sort may revolve on which community
is represented in Congress by persons who cooperate with the presi-

dent. By opening or closing a military base, granting or denying a defense contract, by any one of a wide variety of decisions, the president may deeply affect the fortunes of all sorts of people (especially of economic leaders) who in turn influence their congressional delegation. Government spending and control of the economy is far greater in scope than anything contemplated by the Fathers of the Republic. The power this gives to the executive branch to influence Congress has gone far beyond the bounds intended in 1787 and has completely altered the balance of power between the branches.

The president's discretionary power also includes the power to (1) emphasize certain favorite programs, (2) supervise them perfunctorily, or (3) ignore them (he is not compelled to spend the money appropriated by Congress).

Appointments: Through his power to appoint persons to federal jobs who have been recommended by members of Congress (patronage), the president is able to reward cooperative members. It is estimated that President Carter upon coming to office had available to him around 6,000 patronage positions, which is not many out of a total federal civilian payroll of two and a half million persons, but which, nevertheless, is enough political currency to go a long way. It is true that some appointments are made with the consent of the Senate. But the Senate rarely denies confirmation.

The term patronage in its broader aspects includes all presidential favors. The president's discretionary power, may, as noted above, be used to favor cooperative members of Congress. Congressmen are in almost daily contact with the executive branch in behalf of their constituents who ask them to intercede with this or that agency in every conceivable kind of business from getting a boy out of the army to getting a farmer a federal loan. Presidential blessing may open many agency doors.

Veto: The veto, like patronage, is a classic technique used effectively by presidents long before the twentieth century. It has always been difficult to muster the two-thirds vote needed in both houses to override a veto because most members of Congress normally prefer not to clash directly with the president by voting to override his veto. Today the president's great wealth of powers to reward and punish cause most congressmen to be even less inclined to clash with him. It is almost impossible to get a two-thirds vote on anything the president actively opposes. The mere threat of veto is usually enough to kill it.

President as Party Leader: The United States Constitution was written before there were any organized national political parties, and the Fathers certainly never imagined that the president would be the leader of a national political party which would normally also control Congress. Most matters before Congress are not party line issues because each member, being pretty much responsible for getting himself reelected, must be free to vote on bills as he sees fit. Nevertheless, as party leader the president can employ leverage to win the support of his partisans in Congress. He has something to say about the distribution of certain campaign funds. As the chief campaigner and public figure of his party, the president can take the stump in behalf of cooperative congressmen, can endorse his friends, can even campaign against his enemies (though this is not often done, for practical reasons), can play up and take stands on issues that are central to the campaigns of those he wants to help.

Furthermore, members of Congress of the president's party are motivated to support the president's legistlative program so that the party can build up a legislative record to run on in the next election.

Author of the Only Coherent Budget and Legislative Program: The president exercises influence over Congress when he presents them with the only coherent budget and legislative program they receive—coherent in the sense that all of the various needs of the government are considered by the president (through his Office of Management and Budget) in relation to one another, and in relation to revenue. The Executive Office of the President is the only place in the entire government where total income is related to total outgo and where the requests of one agency are weighed against the requests of another in the light of limited revenue. Congress seems incapable of doing this, and for that reason, among others, is severely impeded as a policy-making body. Fundamental decisions can hardly be made by a government (any more than by a family) without someone being able to survey the total economic and social picture first. Congress acting alone is like a family whose members (the standing committees) write checks without really conferring with each other to see how much money is still in the bank or what expenditures should have priority over others. The standing committees of Congress, each authorizing programs and expenditures without consulting the others, must allow themselves to be more or less guided by the president's budget. Bankruptcy, irrationality, and chaos are the alternatives.

Of course, Congress is not compelled to accept the president's budget. In 1974 Congress established a Congressional Budget Office to free itself, somewhat, from dependence on the president's budget. The CBO has not worked as well as its advocates hoped.

Expertise: A very large part of the knowledge needed to legislate intelligently on just about any subject is within the executive branch of the federal government. Today that branch employs a fourth of all scientists, and a goodly number of the remaining scientists are working in some way on federal projects. Workers in the various executive offices and agencies are, of course, intimately acquainted with the problems of their specialty, and, as specialists, are able to suggest answers. Members of Congress cannot be experts in all the matters upon which they are called to legislate. Senior members with long service on standing committees may be conversant with the main problems before their committees, but even those members are dependent upon outside help for detailed specific information. Often there is no adequate source of expert knowledge outside the government—for example, in a good many armed forces matters. Congress becomes more and more helpless as matters before it become more and more technological. Congress itself has very little staff help, certainly nothing to compete with the bonanza of scientific and technological knowledge housed in the executive branch.

Rule-Making: In this era of technology the executive agencies are in a far better position to legislate than Congress. And, in fact, they do legislate in two ways: (1) indirectly by influencing Congress, and (2) directly, by rule-making. In some ways executive rule-making (quasi-legislation) much overshadows congressional legislation; certainly this is so in quantity, and also perhaps in significance if one discounts the acts of Congress which would never have been passed without executive pressure. Congress has simply been driven to delegate much of its legislative power to executive agencies. Congress has neither the time nor the knowledge to deal with all that needs to be dealt with. The *Code of Federal Regulations* is many times larger than the *United States Code* containing the acts of Congress, and its thousands of regulations affect every individual. Executive discretion in rule-making can affect millions of people and great financial interests.

Prestige of Office: The prestige of the chief executive and of the entire executive branch has soared with the soaring dimensions of the federal establishment. The importance of government in our daily lives, its importance to our economic and social welfare and to our safety has vastly increased, and with it has increased the prestige of the head of that government. The media of mass communication have brought his important role forcefully to everyone's attention, and this in itself lends prestige. The president is news. The White House and the first family are covered every hour of the day and night by a hundred reporters.

Furthermore, the head of the most powerful state in the world is bound to be a person of vast prestige. In a time of continuous national involvement in threatening foreign difficulties, the president becomes a living symbol of the nation. As such, the public more easily falls under his spell in domestic affairs as well. The president can make political hay by approaching domestic political problems in the same mantle of nonpartisan sanctimony used in foreign affairs.

Presidential prestige can be used in all sorts of ways to influence Congress. By simply allowing his picture to be taken with a member of Congress he can greatly reward cooperation. Or the president can woo congressmen by considerate treatment such as having them singly or in small groups to the White House for a private breakfast, or for a walk in the rose garden, or for an intimate conference. These are things that deeply gratify members of Congress and make it possible for them to go home at election time and tell everybody What I told the president last time I was down to the White House for breakfast.

The president's prestige also helps him influence the general public.

In summary, the power of the executive branch to influence Congress can hardly be overestimated. This, of course, is not to say that the executive gets everything it wants from Congress. In recent decades presidents have averaged a box score of about 50 per cent success in getting legislation asked for in messages to Congress. The box score is higher for special pieces of legislation for which the president has launched strong and vigorous campaigns. Still, there is no doubt that a determined minority of well-entrenched congressmen can thwart the president. The power to thwart remains perhaps the most significant function of Congress. But, as a creative body Congress has lost most of its powers and most of its genius to the executive branch.

DEFICIENCIES OF CONGRESS:

What specifically is wrong with Congress? To pinpoint some of its particular ailments one would have to say, first, that its organization is a terrible liability. Everything is stacked against action and in favor of stagnation. The obstacle course over which every bill must run to become law is strewn with traps. The overwhelming majority of bills introduced die early and are buried in mass graves. Of course, most bills deserve a quick death because most of them are introduced as public relations stunts to flatter or appease various eccentric groups back home. We ought not to condemn Congress merely for the volume of *deceased* bills. The important question is how many *significant bills succeed* in their passage over the very lethal congressional terrain. And when we find the answer to that, the next question is to what degree were the bills which successfully passed equipped with presidential armor plate for their journey, to what degree were they protected and escorted along the way by the vast influence of the modern president? A powerful case could be argued that little or perhaps even nothing of significance is getting through Congress without a presidential convoy along the way. The Rube Goldberg organization of Congress almost assures this.

There are many places along the congressional path to kill a bill, so many places to lay booby traps and set ambushes. Congress is a guerrilla fighter's dream, a jungle of opportunities where special and narrow interests can hatchet down the finest samples of legislative manhood. Let us just glance at the way this method of legislative warfare works. How would a lobbyist go about slaughtering a bill? Here are some points of attack beginning in the House of Representatives.

Point 1: If the bill is ambiguously written and concerns something that might be heard by either of several standing committees (a medical education bill, for example, which might go to either the Commerce Committee which handles public health bills or the Education and Labor Committee which handles education bills), try to persuade the Speaker of the House to refer the bill to the committee least friendly to its provisions. Generally speaking, no bill reaches a vote in either house unless approved by a standing committee. Let us assume the Speaker favors this particular bill and sends it to an amicable committee.

Point 2: Try to convince the chairman of the standing committee to kill the bill. This he can attempt to do by piling up other bills on the committee agenda ahead of the bill he wants to bury, and by making doubly sure that the committee's time is entirely consumed on those preceding bills by a long parade of witnesses and questions. The chairman may also call the bill when its proponents on the committee are out of town. Even if a bill should come before the committee, the chairman's hostility to it would severely impair its chances for favorable consideration by other committee members. This is because a committee chairman has many ways of rewarding cooperative members. For example, he may take up legislation that an individual member particularly needs or wants to insure his reelection. Let us assume that the chairman does not object to the bill we are tracing through Congress.

Point 3: Try to persuade a majority of the members of the committee to vote against the bill, or to cripple it with amendments. Let us assume this fails and the bill is reported out. Its next stop is the House Rules Committee.

Point 4: Try to persuade the Rules Committee, whose power to kill or maim is almost total, to do one or the other. If that fails:

Point 5: Try to defeat the bill in the Committee of the Whole where no votes are recorded and where, consequently, a number of congressmen might quietly support you in ways which they could not afford to do publicly elsewhere.

Point 6: Try to persuade the House to defeat or at least weaken the bill.

Points 7, 8, 9, and 10: The bill goes to the Senate where it can be assaulted in the same ways as in the House (except for the Rules Committee and the Committee of the Whole). If the bill is one which some senator or group of senators feel strongly enough about to filibuster, encourage them to do so.

Point 11: If the bill is passed by the two houses in different forms it goes to a conference committee for redrafting in a compromise form. Try to persuade the conference committee to report out the bill in its worst (or most innocuous) form.

Point 12: Try to persuade the president to veto the bill.

Point 13: Try to persuade Congress to sustain the veto.

Points 14–26: In Congress the appropriations process parallels the regular legislative process. Programs are authorized in one bill and the money for them is appropriated in another. An appropriation can be attacked at points comparable to the points in each house where the program itself was attacked.

Experienced lobbyists could no doubt add a good many refined points to this list without any trouble at all.

These multiple opportunities for assault by the enemies of a bill could be cut roughly in half by doing away with one house of Congress. Any political coroner writing up the death certificate of Congress would want to say that it suffered something like a massive coronary occlusion, that its veins and arteries were pinched shut with procedure.

The coroner would also have to say that Congress had long been anemic because of stoppages in the flow of *good* information. Most observers say Congress gets *too much* information, not too little. That is true, but the problem has to do with the *kind* of information. Every session Congress is deluged with reports, letters, testimony, and every known kind of information, but hardly any of it is neutral. The President has two and a half million civilians and three million military persons to gather information for him. He has at his disposal 25 per cent of the nation's scientists. Congress, on the contrary, has no such army of technical specialists working for it. The standing committees have a handful of staff employees to do research, and the various members of Congress also have only a few staff people working for them (mostly keeping track of politics back home). Congress badly needs a way of gathering its own information—neutral, objective information. It could use a vastly greater staff.

The size of Congress is a deadly weakness. If the Senate is abolished (and the reader must understand that I am just tossing off an outlandish remedy here to illustrate the gross character of the malady), then the other House should be cut from 435 to twenty-five members. This proposal does not brush aside the impressive arguments for small constituencies and for representatives who are close to the people who know where the shoe pinches. Nor is this proposal to reduce Congress to twenty-five members made by one who is blind to the view that Congress needs to be large in order to supervise and investigate all the multitudinous government agencies. But the resurrection of Congress as a policy-making body able to compete with the president is far more important than those other lesser benefits that accrue from size.

Five hundred and thirty-five is too many members of Congress today, and the reason has partly to do with a public relations problem. Congress must compete with the chief executive for public attention and must try to match his flexibility, speed, mobility, and intelligence. Public attention gives the president much of his power today. The prestige of Congress is diminished in the eyes of people because the public hardly knows anybody in it. Its members are faceless because there are so many of them that none get national public exposure anywhere near equal to the president's. But in a Congress of twenty-five, every single member would be fairly vivid in the public mind, and the president would find these twenty-five to be effective competitors against him for public attention and respect.

Furthermore, and equally important, a Congress of twenty-five could not be so readily influenced by the president or by any special interest. This is because (1) each of the twenty-five would represent a gigantic constituency so large that few special interests would be powerful enough to touch him, and as a celebrity his views and votes and behavior would be highly visible to the general public which would discourage unreasonable adherence to narrow interests; (2) a Congress of only twenty-five would have to sweep away much of the procedural jungle so adroitly used by special interests to ambush legislation.

If Congress would strip down for action in this way, the remaining members could initiate and legislate major national policy, which is, after all, their salient function.

Without comprehending the full severity of its own illness, Congress has at least sensed, session by session, its own limitations in specific situations and consequently has delegated some of its legislative functions to the president and executive branch. That is why today the *Code of Federal Regulations* (representing the quasilegislative work of the executive branch) is so huge.

If Congress were organized and equipped in the best possible way, it still could not possibly handle all the detail legislation that simply must be delegated to administrative agencies. Indeed, Congress would have to delegate more details than ever before. But, if it were redesigned it could perhaps recapture some of its policymaking role now abandoned to the agencies and to the chief executive.

Standing at the back door of the Capitol in Washington one can look directly across the street to the Supreme Court Building. Nine men working there achieve much more than 535 in the Capitol. Indeed, what they do has been given the label judicial legislation by both the friends and the enemies of the court. Today the court is under siege for doing things that Congress should be doing. The torch of judicial activism looks all the brighter because it burns in the night of Congressional inaction. The glare of what is now called judicial legislation would be far less offensive to the eyes of a good many people if the Congress were doing its job. Consider, for example, the nonfeasance of Congress in the face of our color problem. When in 1954 the court finally did something, its act was condemned far and wide as an unconstitutional usurpation of Congressional power—judicial legislation. But if Congress *had* done the job, the court's decision wouldn't have caused a ripple. A decade passed before Congress was finally prodded into action on the race question by an insistent president. It is Congressional sterility that brightens the judicial image as legislator.

The picture I have painted of the deficiencies of Congress and of the overwhelming power of the president may seem a bit too extreme and catastrophic. Congress is not completely powerless before the executive. Its power, however, is mainly of a no-saying variety despite the fact that it spends much of its time getting around to saying yes to proposals made by administrative agencies. But when Congress expresses its individuality and its power it usually does so by slapping something down rather than by initiating a new idea and seeing it through. Congress does slap a lot of bills down, even major presidential proposals.

Some members of Congress are more immune to presidential influence than others, and sometimes the committees they control are also immune. In part, this immunity, as well as many of the clashes between the president and Congress have to do with the fact that congressmen tend to speak for local interests while the president speaks for national interests. This clash is more evident in some congressional constituencies than in others. There are still a good many congressional and senatorial districts composed of voters who are not the kind of people to whom a president normally addresses his main political appeal, or upon whom a president bases his power primarily. Fundamentally, a president has to speak and act for urban America because that is where the people are, 70 per cent of us, including powerful race minorities. He cannot afford to be against racial minorities or to be weak on urban problems. His message often does not, therefore, appeal to rural districts or to people who strongly object to political equality of the races. Sometimes representatives from those districts hold their seats by opposing much of what the president stands for, and occasionally they (or others willing to fight the president) rise through seniority to control of certain congressional committees.

A few committees of Congress are like feudal baronies ruled by a chairman or by a clique secure in their home constituencies (often constituencies less receptive to presidential appeal than the average district), and secure in their power over the committee (owing

24

partly to the seniority system of Congress) and hostile to the president. For this reason among others, a part of a president's program may be shipwrecked in Congress. However, his problems should abate somewhat as reapportionment progresses under the Supreme Court's one-man-one-vote doctrine, and as race minorities begin to use the ballot where they have not in the past.

The deficiency of Congress lies mainly in its failure to compete with the executive as an innovator, initiator, and creator of policy. Congress is certainly not entirely powerless before the president. It can say no to e president, even on major proposals occasionally, but usually its no is reserved for a lot lesser items for which the president cannot mount major campaigns. Looking at the year 1965, that is, at the first session of the 89th Congress, we see that even a Congress which passed more presidential bills than usual and which was called a rubber stamp Congress by its critics, failed to pass one-third of the president's program. In sixty-three separate documents President Johnson asked Congress in 1965 for a fantastic variety of legislation. Breaking the president's program down into 469 specific legislative requests, *Congressional Quarterly* reported that 321 of these had won approval by Congress. His so-called boxscore was 68.4 per cent.

Even a rubber stamp Congress let about one-third of the president's program fall by the wayside either through outright rejection, or by failure to act, or for other reasons. Some of President Johnson's defeats were, by certain yardsticks, significant. They included, for example, an attempt to repeal Section 14 (b) of the Taft-Hartley Act which permits states to enact right-to-work laws banning the union shop. Repeal has long been a goal of organized labor and failure of the president to persuade Congress to repeal it was considered to be his most significant defeat of the session. Among the other presidential proposals which failed and which were considered significant proposals were included those concerning the minimum wage, unemployment compensation, D.C. home rule, military pay, the army reserve-guard merger, and truth-in-lending and packaging.

Legislative surveillance of administration through budget, hearings, investigations, and reorganizations, is a major fact of life in the administration. Although this legislative oversight of administration may be parochial and although it may be for high purposes or low purposes, still it is there, powerfully there. But its power is not the kind of thing that inspires public esteem, nor is it the kind of thing that can carry on creative policy-making or compete with the president when it comes to matters of gross national interest.

The cracked, leaky, sprung, warped, and defective aspects of Congress are partly evident in all legislative branches (state and local as well as national), as are the strengths of the executive. And the administrative revolution is fueled and inspired as much by the shortcomings of legislatures as by the vigor of executives.

THE COURTS VERSUS THE EXECUTIVE:

Courts have withstood the onslaughts of the twentieth century far better than legislatures. Science and technology have been a warm sun to the executive branch. To Congress they have been a killing frost. As for the courts, the effect of the twentieth century has been to discourage judges from some neighborhoods of the law. Some judicial territory has been ceded to the executive branch. Perhaps the phrase some judicial territory is an understatement. It is a thundering big swath of territory say many lawyers. In any case, administrators are today deciding more cases than the courts, many more. The same juggernaut that has driven Congress and all legislative bodies nearly to the wall also drives back the courts—the same dynamic executive power armed with almost monopolistic control of the key forces in modern society. Yet, despite this judicial retreat, the resiliency of courts in the face of executive power has been quite remarkable, and, like some retreats, it is conceivable that the courts are stronger *because* of their partial withdrawal.

What is the nature of the withdrawal and why has it come to pass?

Hostility of Courts to Positive Aims of Modern Government: In the United States and elsewhere, whether one approves or not, people by the millions are coming to expect more than police pro-

26

tection from government. They want all kinds of services, benefits, and protections above and beyond the cop on the corner. A large part of these services, benefits, and protections are economic, and this jerks government out of its cozy relationship with much of the busine community and propels it toward tax and regulatory policies ot which businessmen often bitterly complain. We will not delay here to explore the intriguing but peripheral question whether this opposition has been short-sighted, whether business is largely responsible for the regulation it so vocally objects to, or whether, in fact, many business interests have nurtured, cherished, and downright begged for certain kinds of regulation, and so on. There is a prevailing tone of opposition to the service state concept among the private owners and controllers of business enterprises.

This hostility is mirrored in the bar and in the courts. The reason for it has much to do with the economics of the legal profession. Remember that lawyers are themselves businessmen. They make almost all of their living by serving other businessmen. A legal practice mainly concerns property and contracts, two subjects so mighty in the first year of law school. It should not be difficult to understand how lawyers over the years come to reflect the economic and political attitudes of the people who pay them. Sociologists report that most of us reflect the dominant values and attitudes of the group we run with (reference group theory, in the jargon).

But how does that explain the attitude of judges? Judges are first of all lawyers and normally they are seasoned lawyers long immersed in the ideological cults of the profession. Second, most judges in the United States are elected (federal judges, however, are appointed). To be elected to practically anything in the United States requires a great deal of money. Those who have money are not likely to spend it on the campaign of a judge who wants to take it away from them. Foursquare faith in capitalism has long been a virtual condition precedent to success at fund raising in most constituencies, although the burgeoning power of organized labor since the 1930's has changed things somewhat. Once elected, a judge (especially one who expects to run for reelection) is strongly impelled to deliver the goods in the form of anti-strike injunctions, maximum sentences for syndicalism, and general hostility toward litigants whose case favors the positive aims of modern government.

To discourage the courts from threatening too seriously what we shall for the sake of convenience call New Deal type programs, Congress has been motivated to transfer to the agencies which carry out those programs much of the power to decide cases arising under them. As we shall see, this has not been the sole motivation of Congress in transferring judicial power to the agencies, but it has been a very important one.

Judicial Lag: It is said that the American legal system is like a car being driven by looking through the rear-view mirror. It is a system in which today's case is decided by reference to yesterday's decision. Stare decisis et non quieta movere (to adhere to precedents and not unsettle things which are established) is the foremost tenet of American common law. "When a point of law has been settled by decision, it forms precedent which is not afterwards to be departed from, and, while it should ordinarily be strictly adhered to, there are occasions when departure is rendered necessary to . . . remedy continued injustice" (119 Fla. 718).

Since stare decisis tends to guide courts along a straight line of precedent, the curves on the road of social change need to be pretty gradual if the courts are going to stay on the road. Actually, social change today is not gradual and the courts consequently are often meandering out in the countryside away from the road of social reality. Today the path of social change curls more and more. We are traveling at high speed on an absolute spiral. As a system of law, stare decisis is poorly designed to accommodate the pace of events. Our judicial system shares some of the inadequacies of Congress in its inability to cope with rapid change.

Thus, courts have been partially retired from jurisdiction over cases in some of the spiraling stretches of our social road. Nor have the courts always protested this. On the contrary, they have encouraged their own retirement from that sector. Naturally, one must understand that the courts in our system of law never *completely* retire from anything, for they must always be in a position to quash illegality of any sort when called upon to do so. What the courts have done is to retire from front line action (that is, from the sector of original jurisdiction) in a number of social and economic areas of adjudication leaving those sectors for administrative adjudication. But the presence of courts always looms in the background to receive appeals from administrative decisions. Appeals, however, are rare. Far from rolling out the red carpet to receive them, the courts are inclined to throw up all sorts of impediments against appeals and prefer to leave administrators alone, though not completely alone.

All of the great regulatory agencies such as the ICC, EPA, SEC, FTC, NLRB, CAB, FCC (the so-called alphabet agencies) carry on adjudication quite comparable to the sort of thing regular courts do, except that they are not in theory bound by precedent and can openly decide cases by looking through the windshield at what lies ahead rather than through the rear-view mirror at what lies behind. They are, in theory, more flexible, less afflicted by judicial lag.

Administrative adjudication is by no means limited to the alphabet agencies, but its development in those agencies (and in all agencies) is partly a response to the need for a new judicial system, free of the old encrusted procedure, free of the old interminable delays, free of exorbitant expense, and so on.

Inflexible Procedures: Some have claimed that 90 per cent of justice lies in procedure. The rules of judicial procedure are a little like Emily Post's rules of etiquette in that they are a set method of seeing to it that no one is hurt in an affair through haste or thoughtlessness. But sometimes people have the uneasy feeling that Emily Post's battalion of rules erect a wall of nonsense between people, and sometimes get in the way of straightforward unaffected relationships. There is a recurrent urge to sweep away good form and hasten on to the matter at hand.

So it is with the rules of judicial procedure. It is alleged that for all their good, they too often delay things and interfere with getting to the real issues. There is suspicion that the legal profession has been interested in something less noble than justice in its campaign for rules of procedure. It has been hinted that lawyers see their own economic security and professional indispensability at stake in a complicated system of judicial procedure. Complex procedure makes longer, more intricate, involved and knotty, and therefore lucrative litigation.

Whether or not lawyers are so motivated, the fact is that the tonnage of legal procedure has grown over the years and whatever justice may be inherent in it there is also monstrous inequity, for procedure can make justice both expensive and slow. "Justice delayed is justice denied" goes the cliché. And there is also something to be said for a system of justice economical enough for the poor. Delay makes justice more expensive.

Certainly we may conclude that one of the forces favoring administrative rather than judicial justice is the belief that one way to escape the delay and expense of judicial procedure is to permit adjudication by administrative agencies whose procedural requirements are minimal (in theory).

The Delay and Expense of Judicial Litigation: Courts of law have become, as emphasized above, pretty expensive places. Lawyers are costly, and the tedious delays now common in litigation can bankrupt any marginal business enterprise or poor person unlucky enough to get caught in the web of a lawsuit.

As Congress has delegated more and more rule-making power to administrative agencies affecting almost all businesses big and little and affecting millions of individuals (the Veterans Administration alone makes rules touching twenty-two million veterans and their families), the result has been a jump in the number of controversies between government and citizens. This has been done partly to make the settlement of these arguments less expensive. It was assumed that economical and speedy justice could be achieved by using informal procedure as much as possible, by deformalizing as much as possible even those procedures which were formal, and by dispensing with the services of lawyers where possible. In most administrative proceedings a party may represent himself, or may be represented by persons other than lawyers, though lawyers often serve as counsel and are by no means excluded.

Inability of a Court to Initiate Action: A court of law cannot initiate proceedings. It is inactive until someone knocks on the court house door and begs for a judicial order of some sort. A court does not hawkishly circle above the country diving at illegality wherever seen. It remains secluded, technically blind and deaf to carnage in the streets and to every other hideous and illegal thing until some-one stumbles to the door with a prayer for help.

An administrative agency, on the other hand, is free to roam far and wide beyond its chambers in search of wrong which it may attack at will. And it can do this quite fearlessly (in theory) against any of the economic beasts of the jungle (perhaps at the secret urging of smaller creatures).

Congress has attempted to curb some of the brass knuckles, thumbscrews, and blackjacks of economic warfare, but has not spelled out exactly what practices are to be curbed. A number of regulatory agencies have been created to make up their own minds what trade practices are unfit, and they are able to bring to justice (often before administrative tribunals) anyone who violates their rules. For example, the Federal Trade Commission bans false advertising and can issue cease and desist orders against offenders and try them if necessary in administrative proceedings.

Why did not Congress simply arrange things so that anyone who is hurt by a lying competitor can go to court and sue his competitor for damages and let it go at that? Why should there be any administrative trial involved? Why should a government agency fight a battle for somebody who could fight his own battle by going to court? One reason is that smaller creatures on the economic terrain might fear to haul their cyclopian competitors into court. To do so might injure future relations with their larger neighbors in the jungle, and would also cost dearly in legal fees. Victory would be unlikely. A wealthy competitor could throw whole firms of lawyers into the litigation and could afford to settle down to endless years of legal combat and bleed white all opposition in the process.

For this reason, among others, it came to pass that responsibility for initiating certain kinds of proceedings was given to the agencies themselves.

Courts Cannot Police and Prosecute: Courts cannot strap on the policeman's club or wear the prosecutor's cap. Administrative agencies can do this, as well as be judge. Indeed, it is the union of policeman, prosecutor, legislator, and judge that so sharply separates administrative adjudication from judicial adjudication. This is a union highly praised in some quarters and vehemently damned in others. Courts have abandoned many sectors of adjudication to administrative quasi-courts which have power to apprehend certain kinds of wrongdoers, bring charges, prosecute them, and finally to judge them. It is, according to some, a very difficult thing to understand why courts of law would bow before such an arrangement that seems to be the essence of evil. How can a policeman and a prosecutor sitting as judge be fair to their own victims? Of course, it should be said emphatically that not all judges nor all lawyers nor all Americans, as we shall see, have acquiesced in that development. But, on the other hand, those who have acquiesced far outnumber and outweigh those who have not. And why?

The union of prosecutor, policeman, and judge, despite all its inherent evil, has struck most observers as the only logical and workable arrangement to get a certain kind of twentieth-century job done: the regulation of huge, complex, rapidly changing enterprises. The three functions of government do not work together smoothly or closely enough under the doctrine of separation of powers. That doctrine envisages the three powers working at cross purposes, competing, struggling with one another—a struggle designed, as we have said, not to promote efficiency but rather to promote liberty. While certain kinds of liberty may be served by separation of powers, speed and efficiency are not served, and it is precisely speed and efficiency that is required for the governance of a great many things in the twentieth century.

In our century the requirements of speed and efficiency in government seems to be on a collision course with the requirements of political liberty. The machinery that can deliver freedom seems unable to deliver efficiency. Of course, we search for middle ground, a little efficiency, a little liberty, but that may not be satisfactory and we may well be headed toward a terrible time as we are driven to a choice. The union of judge, prosecutor, and policeman in our administrative agencies may be a prelude to something worse waiting around the bend. Is there an escape?

Courts Inclined to Consider Private Rather Than Public Interests in a Lawsuit: A court is a little like the umpire in a ball game. Its job, like the umpire's, is mostly limited to looking after the relationship of the two combatants on the field rather than looking after the relationship of events on the field to the public interest. Or to be specific, a fifteen-yard penalty may well square accounts with the other team but may not at all with the general public. Perhaps the game itself is a brutalizing display which should in the public interest be ended.

Suppose, rather than an umpire at the ball game we have a czar of vaster power who could make judgments not alone to satisfy the teams on the field, but to satisfy the demands of the public in the bleachers. Such an officer would have a breadth of power not unlike that of administrative agencies over their areas of jurisdiction. The simile employed above is imperfect, of course, because spectators in a ball park are not quite comparable to the public in, let us say, a gas rate controversy. But the point striven for is that, while this is an era of service government, welfare government, activist government, of government more attentive to the *public* welfare, the courts remain attentive primarily to *private* rights, at least this is particularly so of low level courts. And it is that deficiency in the courts that has helped solidify the trend toward exercise of judicial power by administrative agencies whose orientation is, in theory, toward the public rather than the private welfare, and whose power is correspondingly enlarged.

Courts Are Not Technically Competent in Some Areas of Litigation: Judges are supposed to be experts in law, but to do their work judges also have to become somewhat expert in the various things to which they are asked to apply the law. Consequently, judges and lawyers become very broadly educated persons. Nevertheless, there are some labyrinthine areas of litigation whose network many judges are loathe to enter and consequently there has evolved an increasing amount of case specialization at the bar and on the bench. Indeed, a trend toward specialized courts (such as the Tax Court of the United States) is well under way in this country. There are several such courts now, and every year suggestions for more of them are offered Congress.

It is only a short step from specializing a court to the next stage which is making a court out of specialists, or at least making a quasi-court out of them. The latter is done very frequently these days by giving administrative agencies which are expert in some particular matter the judicial power to decide certain cases within their specialty and to spare the regular courts. There is a strong assumption, furthermore, that the officers of government whose duty it is to regulate some aspect of society are the very ones best suited to decide controversies concerning their own work (at the early stages of litigation at least). Students no doubt understand, for example, the value and convenience of allowing a professor who gives a test to adjudicate any questions that may come up concerning the grading of the test. He knows best the mechanics of his own grading system and the components of a good answer. This same principle operates on a massive scale throughout the government, and is partly (and powerfully) responsible for the retirement of courts of law from the area now occupied by administrative adjudication. Perhaps this is the most compelling reason for the great growth of administrative adjudication, though it is probably a mistake to assign any one cause a superior rank.

Courts Would Be Swamped by the Volume of Adjudication Now Handled by Administrative Agencies: The words one selects to describe the volume of cases decided administratively today depends quite naturally upon how such adjudication is to be colored. One might say it is obese, overgrown and even bloated, or, on the other hand, that it is mighty and magnificent, or, perhaps in more neutral tones, that it is simply colossal. In any event there is a lot of it and it far exceeds in volume the litigation before courts. Its evolution outside the regular court system is explained by the reasons set forth above, and its volume has grown swiftly during recent decades and now the very mass of it becomes a final justification for continuing to keep it outside the courts.

Chapter 2

How Has the Administrative Process Failed?

☆ ☆ ☆

The enemies of the administrative process never did see any good in it and wanted to hang the label, hatchet murderer, on it even before the first robin was killed. Now the obvious deficiencies of the system have fueled their suspicions. Even the begetters and advocates of the administrative process have doubts, although they are not throwing up their hands yet.

Any jury weighing the administrative process would want to keep in mind the hostility which that system has long put up with from its enemies who only saw the worst in it and who snatched every opportunity to lay obstacles in its path. It is appropriate to begin the following list of difficulties suffered by the administrative process with that problem.

THE ADMINISTRATIVE PROCESS HAS BEEN HOBBLED BY ITS OPPONENTS:

A tool has no preference among its users. Screwdrivers and hammers are neutral. The administrative process is a tool and it is freely available to any cause high or low. But some of the enemies of the administrative process have mistaken the tool for the artisan, and attack the tool rather than their real targets who are the ones who currently use that tool in behalf of the service state, welfare state, business regulation, and so on.

Admittedly, a tool, no matter how neutral it may be, is by its very nature designed to do certain kinds of work. A hammer is better than a hoe for driving nails. Probably, the administrative process by its mobilization of legislative, executive, and judicial power into the same hands is best designed to do what it is doing. The speed and mobility of the administrative process are needed for achievement of service state goals. Conservatives may not miss the mark too far when they condemn both the service state and the administrative process in the same breath.

Those who oppose the goals of the administrative process have naturally concentrated on hobbling the efficiency of that process. Ideally an administrative agency is flexible in its procedure, speedy, inexpensive, creative, energetic, and fair. Opponents try to prevent it from being those things, and try to kill the administrative process as an effective tool. Two examples follow:

Preventing Agency Reorganization: Interfering with agency reorganizations is a time-honored political tactic. Every organization periodically needs reorganization to accommodate the natural evolutionary changes in the size and nature of its job. Interference with reorganization is like interference with breathing. It is a form of strangulation useful against programs or agencies which are too popular to be directly attacked. For example, opponents of the National Labor Relations Board opposed legislation authorizing reorganization of the NLRB. The reorganization was designed to help that agency handle its huge case load. The object of those who opposed the reorganization was, at bottom, to embarrass the fundamental principle of the National Labor Relations Act which was that collective bargaining should be the foundation of labor-management relations in the economy.

Budget Difficulties: Starvation is another popular and quiet method of hobbling the efficiency of an organization. Money is food and, of course, as everyone knows public agencies never count calories. They wolf down anything set before them and still cry starvation. But in truth, some are really languishing, and like the Federal Trade Commission, cannot afford to hire enough people to carry on assigned functions. This inability is just fine in the eyes of those to whom inefficiency in the FTC is a virtue, or inefficiency elsewhere.

THE ADMINISTRATIVE PROCESS MISUSED BY SPECIAL INTERESTS:

Down from Virtue: In the beginning (i.e., the 1930's) the administrative process was like an innocent girl alone on the streets of a bad neighborhood. It got whistled at, pinched, and even raped from time to time. But still it went on, bright-eyed, undismayed, virtuous. After a while it got used to being outraged: the whistles, pinches, and attacks seemed less wicked. Then, finally, all these things seemed natural and normal. Then downright pleasing.

The administrative process has evolved from bright-eyed purpose to something less to something far less. This backsliding out of virtue began in the 1930's. Although the administrative process is as old as the Republic, it was during New Deal days in the 1930's that "high-purposed" people turned most enthusiastically to it as an instrument of social reform. The New Deal transformed government into an active agency of reform, and attracted to government service many social redeemers, professors, and other intelligent, lively, and earnest idealists. Public feeling for the New Deal was high, and public attention to its efforts was also high.

During those exciting days many new agencies were created to regulate business and labor and to dispense service. These agencies (many of which are still with us, or at least their descendants are) began their careers with an aggressive spirit. Their chief officers were daring and inventive (by bureaucratic standards) . They were backed by sympathetic political leadership, and by strong public interest and support.

A new and higher breed had ventured upon the streets of political and bureaucratic leadership. They crusaded against the depression, the farm problem, the drought, and many other distressing problems. A plethora of alphabet agencies (AAA, NRA, CCC, WPA, NLRB, and others) armed with legislative, judicial, and executive power, were thrown into the field to battle titanic problems.

There was opposition to all this uplift effort. Conservatives waged war on it. They were defeated in the deluge of 1932 (Roosevelt's election) and by successive deluges throughout the thirties and forties, but they kept up a stout battle, snapping all the while at the heels of professors and redeemers and socialists and everybody else whose welfare statism was leading us "down the road to serfdom."

During the early days of the depression, as mounting distress led to passage of reform legislation, conservatives were able to force New Dealers to write their bills in vague language. This prevented plain and lucid legislative mandates, and opened everything the agencies did to legal challenge on grounds that what they did was outside the scope of their vaguely defined authority.

To the uplifters, that was only a mosquito to be slapped. New agencies went right ahead skipping down the street of reform. Their leadership was somewhat inexperienced politically, their relationships with Congress were somewhat uncertain, and their legal powers were unclear and untested. In all the alleys and doorways along the way there were well-organized, well heeled groups (the ones to be regulated in theory) carrying on a campaign designed to insure the fall and failure of those high-minded agencies.

Darkness and Public Apathy: One of the worst troubles a politician can have is to be forgotten by the public. The same is true of administrative agencies, for they live a highly political existence. Their success in getting money and legislation from Congress often depends upon the one thing congressmen respect most: pull with

the electorate or pull with persons who can influence the electorate. The same is needed to get presidential support, for he is
interested in votes too. Nothing is worse than being unknown and
without means of becoming known.

As every politician and actor knows, it is extremely difficult to
be known by a large general public. The competition is rough.
Literally everybody is trying to get the public's attention. Every
government from mosquito control district to federal government
would like to explain itself to the general public, and every agency, bureau, office, section, and division of every government would
like to do the same. Every housewife, for that matter, would like
to tell her story to the world. But the public's attention is limited.
Competition for it supports whole firms of Madison Avenue public relations experts whose purpose in life is to dream up ways of
kidnapping our attention for twenty or forty or sixty seconds. As
competitors for public attention with Lucille Ball, Red Skelton, the
Beach Boys, and Dippity Do Hair Dressing, government agencies
are outclassed. Consequently, parents do not know anything about
their school district, property owners do not know anything about
their planning commission. Not one in ten thousand ever heard
of the Food and Consumer Service of the U.S. Department of
Agriculture, the Ocean Mining Administration of the Department
of Interior, or of the Employees' Compensation Appeals Board of
the Department of Labor.

Loss of public interest and attention is one of the fatal difficulties encountered by that bright-eyed clavern of idealists we left
skipping down the street of social reform with their exciting new
agency in the sunlight of public esteem. The sun set, and when it
did, all those creatures in the alleys and in the doorways came out
and did a whole catalog of unmentionable things. The sun of public
attention set. That is the saddest story known in any language for
any reform. Reform so often runs only a brief hour against
established power. After reform has had its moment, people lose
interest, and when that happens the old powers crawl back.

Most agencies never had any public acclaim at all and never will.
Most live out their lives in a long night of public apathy. The
night is never completely dark, of course. There is always a narrow
blinding ray streaming in on each agency, piercing the blackness

like sun through a crack in the dungeon wall. That ray is the eager attention which regulated or client groups focus upon their regulators. When everyone else has forgotten about the Interstate Commerce Commission it will have at least one band of eternal friends: the railroad managers. They are ready in the dead of political night to see to it that the "right" people get appointed to the commission and that the "right" laws get passed affecting the commission, etc. In the absence of any popular agitation to the contrary, Congress or a president will give durable power interests what they want. What they want is strangulation, starvation, or death to enemy bureaus; food, light, and air for friendly bureaus. Politicians hesitate to be identified as champions of reform except in periods when public support for reform is overwhelming, or potentially so.

That is how and why a regulatory agency passes from the status of regulator to regulated, captor to captive, reformer to reformed, and from high minded to low minded.

Private Government: In some cases regulation is imposed upon an industry, profession, or activity to stop various evils. The Interstate Commerce Commission is a case in point. The evils being perpetrated by the railroads so outraged people back in the 1880's that regulation was demanded by farm groups and others injured. In those days the railroad was the only practical way a farmer could move his crop and livestock to market. Furthermore, it was the only practical way for people to travel long distances. The railroad was an absolute monopoly and a natural one, since competing lines did not and would not run next to one another. Businessmen could not send or receive goods from distant points except by railroads in most cases. Inland and coastal waterways offered some competition, but these had their obvious limitations. Railroad companies could and did charge exorbitant prices and win political power in cities and states by threatening to charge even higher rates to anyone who did not cooperate, and by giving lower rates to those who did, and by all sorts of other means. Railroads came to hold political and economic power over broad areas.

To curb the railroad monopolists, regulatory agencies (often called railroad commissions) were set up in most states, and the federal government in 1887 created the first of the great independent regulatory agencies, the Interstate Commerce Commission. (Today, of course, railroads do not enjoy the same monopoly they held ninety years ago. Trucks, cars, busses, and planes have broken it.)

Evils afflicting many other businesses and activities have lead to similar regulation: high monopolistic prices in utilities, fraud in medical practice, deception in the manufacture and distribution of drugs, false labeling of food, and so on. Most regulation came first to answer a need for protection of some sort. The basic goal of most regulation is reasonably well accomplished. There *is* reasonably pure milk, food *is* more or less honestly labeled, and so are drugs, the medical profession is reasonably free of fraud, etc. Regulated groups have often been cooperative with the regulators because ordinarily the people being regulated share the goals of regulation. That is to say, doctors are against medical fraud, milk producers are against watering down milk, and so on. This oneness of interest produced a very cozy relationship between the police and the policed, a relationship made still cozier by cultivation. Furthermore, the regulators need the help of the regulated— their judgment, their facts—to do a good job.

Not only have regulated groups often been extremely cooperative with their regulators, but also persons in regulatory agencies have found that there are rewards for being cooperative with the regulated. A railroad can do things for a bureaucrat, can invite him to give a speech and pay a thousand dollars, can open executive positions with the railroad to friendly commissioners, can arrange for bureaucratic promotions for cooperative bureaucrats.

All in all there has been a mutuality of interest between regulators and regulated. Railroads need the ICC and the ICC commissioners need the railroads. So it is with most regulatory agencies and their client groups. The profit for both sides can be enormous.

So rewarding has regulation been to the regulated, that practically everybody wants to be regulated today, and practically everybody is being regulated. For example, barbers in almost every state are now regulated by a state board of barber examiners (or by some agency). Ostensibly the purpose of such regulation is to protect the public against ill-prepared and unsanitary barbers, but another important purpose (probably the main one) is to keep down the supply of barbers and keep up the price of haircuts. This is accomplished largely by requiring unreasonably long periods of schooling as a prerequisite to licensing. Barbers must learn not only how to cut hair but also what hair is and what makes it grow.

The same sort of tactic is followed by the legal profession, which, despite its traditional conservatism and despite the very loud condemnation by some lawyers of labor unionism and business regulation, has lost no time and spared no effort to get itself regulated (which is now done in every state). Lawyers have not been able to justify this regulation in terms of public health, but they do claim that regulation is necessary to save the people from ill-trained lawyers. Not very many years ago lawyers learned law by reading it in the office of established attorneys. Anyone could be a lawyer by just hanging out a sign. Consequently, there were so many of them that it was hard to make a living. And so the profession gladly embraced regulation which in effect gave bar associations power to license attorneys, impose bar examinations, and to set other difficult standards for admission to the bar designed in large part to thin out the ranks of lawyers and make their services dearer. Of course, none of this is intended to deny or depreciate the fact that regulation of the bar has benefitted the public by vastly improving the quality of lawyers in this country.

The bar associations are in effect powerful labor unions which do not need the power to strike so long as they can control with government power entry into the profession. Other professional and occupational groups use the same tactic. Almost every group hankers to be regulated and to control the board that regulates it. Many do control the board, and that control constitutes private government. Here are some of the agencies that regulate professions and occupations in California:

Board of Dental Examiners of California
Board of Medical Quality Assurance
Board of Osteopathic Examiners of the State of California
Board of Registered Nursing
State Board of Optometry

California State Board of Pharmacy
Board of Examiners in Veterinary Medicine
State Board of Accountancy
California State Board of Architectural Examiners
State Board of Barber Examiners
State Board of Registration for Civil and Professional Engineers
Registrar of Contractors
State Board of Cosmetology
State Board of Funeral Directors and Embalmers
Board of Examiners of Nursing Home Administrators
State Board of Registration for Geologists and Geophysicists
Board of Behavioral Science Examiners
Department of Real Estate
Insurance Commissioner
State Board of Fabric Care
State Board of Chiropractic Examiners
Board of Vocational Nurse Examiners of the State of California
Certified Shorthand Reporters Board
Bureau of Collection and Investigative Services
California State Board of Landscape Architects

Many of these agencies are totally captured by their clients. Agencies which regulate other kinds of business are also frequently more or less captive, at all levels of government. It is alleged, for example, that the Civil Aeronautics Board is the instrument of the dozen leading airlines in the United States. It is said that the CAB prevents the establishment of new major airlines and keeps long distance air hauling the monopoly of big operators now in the business. To cite another example, it is charged that the Federal Communications Commission is the captive of the large networks whose purpose is to prevent establishment of new networks and other disrupting developments such as censorship of programs. And another example: it is charged that the Federal Power Commission was the captive of big gas producers. And so on down the list. Whether these charges are true cannot be proven, although there is plenty of smoke to suggest fire.

A captive regulatory agency may still advance and protect the public interest. A business, profession, or occupation is often improved by regulation (even when that regulation is in effect self-regulation) through the curbing of bad practices and substandard members. American medical practice has no peers in the world, yet this has been accomplished with the help of captive state boards of medical examiners which have tried to make the medical business profitable by cutting down the supply of doctors which has been done in part by imposing higher and higher standards for entry into the profession. The character of the legal profession has, to repeat, also been improved. While many other similar examples of improvement can be cited, it cannot be said that all regulation has been beneficial. A case can be made, for instance, that railroads, airlines, and other modes of transportation have suffered by being too well protected from competition by the regulatory agencies that supervise them.

COMPLAINTS ABOUT THE EXPERTNESS OF THE EXPERTS:

One argument for the administrative process has been that it gives power directly to experts. Yet it is widely known that persons vested with authority to make rules and decide cases are very frequently not experts at all. Usually the members of regulatory boards are lawyers and/or politicians, although state professional and occupational licensing boards tend to be made up of members of the profession regulated.

Whatever expertise the heads of administrative agencies may develop through experience and service in the agency itself is for the most part lost through turnover. Service on the boards of the great federal regulatory agencies is considered to be a stepping stone to higher and better things by many who receive such appointments. This is also true of the more important state boards.

Many agencies vested with rule-making and adjudicatory authority employ staffs of experts, sometimes hundreds of experts. But agencies seldom have enough experts partly because client groups often do not want their regulatory agency too well equipped. An agency shorthanded on staff will quite naturally turn to people in the community who are expert, and those people are most likely the ones being regulated—a dubious source of neutral information.

Lawyers harbor some complaints against agency staffs, complaints that go to the heart of the legal process. They say that experts behind the scenes have too much to say about the decisions made in cases litigated before the agency. Lawyers accustomed to practice before courts of law are accustomed to having the judge who hears the case actually decide the case. But in the administrative process lawyers are often in the curious position of addressing their arguments to anonymous "judges," for no matter who presides over the hearing, the actual decision is often drafted, if not made, by anonymous staff experts. This is especially so of decisions on technological matters.

It is also alleged that agency heads occasionally use their expert staff to dress up biased policy decisions and camouflage them to look scientific. The expert staff, according to this theory, is used ex post facto to think up reasons why the agency made the "right" decision. It is well known that many larger agencies use opinion writers to draft decisions which are then quite often delivered by agency heads verbatim as their own. (These opinion writers may learn what they are to prove by sitting with the agency heads when cases are discussed.) Thus, to some degree, the manner in which agencies use experts may be compared to the way private parties use lawyers to marshal arguments. Indeed, there has been some sentiment among agency heads that if the parties litigating cases before them can use attorneys to think up arguments, the agency itself has the right to use experts to think up arguments, especially since the agency itself is usually one party in the litigation (the agency being both a judge and a party).

The complaint is also heard that staff experts and agency heads are reluctant to establish any firm policies as guidelines for deciding cases. It is charged that they do not want to write opinions in a way that would bind their hands in future cases. The technique, according to this line of attack, is to keep open plenty of back doors so that opinions will not clash: avoid general statements, pile up a mountain of facts so confusing that nobody can make head nor tail of it, then just come to a conclusion and say the facts support the conclusion.

The massiveness, incomprehensibility, and vagueness of opinions and the absence of agency policy are other complaints closely related to what has just been discussed. Sometimes bias and absence of any clear, consistent agency policy masquerade behind what appears to be just the reverse. The Federal Communications Commission has been accused of this. The FCC has an apparently clear-cut set of about eight yardsticks or policies by which it determines who shall be awarded television and radio licenses. Each applicant is measured by all eight, and the one who comes up with the best score wins. However, it is alleged that from day to day the agency favors different yardsticks. Special strength in number 3 could be the turning point in today's case and number 7 in tomorrow's case. The yardsticks could be like eight mouseholes through which the agency could run toward any decision that its allegedly biased judgment may wish to take it. The experts could make just about any case they want by playing on those eight yardsticks.

INCOMPATIBLE FUNCTIONS:

Combining judicial and legislative functions is difficult. A judge is supposed to decide cases almost solely on the basis of evidence put into the record during the trial. He is not supposed to let any other evidence (except that officially noticed) influence his decision in the case. In other words, ex parte evidence is not to be received. Evidence considered by the judge should be known by both sides and should not be introduced by or for one party only (ex parte).

But this is difficult in administrative adjudication because the judges are also lawmakers and as lawmakers they are constantly in communication with all sorts of people about all sorts of problems within their subject matter jurisdiction. This is as it should be. Yet, how can an administrative "judge" expunge from his mind the information acquired in his legislative capacity? A Civil Aeronautics Commissioner goes about the country in his quasi-legislative capacity finding out about the air transport business and getting personally acquainted with airline executives who will later stand before him in his other capacity of judge. A judge in a court of law is not supposed to discuss a case before him with anybody except in open court or in conference where all parties are present. But an administrative judge cannot stop being a legislator even *during* litigation, for some aspect of nearly every problem and many of the people he has to deal with as legislator are in some form of litigation before him most of the time. Furthermore, as a legislator, the administrator in practice must frequently (too frequently) rely upon the people regulated for information. This puts the agency and its clients into a familiar relationship, made still more familiar by efforts of client groups to win the friendship of agency heads. Familiarity is altogether incompatible with the aloofness and neutrality incumbent upon a judge.

Yet, if an agency head were to maintain the social distance demanded by his judicial role, then he could not do his legislative job, a job which requires free flow of information and personal interaction with client groups.

The role of administrator (including policeman) is also quite incompatible with that of judge for reasons already discussed.

And so the administrative process which features the union of legislative, judicial, and executive functions is criticized for the many outrageous contradictions which flow inescapably from that union of functions. There is a great deal of talk about ethical problems in the administrative process. It is said that codes of ethics need to be written to restore the purity of government, to discourage administrators from receiving ex parte evidence and to discourage them from being biased in favor of the prosecutor (themselves). But these are not really ethical problems. They are organizational problems. Every administrative agency with legislative, judicial, and executive powers combined is forced to sin because these powers are so incompatible.

POLICY BIASED ADJUDICATION:

It is plain to see that when a judge is also a prosecutor he is going to be biased in favor of the prosecutor. A reasonably successful effort has been made to cure that problem through internal separation of functions. But there is another kind of bias that is more difficult to cure because it is not really a disease, although it is believed to be a disease by many: the bias of the administrative judge toward whatever *policy* he happens to favor. This bias is a natural part of the administrative process because, curiously, the purpose of much administrative adjudication is not justice at all, but the creation of policy. The basic purpose of much administrative justice sharply differs from the basic purpose of judicial justice. The purpose of a judicial trial is justice to the parties; the purpose of administrative adjudication is often legislation (in the guise of adjudication). While courts of law also legislate, legislation is not their acknowledged purpose. Legislation *is* a central acknowledged purpose of much administrative action.

Here is an example of legislation disguised as administrative adjudication. Suppose the Federal Communications Commission holds a hearing to determine which one of several applicants shall be given a television license. That hearing is adjudication, and the case is called an application case. If the current policy of the FCC is to discourage persons who already own one station from acquiring other stations, and if there is only one applicant who does not already own another station, then that applicant will get the license. The decision enunciates a policy and enforces it. The question is not, "What is the just way to treat these applicants?" but rather, "What policy do we want to set forth today?" In one sense, the question is not wnat is good for the applicants, but what is good for the public as viewed by the agency.

Some agencies do much or all of their policy-making through the vehicle of adjudication. The Federal Trade Commission, for example, usually makes and/or changes a policy after an administrative hearing to determine whether the respondent did or did not do something of which the FTC ought to disapprove. The decision is in effect an announcement of policy.

Some agencies use a combination of formally announced rules, supplemented by decisions in adjudicated cases which spell out details. For example, a board of medical examiners may make a rule forbidding advertising by doctors, leaving the whole question of what constitutes advertising to be determined by decisions of the board in cases where specific doctors are tried for specific acts. The board is not governed by stare decisis as a court of law is supposed to be. Thus, it might decide similar cases differently according to its policy shifts without offending any hoary traditions of conformity to policy.

It is not intended here to suggest that administrative agencies have no policies. They do have policies, they do often try to stick to the same policy. This is natural. It makes deciding easier, and it satisfies the sense of justice. Indeed, there is a war between the need for administrative flexibility on the one hand, and the yearning for stable policies on the other.

Lawyers have been particularly vocal in clamoring for stable administrative policies. The traditions of the legal profession in this regard are at odds with the fundamental purpose and technique of the administrative process. The bar thinks quite naturally in terms of justice to private litigants. But the administrative process focuses on policy-making and enforcement. The bar wants the agencies to announce their policies in advance like legislatures, and when agencies adjudicate the bar wants decisions based on prior decisions. But one of the major reasons for use of the administrative process is to free government from the shackles of stare decisis, and from legislative immobility. The administrative process is designed to be agile, brisk, and lithe. The times demand it. But ordinarily, justice to private parties demands consistency, steady adherence to steady policy. There we come to an impasse, to a very troublesome problem.

The problem is made worse by the fact that administrators who are really supposed to be biased in favor of agency policy, can show an improper personal or political bias which is difficult to distinguish from the other kind of bias. The ease with which unethical bias hides behind legitimate policy bias sharpens demands for elimination of *all* bias. But that would eliminate the administrative process.

DELAY:

Delay in settling administrative cases is often as great as delay by courts of law. Hundreds of cases before regulatory agencies pend for three years or more. Delays for one or two years are routine. The reason most commonly offered for delay is too little staff. A few years ago the Federal Power Commission shocked people by announcing that it would require thirteen years with the staff it had at that time to clear up 2,313 producer rate cases pending as of July 1, 1960, and that with the contemplated 6,500 cases that would be filed during that thirteen-year period it could not become current until the year 2043 even if its staff were tripled.

There are instances of ten and fourteen years elapsing before final determination of some cases by certain agencies.

A staff shortage is often a *symptom* rather than a *cause* of trouble. A deeper cause of staff shortages and delay common in the administrative process is judicialization of the administrative process. Lawyers in particular have campaigned to make administrative adjudication as much like that of ordinary courts of law as possible. The American Bar Association has ceaselessly fought for reform of the administrative process. During the 1930's the Association gave its support to several bills proposing to strip administrative adjudication completely away from administrative agencies and vest it in an administrative court. Those bills failed and the Association then supported the Walter-Logan Bill which would have greatly increased the judicial review of quasi-judicial determinations. That bill passed both houses of Congress only to be vetoed by President Roosevelt who said the legislation would hamstring the agencies. Thwarted by the Walter-Logan veto, the Association then spawned proposals for a federal administrative procedure act to make the quasi-judicial procedures of agencies more like those of regular courts. Congress enacted an administrative procedure law in 1946, culminating a journey begun years before at state as well as national levels.

The agencies themselves have continually encrusted themselves with more and more formalism and procedure over and above that imposed on them by administrative procedure acts.

One of the main accomplishments of some administrative procedure acts is internal separation of functions, that is, the separation of judicial functions within the agencies from prosecuting, investigating, and legislating functions. This is done primarily through the establishment of independent hearing officers who act within the agency as independent judges much as the courts of law act independently within the government at large. This is a long step toward judicialization. Independent hearing officers begin to think of themselves as regular judges and tend to bring along lots of baggage including rules of evidence, cross examinations, stare decisis, and the rest.

Furthermore, hearings are too often unreasonably lengthened by the unwillingness of hearing officers to discipline factual inquiries.

Evidence may be allowed to pile up far beyond what is necessary to prove whatever the evidence is supposed to prove. Hearing officers may permit parties to filibuster a proceeding with endless repetitive superfluous presentations of evidence.

Another source of delay is that the hearing officer's decision is only a recommendation to the head of the agency. Many cases have to be tried twice, once at length before the hearing officer, and a second time before the head of the agency.

Another source of delay is the piling up of opportunities for appeals within the agency. Fairness, of course, seems to call for some sort of opportunity to appeal, but since speed and simplicity are supposed to be among the primary benefits of administrative adjudication it is best to settle things with as few appeals as possible.

Still another impediment to speed is the liberality with which people are permitted to intervene as parties in cases before agencies. Those who are indirectly affected and who perhaps are not necessary parties to a case frequently desire to intervene and offer proof and argument. An example of an indirectly affected party is a public utility whose profits would be affected by the outcome of a hearing to determine whether to license a new competitor. Another example might be a labor union which is interested in the outcome of a workman's compensation case that involves a statutory construction that would affect future cases.

Responding to pressure as well as to a sense of fairness, agencies tend to liberally allow interventions. Their liberality is also motivated by uncertainty about the intricate law governing which parties are necessary parties without whom the proceeding would be invalid. Agencies that try to limit the number of parties to an adjudicatory hearing promptly become enmeshed in that law as they try to determine which potential parties have a legal interest or a legal right to be parties. The easy way is to open the doors and let almost anyone intervene. Some agencies, however, try to be selective. But in 1946 the U.S. Supreme Court handed down a decision that inhibited the power of agencies to narrow down the number of parties to cases: *Ashbacker Radio Corporation* v. *Federal Communications Commission*, 326 U.S. 327.

Sometimes intervenors pile into a case for the sole purpose of delaying a decision and making the proceeding too expensive for some competitors. Intervenors impede the hearing and confuse the issues by long, complicated and often needless cross examination and other presentations of evidence. In the Civil Aeronautics Board's *Seven States Case* there were 225 parties and intervenors. One hundred and ninety-four witnesses testified before the hearing officer and they filed over a thousand exhibits. When the hearing was over the examiner sat down with a pile of proceedings, transcripts, exhibits, and briefs five and a half feet high. It took him over a year to read it and make his decision, which alone ran 658 pages. (Initial Decision, No. 7454, CAB, 1957.) Then the whole case was heard over again by the Board, which took only four days. They rejected the examiner's plan, and, working largely on the basis of what they heard during four days, came up with another plan. The whole proceeding took over three years, most of which was the examiner's long, complicated, expensive, and almost futile hearing.

The practice of making policy through the vehicle of adjudication is another cause of delay in the administrative process that might be corrected. If, for example, the Department of Alcoholic Beverage Control in a certain state would elaborate on its rule that no alcoholic beverage may be sold within one block of a school so that the rule would clarify whether one block means one block as the crow flies or one block following the sidewalk, and also explain how many feet constitutes a block, and so on, it would not be necessary for the Department to litigate the definition of one block. Foggy policies and imprecise rules lead directly to litigation and to the expense and trouble and delay associated therewith.

COST:

Delay and formalism raise the cost of administrative adjudication frightfully. Preparing exhibits, hiring experts such as engineers and accountants, retaining lawyers, and housing and feeding this collection of persons is costly especially when the hearing lasts for weeks. In the Phillips Petroleum Co. rate case before the Federal Power Commission, seventy-six lawyers entered appearances for thirty-three parties and intervenors and the hearings consumed eighty-two days. Total costs ran into millions. The Phillips case began in 1948 and was not settled until 1960. The cost of the record alone was monumental. (Records cost several dollars a page. Some records run as high as 20,000 pages.)

Delay and formalism is costly in other ways. For instance, while a case is being delayed, business decisions are also being delayed and the profits which might have flowed therefrom are partially lost. Delays by the Federal Power Commission in the establishment of rates for transportation of gas have held up programs for expansion. Delays by the Civil Aeronautics Board have held up procurement policies for commercial air lines.

Delay in administrative adjudication is costly to governments too, for they are compelled to spend more money over a longer period of time for lawyers, hearing officers, and so on.

AGENCIES HAVE LOST THEIR CREATIVITY:

During the 1930's the federal government under leadership of a president willing to try new paths embarked upon what to many people was an exciting adventure in solving some of the nation's economic and social ills. Whether these new paths were good or bad, they were at least *new*, and the President attracted intellectual pioneers and creative people into government service. The administrative process was to be an important instrument, and many new agencies combining legislative, judicial, and executive power were established under the New Deal.

Since the 1930's there has been a steady decay of creativity. This is partly for reasons already described, especially the loss of public support by regulatory agencies and their capture by special interests. Creative people have not been attracted to government service as they were in the 1930's. Prosperity has produced complacency. With a return to normalcy came a decline in the sense of national emergency. Many inventive and adventuresome spirits attracted to government service by that emergency began to depart the federal establishment (including, it is said, a departure of the same sort of people from the White House). Government service has not been the bright opportunity for service to humanity that many creative people conceived it to be thirty years ago. Furthermore, there have been many good jobs in private enterprise for creative people.

Rapid turnover in high level government jobs has also bled

government service of creativity. Partly in consequence of complacency, key government jobs have been used as stepping stones to better jobs in government or higher paying jobs in client industries. The heads of regulatory agencies, as well as high staff officers in those agencies, have often sought jobs in the industries regulated by their agency, and of course those industries have been only too eager to hold open the possibility of such employment as a means of controlling the agency. Furthermore, client industries profit by hiring persons with knowledge of the internal operations of the agency who have contacts in the agency and perhaps knowledge of confidential agency plans.

Rapid turnover is fostered by other factors, including, for example, the level of government pay (which is low compared with industry); and the political ambition of many agency heads which motivates them to use their positions as stepping stones to something else.

A government official who sees his job as temporary is not at all likely to have a devotion to the work of his agency. Probably all he wants to do is keep the lid on until he gets out. That means he usually defends the status quo. He usually opposes anything that might rock the boat, cause controversy, draw fire, or bring unfavorable publicity. Nor does he want to waste his vital energies thinking out novel or improved solutions to the problems with which his agency is supposed to deal. He is a time server in the purest sense of the word. There are, of course, individual exceptions to this pattern of mediocrity. But creative individuals today are apt to be overwhelmed and driven to despair by the dead weight to which they are bound on all sides.

Bureaucracy itself is a terrible blight to creativity. Bureaucracy must work by orderly procedures, and where there is weak or dispirited leadership at the highest levels these procedures can become virtually an end in themselves, piling up to the point where the goals of the agency are lost sight of while everybody's attention is riveted on the red tape. Bureaucracy in routine times can be lethal to a creative soul.

Judicialization of the administrative process is a symptom or perhaps an actual cause of uncreativity, particularly the use of adjudication in place of clear and thoroughgoing regulations.

Rather than turn their heads to serious thought about the work of the agency, and rather than draft clear policy statements, agency heads today often seem to prefer to sit back and adjudicate cases, which is an activity that takes less energy and puts the burden on the lawyers who argue the case.

Creativity is also said to be impaired by the secret desire of agency heads to keep their policies cryptic, undecipherable, and foggy. So long as an agency is deciding cases one by one and being careful not to decide them in terms of any clear policy, the agency is in no danger of criticism for erroneous policy. If nobody knows what your policy really is, then nobody can criticize it. Congress cannot raise a storm about a policy that does not exist. Such a desire to avoid policy might well dampen creativity.

Creativity by boards is also impaired by the practice commonly employed by boards of handing down unsigned decisions for which no one takes personal responsibility. (However, the Freedom of Information Act of 1966 [5 U.S.C. 552] apparently now prohibits unsigned opinions at the federal level.) Furthermore, boards are by their nature uncreative. An *individual* can be creative, but a board has to produce a collective decision, and most collective decisions are cautious ones, flavored with compromise, and devoid of anything that might smack of being new or radical.

INDEPENDENCE: TOO MUCH AND TOO LITTLE:

Judges in courts of law should not have to fear that they will be fired if they make a decision against powerful interests, or make an unpopular decision. A judge needs to be independent, and elaborate provisions have been made to insure the independence of federal judges. Justice fears a fearful judge. Federal judges are for that reason appointed for life and can be removed only by impeachment. In other words they have tenure so that they can call them as they see them without fear or favor. Only four federal judges in American history out of thousands who have served have been removed by impeachment. The federal constitution also prohibits the reduction of a federal judge's pay during his service.

Administrative adjudication is criticized because most agency heads do not have that kind of independence. Most high level government officials are political appointees who can be removed at will by the president and whose duty it is to do what they are told when and if they are told. When they sit as judges in the quasi-judicial cases litigated before them, they are subject to an array of pressures from which federal judges are largely immune. Part of the problem is that hardly anyone thinks of an agency head as a judge. He is quite rightly viewed as a political executive. This is part of the picture of conflicting roles so evident in the administrative process in which the same people try to carry on several kinds of incompatible jobs all at the same time. Congressmen and others will freely try to influence an agency head as to cases he is adjudicating, and do so in blatant ways that they would hardly dream of doing if the case were before a court of law. Furthermore, most federal judges have strong codes of ethics about receiving ex parte evidence. Such a code is not standard equipment for political bureaucrats, and if it were much of their work as bureaucrats would be impossible.

One of the reasons for the independence of the so-called independent regulatory agencies is to give the heads of those agencies more independence in their quasi-adjudications. Among the independent agencies are some of the biggest and most important in the federal establishment: the Federal Trade Commission, the Federal Communications Commission, the Securities and Exchange Commission, the Environmental Protection Agency, the Interstate Commerce Commission, the National Labor Relations Board, the Civil Aeronautics Board. They regulate large sectors of the nation's economy. They are called independent because the heads of the agencies cannot be fired by the president, except for cause. They are said, therefore, to be independent of the president. They serve for fixed terms of several years.

Independent agencies are not as independent as they may seem. The president has many ways of influencing them. (1) Their budget requests to Congress are included in the general budget prepared by the president's budget bureau. Although the president's budget is only a recommendation to Congress, it is a powerful one which in its broad outlines is generally adhered to by Congress. A president can make monetary threats, or hold out financial rewards depending on whether an independent agency is hewing to his policies. (2) While the president cannot remove the head of an independent agency as easily as he can the head of other executive agencies, he does, nevertheless, have authority to remove the head or any other member of an independent agency for cause. This is rarely done, but can be done for gross neglect of duty and for other reasons specified by Congress. This is probably the least of his powers over independent agencies, but it is there. (3) Occasionally an agency head may look forward to reappointment for another term, in which case he will want to make himself worthy of reappointment by avoiding too much independence of presidential policies. (4) Many agency heads use their jobs as stepping stones to political advancement and will not want to cross the president from whose generosity political advancement may come. (5) The president names the chairman of independent boards. (6) A government agency cannot appeal an adverse court decision without the consent of the Solicitor General who is appointed by the president. If an agency policy which is at odds with presidential policy falls into legal difficulty, the Solicitor General may not be inclined to appeal it.

Of course, the so-called independent agencies are not altogether independent of Congress either. Congressional committees and individual members of committees overseeing an independent agency can exercise powerful influence over those agencies through the threat of investigation, through power of the purse, and through power over the organization and authority of the agency, and by all the techniques of political pressure on ambitious agency heads.

And so it is clear that independence in an agency does not really produce independence. Without curing the evil it was intended to cure, independence produces some new evils of its own. The independence of the independent agencies is therefore another criticism of the administrative process. One evil of independence is that it somewhat isolates the agency from the president and leaves it more vulnerable to pressure and capture by client groups. It is somewhat more difficult for a client group to capture an agency which is directly under the president (who can get rid of a captured agency head if he really wants to badly enough). The head of an independent agency can sell out to a client group and still hold his job even against presidential disfavor. A second evil of independence is that it complicates the job of coordinating national policy on various matters. For example, the coordination of civilian and military aviation is made more difficult by the fact that each is supervised by different government agencies, one of which is independent. The agencies may have conflicting policies. The same problem exists in regard to anti-trust activity, some of which is controlled by the Anti-Trust Division of the Department of Justice and some by the Federal Trade Commission, an independent agency. Development of a national transportation policy is made difficult by the fact that different forms of transportation are regulated by different independent agencies. There are many comparable problems.

PROCEDURAL INFLEXIBILITY:

Perhaps flexibility is the central characteristic which the administrative process is supposed to exhibit—the central purpose for which it was created—the central good to be enjoyed in exchange for the evils inherent in the administrative process. Flexibility, freedom of movement, ability to give continuous supervision to galloping events: these are the main plusses of the system. The administrative process with its union of executive, legislative, and judicial power was to have been an armored division in the war for good government—loose, free, agile, capable of wide sweeps with mobile equipment, of sudden coordinated attacks from all sides, of outflanking movements against the elusive problems of technological society. To carry on mobile warfare, the administrative process claims to have stripped itself of excess baggage, abandoned tedious procedures, abandoned the cumbersome methods of passing laws, abandoned stare decisis, abandoned the rules of procedure and evidence so oppressive to courts of law. As we have seen, the administrative process has not been freed of these impediments anywhere near to the degree that many desired. The administrative process has often failed to achieve flexibility.

To say that the administrative process has failed to achieve flexibility, or to exhibit speed, mobility, agility, and maneuverability is to charge it with the greatest sin of which it could possibly be guilty—measured by its own goals.

Chapter 3

What and Where Is Administrative Law?

DEFINITION:

Administrative law is law governing the legal authority of administrators to do anything that affects private rights and obligations. It limits not only scope of authority but also the manner in which that authority is exercised. The main enthusiasm of most persons interested in administrative law is in the latter, that is, in fair procedure and in remedies at law for unfair procedure.

One may wonder how administrative law can focus on authority and at the same time concern procedure? It is because no one has authority to act by illegal procedure. And so authority (vires) is the central concern of administrative law; and ultra vires behavior, whether substantive or procedural, is the central wrong.

Administrative law is not, by this definition, the substantive rules made *by* administrators, nor is the adjudicative decisions they make. If the Federal Aviation Administration makes a rule forbidding passengers on airlines to carry guns, that rule would not be

59

administrative law. However, administrative law would touch on the authority of the Federal Aviation Administration to make the rule, and upon the procedure employed in making it.

American legal writers generally define administrative law as I have, and they tend to concentrate their attention on procedural fairness. Most textbooks on the subject are divided into three parts: rule-making procedure, adjudicative procedure, and judicial review. Judicial review is included because courts are the final judges of the fairness of administrative procedure and other questions. Therefore a great deal depends upon the willingness of courts to review and upon the kinds of things they will look at when a litigant complains of unfair administrative procedure or some other wrong.

Many administrative law texts include chapters on tort liability. These subjects are included because judicial review of administrative unfairness is not always an adequate remedy for a party. It is often not enough for a court to declare that an agency or officer has acted illegally. The illegality may have done harm, as when health authorities erroneously kill healthy cows mistaken for sick cows. The owner of those animals may surely wish more than mere judicial review of authority. He may wish to sue the government or sue the officials. Liability of government and of its officials for tort is a corner of the general law of liability, a corner assumed by some writers to be part of administrative law.

Administrative law comes into play, as was pointed out several paragraphs above, when administrators undertake to affect rights and obligations. These rights may be private (the right to property, for example) or they may be civil (the right to speak, for example). They may be individual rights, or they may be the rights of companies, corporations, the general public, or other groups. All these rights have, by some writers, been lumped under the heading private rights. Or in the case of obligations, private obligations.

One may wonder where administrative law ends and other kinds of law begin. Where, for example, does the law of civil rights leave off and administrative law begin? The answer to that cannot be supplied any more than an answer to the question where blue ends and purple begins. Administrative law is not a thing of clear boundaries, nor is any other branch of the law, for they are all *neighborhoods* in the world of law which fade into one another block by block. The central business district of administrative law is fair administrative procedure.

TYPES OF ADMINISTRATIVE LAW:

Administrative law is found wherever law is found. It is in the United States Constitution and in all the state constitutions. It is in the form of statutes—state and federal—and in the form of local ordinances. Every or nearly every unit of government, from mosquito control districts up, has enacted some administrative law. Furthermore, administrative law is in the form of common law made by courts and it is in the form of procedural rules made by administrative agencies themselves.

Constitutional Administrative Law: The entire U.S. Constitution is, in a sense, administrative law for the constitution is a limitation upon government. Its purpose is to say what government may and may not do, and also to say what the various branches of government, such as the executive, may and may not do. This is also true of state constitutions.

If any part of the U.S. Constitution may be singled out as most significant to the administrative lawyer, it is the due process clauses of the Fifth and Fourteenth Amendments. These clauses are important because they say that no governmental action denying life, liberty, or property in the United States is legal if it is unfair. Of course, the Fifth and Fourteenth Amendments do not use the terms fair or unfair. But if there is any one word in the English language that sums up what the law courts over the years have held is the meaning of due process of law that word would be fair. The Fifth Amendment says the federal government may not be unfair: "No person . . . shall be deprived of life, liberty, or property, without due process of law." The Fourteenth Amendment says the states may not be unfair: "No state shall . . . deprive any person of life, liberty, or property without due process of law." These guarantees of due process will be discussed later.

The constitutional doctrine of separation of powers has also played a large role in the development of administrative law. The quasi-legislative rule-making powers of agencies have repeatedly been condemned as an invasion of legislative power given to the legislative branch, and the quasi-judicial power of agencies has been condemned as an invasion of power given to the judicial branch.

Statutory Administrative Law: Very frequently statutes which establish an administrative agency will also say something about how they are to proceed. The Clayton Act of 1914, for example, established the Federal Trade Commission and in Section 11 provides for the way in which its authority is to be exercised. I quote one sentence of that section for illustrative purposes:

> Whenever the commission or board vested with jurisdiction . . . shall have reason to believe that any person is violating or has violated any of the provisions of sections two, three, seven and eight of this Act, it shall issue and serve upon such a person a complaint stating its charges in that respect, and containing a notice of a hearing upon a day and at a place therein fixed at least thirty days after the service of said complaint.

The United States government and many states have also enacted administrative procedure acts. These are attempts to provide some uniformity of procedure among the rule-making and adjudicating agencies in the exercise of their powers.

The federal government and many states have also enacted tort claims laws which say something about the circumstances under which a citizen may sue a government or a government employee for tort.

There are many other federal and state and local statutes and ordinances which set forth administrative procedure and which provide remedies for administrative wrongs.

Common Administrative Law: Common law is made by courts and it results from their habit of repeating themselves. Because courts will ordinarily decide today's case the same way they decided yesterday's case if it involves comparable fact situations (we call that habit the principle of stare decisis), we have a whole lot of hints as to how courts will decide cases, and this collection of hints is called common law. Common law prevails on a point of law so long as there is no statute or ordinance or constitutional provision which contradicts it. Judicial interpretations of statutes, ordinances, and constitutional provisions are also part of the common law and they too prevail until reversed by the makers of those laws. Much administrative law is in the form of common law simply because formal law does not regulate every niche of administrative authority and procedure and because the courts have often interpreted the formal law that does exist.

Much of what I earlier described as constitutional administrative law is, in fact, common law because the federal constitution and to a lesser degree state constitutions are very brief and vague and are, therefore, often interpreted by courts. It is fortunate that constitutions are vague. This enables each generation to mold its constitution to accommodate social change. Most of the molding process is done by courts through the process of constitutional interpretation and reinterpretation. The U.S. Constitution speaks, for example, of "due process of law" and from those rather mystic words has sprung a whole universe of meaning encased in hundreds of judicial decisions which constitute both common law and constitutional law.

Administrative-Administrative Law: It may at first seem odd that some of the administrative law which governs administrators is made by administrators themselves, but it is really no more odd than the fact that much of the law which each person in his personal life lives by is self-imposed. One may argue that the latter, the personal self-imposed rules, are really more or less forced upon us by society, or urged upon us by parents, or urged upon us by considerations of health, etc., and that they are not entirely self-imposed therefore. The same may be said of administrative agencies which seemingly bind themselves with procedural rules. Though apparently self-imposed, the procedural rules of administrative agencies are in no small degree imposed or impelled by public pressure and by public expectations exerted through so many arteries of the political process. That is one reason why the cause of fair administrative procedure is served by teaching students and the general public what fair administrative procedure can and should be.

The procedural rules which agencies impose upon themselves are often found in the same book along with all the other rules and regulations made by the agency. The Federal Communications Commission, for example, publishes a ten volume book called *Rules and Regulations*. Part I, Volume I, called "Practice and Procedure," is eighty pages long.

These rules of practice and procedure may also be found in the *Federal Register* along with the other rules made by federal agencies. It is not difficult to see why lawyers become impatient and exasperated about the procedural rules made by agencies. There are hundreds of agencies and if they all have their separate procedures it becomes confusing to lawyers. That is one reason the American Bar Association supported federal and state administrative procedure acts. Lawyers hoped that administrative procedure acts would impose at least some uniformity of procedure on the agencies. Yet there remains much divergence.

WHERE AND HOW TO FIND ADMINISTRATIVE LAW:

Administrative law is found in the same places and in the same ways that one finds the rest of the law. The law is magnificently organized, indexed, digested, and commented upon. An important part of any lawyer's tool kit is his ability to track down a fugitive point of law in the congested world of law. He needs to know about all the aids to legal navigation. Law schools offer courses on how to find the law, and some good textbooks have been written about legal research. One of the best is *How to Find the Law*, 7th ed. (St. Paul, 1976). Another is *Effective Legal Research* by M. O. Price and H. Bitner (Boston, 1962). In general they describe how to use and/or how to find legal encyclopedias; digests; court reports; statutes; rules, decisions, and other publications of administrative agencies; loose-leaf services; periodical literature; treatises; restatements; uniform state laws; dictionaries; citators; nonlegal materials related to law; foreign law; card catalogs; and law libraries in general.

We cannot go into all the details of legal research here, but there are some bits and pieces of basic advice that can be offered to people who want to stick a toe into the sea of legal materials. First, it is very nice to have a dictionary that defines words commonly or uncommonly used in the jargon of lawyers. The one most commonly used in the United States is *Black's Law Dictionary* (St. Paul, 1979) which weighs six pounds, ends on page 1,511 and begins by discussing "A" as a nundinal letter, a dominical letter, as a symbol, as an abbreviation, as an indefinite article, and goes on to describe its use in Latin, French, and Roman law, and tells how to spell "A." The dictionary cites cases in which judges have used and defined the various terms.

There has been a lavish outpouring of magazine articles on nearly every imaginable legal subject. The best place to find out what has been written and when, where and by whom, is the *Index to Legal Periodicals* which covers the main legal and semi-legal periodicals of the English speaking world. There is also an *Index to Foreign Legal Periodicals* and an assortment of other indexes. Since law splashes over into practically everything else, there are many articles about law (or related to law) in an array of nonlegal periodicals. Much of this is traceable through the *Reader's Guide to Periodical Literature* (available in almost all self-respecting libraries), the *International Index* (which is a guide to periodical literature in social sciences and humanities), and the *Public Affairs Information Service Bulletin* (which selectively indexes around one thousand periodicals mainly in the social sciences).

There are dozens of law reviews published by law schools. Among the best are the *California Law Review, Columbia Law Review, Cornell Law Quarterly, Harvard Law Review, Michigan Law Review, Minnesota Law Review, New York Univeristy Law Review, Northwestern University Law Review, Stanford Law Review, Texas Law Review, Virginia Law Review*, and the *Yale Law Journal*. Also there are a drove of other law periodicals published for specialized clientele such as (to cite two of the most respected) the *American Bar Association Journal* and *Judicature* (the latter published by the American Judicature Society). Dan F. Henke, law librarian at the University of California at Berkeley said in 1963 that his library was receiving about 541 Anglo-American legal periodicals and 283 foreign legal periodicals (*Legal Research Guide for California and Federal Law* [Berkeley, 1963], p. 75). This suggests that hardly anything legal can avoid exposure in the pages of some magazine somewhere.

There are textbooks (often called treatises) on administrative law. One of the most grandiose and best written is by Kenneth C. Davis, *Administrative Law Treatise* (St. Paul, 1958). It runs four doctrinaire volumes. Some of the best literary stylists among textbook writers today are writing about administrative law. Besides Davis in that category is Bernard Schwartz, author of many lucid and provocative works in administrative and comparative law. Frank E. Cooper's works are also especially well written.

Besides treatises there are also casebooks on administrative law. The difference between a treatise and a casebook is that a treatise describes, explains, discusses, and offers suggestions and criticism; while a casebook presents the leading decisions of courts, usually pruned and shortened and briefly commented upon by the editor. There are a number of casebooks in administrative law, including these authors: Kenneth C. Davis, Walter Gellhorn and Clark Byse, Louis L. Jaffe and Nathaniel L. Nathanson, Carl McFarland, and Bernard Schwartz. There are others, of course. Some law students have a vicious habit of buying "canned briefs" of the cases in casebooks. These briefs attempt to boil down, usually to one page, the action, facts, contentions, issues, holdings, and reasoning of the court in a particular case at law. Such briefs are often misleading because of their brevity and because of the amateurishness of their authors. But, no doubt, it is possible to get through some law schools on the strength of canned briefs.

Legal encyclopedias are also helpful for getting an overview of administrative law or of any other subdivision of the law. Some encyclopedias attempt to cover the entire law. The two most famous American encyclopedias are *American Jurisprudence* and *American Jurisprudence, Second Edition* (cited *Am. Jur.* and *Am. Jur. 2d*), fifty-eight volumes; and *Corpus Juris* and *Corpus Juris Secundum* (cited *C.J.* and *C.J.S.*), 101 volumes. Every so many years a massive effort is made to revise and update these collections, and between times pocket parts are supplied to be inserted in the back of each volume. The pocket parts discuss developments since the series was published. Lengthy as they may be, these encyclopedias cannot do more than supply a rather superficial description of the law on various subjects. Both sets discuss the law under about 400 separate headings. Administrative law is discussed by *American Jurisprudence, Second Edition,* under the heading "Administrative Law," *Corpus Juris Secundum* does so under the heading "Public Administrative Bodies and Procedure."

Most administrative law is in the form of common law and this is true for the same reason that 90 per cent of American law is common law. Common law is a collection of past court decisions on a given situation or subject. These past decisions are called law because Anglo-American courts base their present decisions for the most part on principles laid down in their past decisions. Therefore, the past decisions are law in the sense that they tell how future cases are probably going to be decided. In addition to common law there are constitutions and formal enactments of legislative bodies. In the process of enforcing them, they are interpreted by courts. Those interpretations are part of the common law just as much as other judicial opinions which are not interpretations of statutory law. Much of the common law is built upon statutory law. (For the sake of convenience, constitutions are usually included within the definition of statutory law although a statute is generally considered to be an act of a legislative body.)

How are the opinions of courts found? To begin with, one is probably going to be interested in the decisions of higher level courts (appellate courts) simply because they have the last word on controversies about what the law means. Most so-called leading cases are either federal or state supreme court decisions, or are cases a supreme court has declined to review and has permitted to be the last word. A leading case is a decision that first enunciates some principle of law and which is followed by other courts in deciding cases with the same or similar fact situations. Thus, in administrative law, one of the leading cases is *Humphrey's Executor* v. *United States,* 295 U.S. 602; 55 S. Ct. 869; 79 L. Ed. 1611 (1935) which stands for the principle that federal officers exercising quasi-legislative and quasi-judicial powers (presumably meaning members of regulatory commissions) may not be removed by the president except for reasons specified by Congress. The case was decided by the U.S. Supreme Court. The next time the president tries to fire a member of an independent agency solely because the member's economic philosophy differs from that of the president the case may not need to go to the supreme court because the lower courts will in all probability decide by reference to *Humphrey.* Thus, the casebooks that burden law students with their weight and expense are for the most part filled with supreme court decisions like the *Humphrey* case, or with other appellate court decisions.

Court decisions are published, sometimes by government, sometimes by private publishers, sometimes by both. By now the number of volumes containing the decisions of all the state and federal appellate courts in the land is astronomical and sags many hundreds of yards of library shelves. The United States probably has more courts per square mile than any country in the world owing to its federal system, and to its passion for settling disputes by lawsuit. These courts have been producing decisions since their beginning, which means since 1789 in the case of federal and some state courts. Furthermore, American case law rests upon the pre-1789 case law of Britain, which in turn rests on miscellaneous law going all the way back to Roman times and before. The law is a great storehouse from which lawyers can pick and choose citations of an infinite variety to support their contentions in court.

U.S. Supreme Court decisions are published in three different collections or series. One is an official series which means it is published by or for the government, and the other two are unofficial and published by private firms. Often the location of a U.S. Supreme Court decision will be cited in all three series, as I did in citing the Humphrey case above. The accepted style of citing cases is to give the name of the case, followed by the volume number, followed by the series designation, followed by the page on which the case begins in the volume, followed by the year that the case was decided in parentheses. For example: *Morgan* v. *United States,* 298 U.S. 468 (1936) . The official series of U.S. Supreme Court decisions is known as *United States Reports* (cited *U.S.*) flanked by volume and page. If a case appears in a volume before 91, the name of the court reporter (thus immortalized) is used rather than the series designation "U.S." Thus, volume one of the official series would be cited 1 Dallas. The official series simply presents cases chronologically without comment.

The two unofficial series do the same thing but include some very important aids to law practice. The *United States Reports, Lawyers' Edition* (cited *L.Ed.*) helps lawyers because it is annotated, that is, it contains notes relating to many of the cases. The notes highlight the outstanding points of the case and cite other federal cases bearing on the point highlighted. Another unofficial series is the *Supreme Court Reporter* (cited *S. Ct.*). It includes supreme court cases back to 1882, and it also includes supplementary information helpful to lawyers primarily by being hooked up to an indexing system of grand proportions known as the Key-Number System.

Perhaps the best way to get hold of the decisions of all the supreme courts and intermediate appellate courts in the land is to use the National Reporter System. It is an unofficial publication of cases but is rated even more reliable than the official reports. The National Reporter System is composed of several series of books containing the appellate court reports of all the states in the general region of the United States covered by the series. For example, the *Southern Reporter* reports the cases of the appellate courts of Louisiana, Mississippi, Alabama, and Florida. There is also a *Pacific Reporter,* a *North Western Reporter,* a *South Western Reporter,* a *North Eastern Reporter,* an *Atlantic Reporter,* and a *South Eastern Reporter,* as well as a special *New York Reporter* and *California Reporter,* and also a *Federal Reporter* containing decisions of the U.S. Courts of Appeals. There is also a *Supreme Court Reporter.* The chief merit of the National Reporter System is that the whole system of regional reporters together with the federal reporters is bound together with a system of indexing known, as mentioned above, as the Key-Number System which relates points of law in one case to the same or similar points of law in other state and federal cases.

This brings us to the subject of digests. The function of a digest is to lead you to the precise cases that illustrate particular points of law. Of central importance to the use of some digests is the Key-Number System. The law has been arranged under seven basic categories and further subdivided into around 421 topics which are further subdivided into specific points of law, and each of those points has a Key-Number. All a researcher has to do is go to one of the digests employing the Key-Number System and look under the Key-Number where he will find summaries of the facts and holdings of pertinent cases.

There are other kinds of digests or indexes besides those based on the Key-Number System. For example, there is one employing words and phrases. It lists cases pertinent to each word or phrase. Another extremely useful research tool is a series of books called the *American Law Reports* (cited *A.L.R.*). The editor of this series has selected a large number of federal and state cases on subjects of current interest and has reported them together with a thorough annotation. The annotation digests every American case known to the editor which bears upon the subject and gives other information. Although *A.L.R.* does not attempt to cover the law like an encyclopedia, its annotations are very much like an encyclopedia on the points covered.

Citators are also valuable tools for locating the law. A citator will tell you the history and treatment of a case or of a statute or of a constitutional provision. If you want to know whether a case has been affirmed, dismissed, modified, reversed, superseded, criticized, distinguished, explained, followed, harmonized, limited, overruled, questioned, or several other things, you can go to an appropriate recent citator, look up the case in question and read a list of citations in which those various things may have happened. In essence, a citator helps you evaluate a case by telling how it has been treated since it was handed down. A citator will even tell you where it has been discussed in law reviews, etc.

In separate volumes citators also cite the treatment of statutes, constitutional provisions, certain agency rules and orders and even some ordinances of local governments, and tell the instances in which a particular section of a statute, constitution, rule, order or ordinance has been construed, applied, cited, or affected by subsequent legislation. Since Shepard's Citations of Colorado Springs, Colorado are leading publishers of citators, it is said you are shepardizing a case or a statute when you use the citator. If you want Shepard's citations for cases and statutes of a state just ask for state-so-and-so citations (*Massachusetts Citations,* for example). If you want citations of the federal constitution, cases and statutes, ask for *United States Citations.* If you want citations of cases in the National Reporter System just ask for so-and-so reporter citations (*Atlantic Reporter Citations,* for example).

Statutory law, measured in pages of print, is small compared to the quantity of case law. Nevertheless, the revised codes of the fifty states plus the federal government would add up to several hundred large books. There may be as many as sixty or seventy thousand pages of new statutes every year, including local ordinances.

Congress passes myriad laws every session and at the end of the session these are simply piled into a book called the *Statutes at Large.* Before they get into that book they are called slip laws (because they are on slips of paper). These slip laws are numbered consecutively: their public law number, if they are public laws. Private laws have a private law number. Although the *Statutes at Large* is like a child's room before mother has picked up, the *United States Code* (cited *U.S.C.*) is a more orderly arrangement. The statutes are arranged by subject, fifty titles. *U.S.C.* is published roughly every six years and tells you what federal statutes are currently in effect as of the date of printing. If you want the code annotated there is another set of books called the *United States Code Annotated* (cited *U.S.C.A.*) running around eighty volumes which refer you to cases touching on the various sections of the code and other material. There is a thoroughgoing index of the code in the last four volumes of *U.S.C.A.*

The enactments of state legislatures, known popularly and sometimes officially as session laws, are also bound at the end of each session and then periodically codified into state counterparts of *U.S.C.* and/or *U.S.C.A.* As for local ordinances, they may or may not be codified. In the larger places they are. Where they are not codified, it is a harrowing job to find anything.

The U.S. Constitution is easy enough to find. The first four volumes of *U.S.C.A.* has both the constitution and digests of cases which construe its various sections. Another very useful and convenient source is *The Constitution of the United States of America: Analysis and Interpretation.* It is a thoroughly footnoted attempt to explain what the constitution means in the light of judicial interpretations. State constitutions can be found in the state codes, often in the first volume of such codes, in some cases annotated with index. City charters, which are in a sense city constitutions, are also found in the state codes because they are really only enactments of the legislature in most states.

Rules made by administrative agencies are also part of the statutory law of federal, state, and local governments, although rules cannot be found in the codes discussed above. You are plunging into something pretty hair-raising in some states and in most local governments if you want to find a rule. Most states at least require filing of state agency rules with the Secretary of State. In a few states and in the federal government there is a systematic method of collecting and codifying rules. The federal system works approximately this way. (Keep in mind that literally hundreds of agencies are making rules.) When an agency makes a rule it is published in the *Federal Register* before it becomes effective unless it is an emergency rule in which case it is published but not necessarily before it becomes effective. The *Federal Register,* a quasi-legislative cousin of the *Statutes at Large,* is a daily publication (except Sundays, Mondays, and the days after holidays). The daily issues are bound annually (actually a new volume of the *Federal Register* is started every year) and there is an index published monthly, quarterly, and annually (in fact, each daily issue is also indexed).

If you are looking for a rule on a subject, do not start with the *Federal Register.* Begin with the *Code of Federal Regulations* (cited *C.F.R.*) which is a codification of quasi-legislation and is put out every half-decade or so. *C.F.R.* is comparable to the *United States Code.* It codifies the *Federal Register* like the *United States Code* codifies the *Statutes at Large.* In fact, *C.F.R.* is arranged into the same fifty titles that the *U.S.C.* is arranged into, and it has a general index which is a master index to the entire *C.F.R.* set. That is where to start looking. If you cannot find what you want in *C.F.R.* (not overlooking its pocket parts) then go to the annual volumes of the *Federal Register,* then to the quarterly, monthly, and daily indexes of the *Federal Register* since the last *C.F.R.* pocket part was published.

Several states have comparable systems for publishing and codifying their rules, but in most states the situation is less convenient.

Presidential proclamations and executive orders (there is no legal difference between them) are also found in the *Federal Register*. They are simply the rules issued by the president. A proclamation may be used for something flamboyant like a day of prayer for peace and love. Executive orders are usually more work-a-day.

Some agencies also publish their regulations (and miscellaneous other information) in separate booklets or loose-leaf collections. Also there are some loose-leaf services privately published to keep practitioners up-to-date on rules and other matters of interest in certain subject areas such as tax and labor.

As for the quasi-judicial decisions of agencies (called orders by the federal Administrative Procedure Act), the best place to get them is from the agency itself, most generally. Some agencies publish their orders (which are often reasoned decisions comparable to court decisions) in bound and indexed volumes that look very much like the reports of a court. (The *Civil Aeronautics Board Reports*, for example.) However, in some state and local jurisdictions you will be lucky to find anyone who remembers which desk drawer the decisions have been thrown into.

It might be worth pausing to note some other publications useful to persons trying to find their way through the bureaucratic maze. If you want a detailed organizational outline of the federal government and want an explanation of what the function of each agency is, the names and titles of its leading officials, and the statutes that created the agency, go to the *United States Government Organization Manual*, published annually by the United States Government Printing Office. Most states have similar manuals or books. Also the Council of State Governments publishes *The Book of the States* which gives information about the organization of state governments and about the officers and functions of various state agencies and other useful data about states. Another interesting source of information about the personnel and organization of a government or agency is the phone book. Many larger agencies have their own phone book, as do some state and local governments.

Both federal and state governments publish a stupefying variety of books, pamphlets, reports, and what not. The United States Government Printing Office issues a *Monthly Catalog* of government publications which lists the publications of the executive, judicial, and legislative branches of the federal government. There is also an annual index made of the *Monthly Catalog*. As for state publications, one of the best ways to find out what has been whelped is the *Monthly Checklist of State Publications* prepared by the Library of Congress.

Chapter 4

Do the Doctrines of Separation and Delegation of Power Still Prevail?

☆ ☆ ☆

SEPARATION OF POWERS: HOW MUCH?

Drafting the Constitution of 1787, the Fathers of the Republic had before them a classic problem: how to give government the power to do the things it needs to do, yet prevent it from growing tyrannical. The Fathers found an answer, at least part of an answer, in separation of powers: division of power among competing branches of government—legislative, executive, and judicial. Each would contest with the others for power and in so doing check and limit one another.

The Constitution of the United States does not use the phrase separation of powers. The idea that each of the three branches should have exclusive control over its own peculiar variety of power is, one might think, implied from the first sentence of Articles 1, 2, and 3. Article 1 begins with the words, "*All* legislative powers herein granted shall be vested in a Congress of the United States which shall consist of a Senate and a House of Representatives." The key word is *"all."* Article 2 begins with a similar sweeping statement, "The executive power shall be vested in a president of the United States of America." It does not say "most" of the executive power, or "some" of it; it is a simple and all-inclusive statement. Article 3 asserts, "The judicial power of the United States shall be vested in one supreme court, and in such inferior courts as the Congress may from time to time ordain and establish." Clearly the Fathers intended a separation of powers even though they nowhere used the phrase.

Similar statements are made in the constitutions of most states, sometimes with high eloquence. The Constitution of Massachusetts, for example, provides for separation of powers in Article 30 of the Declaration of the Rights of the Inhabitants of the Commonwealth of Massachusetts:

> In the government of this Commonwealth, the legislative department shall never exercise the executive and judicial powers, or either of them: The executive shall never exercise the legislative and judicial powers, or either of them: The judicial shall never exercise the legislative and executive powers, or either of them: to the end it may be a government of laws and not of men.

The Declaration of Rights of the Maryland Constitution says in Article 8:

> That the Legislative, Executive and Judicial power of Government ought to be forever separate and distinct from each other; and no person exercising the functions of one of said Departments shall assume or discharge the duties of any other.

The separation of powers idea has never been rigidly enforced at any level of government. Administrators have always been asked by legislatures to perform various discretionary duties, have always been given the job of making rules, of deciding when to apply or enforce certain laws, of filling in the details of statutes. This is not a new thing nor is it avoidable. Governments cannot operate with absolute and total separation of powers. Absolute separation of powers would cause a chronic governmental lockjaw if it were tried. But, of course, it has never really been tried and never will be, because total separation of the three powers of government is impossible. It is logically impossible because people working on the same job (whether raking leaves in the front yard or running the government) must work in some sort of concert. Furthermore, it is hard to tell whether a given act (in the front yard or in a government) is legislative, executive, or judicial. This has been obvious to the courts since the dawn of the Republic and they have never attempted so foolish a thing as to try separating what is inseparable. Even the words legislative, judicial, and executive are incapable of precise definition, and, if defined, are defined falsely or inadequately.

The federal Constitution so often speaks in superlatives, and so often merely intends to suggest a direction in which to travel. It commands freedom of religion without pausing to omit human sacrifice; freedom of speech without pausing to omit conspiracies; separation of powers without pausing to omit its multitude of exceptions and impossibilities.

Administrators simply must make certain decisions of both a semi-legislative and semi-judicial nature. Consider, for example, the 1895 case of *In Re Flaherty*, 105 Cal. 558, in which a man was sent to jail for beating a drum on the streets without a permit. A city ordinance made it an offense for any person to beat a drum on the streets of the city without a special permit in writing to do so from the president of the board of trustees of the city, and gave him authority to grant these permits whenever in his judgment the issuance would not imperil the public safety. (In those days it was feared drums would stampede horses.) Note the discretion this ordinance gives to an administrative officer either to issue or not issue depending on his judgment of the situation. In effect he was delegated power to make a law or rule to fit each situation as it comes along, a semi-legislative power of a common type.

The local legislature could not foresee in advance whether beating a drum on a particular occasion would threaten the public safety, and so it gave discretion to the officer. Legislative bodies at all levels of government have always done this kind of thing. In the drum case, it was claimed by the victim that a law giving this kind of discretionary authority to an executive officer was a violation of separation of powers and therefore unconstitutional. The court upheld the law, however, declaring it to be a proper delegation of authority.

Municipal governments are constantly giving authority to administrators to determine such things as whether a building constitutes a fire hazard or whether it is unsafe or unsanitary, etc. To pick a case at random, *Gaylord* v. *The City of Pasadena et al.*, 175 Cal. 433 (1917), illustrates a controversy between a city and a citizen over the authority of the city electrician. Pasadena gave to its electrician the authority to determine when electrical connections in buildings were unsafe and in need of repair. That is, the electrician was authorized to exercise a kind of legislative function in determining precisely what was safe or unsafe and to enforce those judgments as law.

He found defective connections in property owned by Gaylord, who promptly went to court charging that the city council had no right to delegate such discretionary authority to a city official. Of course, the court upheld the council's right to delegate that quasi-legislative power, saying,

> even a casual observer of governmental growth and development must have observed the ever increasing multiplicity and complexity of administrative affairs, national, state, and municipal,— and even the occasional reader of the law must have perceived that from necessity if for no better grounded reason, it has become increasingly imperative that many quasi-legislative and quasi-judicial functions which in smaller communities and under more primitive conditions were performed by the legislative or judicial branches of government, are entrusted to departments, boards, commissions, and agencies.

In 1888 the Minnesota Supreme Court provided us with a classic defense of the now familiar pattern of business regulation by commissions exercising all three functions of government. In *State of Minnesota* v. *Chicago, M. & St. P. R. Co.*, 38 Minn. 281, the Minnesota court said regarding railroad rate regulation by commission:

> If such a power is to be exercised at all, it can only be satisfactorily done by a board or commission, constantly in session, whose time is exclusively given to the subject, and who, after investigation of the facts, can fix rates with reference to the peculiar circumstances of each road, and each particular kind of business, and who can change or modify these rates to suit the ever-varying conditions of traffic.

In recent times, more and more legislative and judicial power has been delegated by national, state, and local legislatures to administrative agencies. This has been necessary because of the ever-increasing areas of social and economic life that are supervised by government. Legislatures simply do not have the time, knowledge, or ability to devise detailed rules (or even broad policy in some cases) for the many areas over which law must operate. Consider, for example, railroad regulation. The national government wants safe railroads, but Congress has neither the time, nor the technical knowledge to debate the merits of particular safety devices. It has turned the job of formulating precise safety rules over to the Interstate Commerce Commission, which does the debating and the rule-making guided only by the general intent of Congress. Many other regulatory agencies at all levels of government are operating likewise. Civilized twentieth-century government could not function if a strict separation of legislative, executive, and judicial powers were maintained. Nor for that matter could any government function.

DELEGATION OF POWER:

The rule against delegation of powers is often, and perhaps understandably, confused with the doctrine of separation of powers. The reason for this confusion lies in the fact that when one branch of American national or state government delegates its power to another branch, this is a violation of both the separation of powers doctrine *and* of the rule against subdelegation of delegated powers.

The latter rule, which lawyers are pleased to know in Latin as delegatus non potest delegare (a delegate cannot delegate), is a legal doctrine lifted directly out of the private law of agency and applied to public affairs. It is not difficult to understand that an individual who authorizes another person to act on his behalf would object to having that other person (his agent) subdelegate the power without his permission. Agency law forbids it.

The United States Constitution begins with the words, "We the People of the United States . . . do ordain and establish this Constitution. . . ." This means the *people* establish the government and delegate certain powers to it. The government is the people's agent, and the people have said in their constitution that *all* legislative power shall be vested in Congress. Congress is the people's agent in legislation, and may not subdelegate the people's power to others without the consent of the people (requiring a constitutional amendment).

The law of agency does not interfere with delegations of government power in England because England has no formal written constitution vesting power in the people, and because, furthermore, Parliament acting through the crown is assumed to be supreme and sovereign possessing all the authority which in the United States is presumed to rest ultimately with the people. Parliament and the crown are principals, not agents, and as such may delegate as they wish.

The doctrine of delegatus non potest delegare has been used in the United States to assail the authority of various agencies, but neither it, nor the separation of powers doctrine, have enjoyed much success as legal hammers with which to beat down the administrative process.

Governments at all levels flout the doctrines of separation of powers and nondelegation of powers. All kinds of legislative (and judicial) power is being given to executive agencies. It is not *called* legislative power, but rather *quasi*-legislative power. *Quasi* is a facade which makes it easier for the courts to uphold such delegations in the face of hostile constitutional principles. However, someone has said that if a person is sent to jail for violation of a quasi law, the prison cell will not be a quasi cell.

Laws made by administrative agencies are called *rules* rather than *laws*. So we refer, in the field of administrative law, to rule-making power. The legal effect of a rule is precisely the same as the legal effect of a statute according to the United States Supreme Court. Several years ago a Florida Game and Fresh Water Fish Commission rule was declared by the Supreme Court to be a law of the state. The case developed when a defendant was charged with a violation of a federal statute making it unlawful for any person to deliver for transportation across any state line any fish, if such transportation was contrary to the law of the state. The court found the Florida rule against such transportation to be a law of the state (*United States* v. *Howard,* 352 U.S. 212 [1957]).

Judicial power is similarly masqueraded behind the word quasi. The punishments imposed by quasi-judicial agencies are called sanctions.

These twists of phraseology have helped ease the pain, grief, and torment that judges may feel in burying the venerable principle of separation of powers.

THEORY VERSUS PRACTICE:

Legislative Powers:

CRIME: Courts ordinarily refuse to recognize as valid any attempt by a legislative body to delegate the power to determine what shall be a crime. A crime is an act usually punishable by fine or imprisonment. Any law which allows an administrative officer to determine that speeding is a crime would probably be struck down as an unconstitutional delegation of legislative power. Only a legislature may make it a crime to speed, though it may leave the determination of what constitutes speeding on a particular piece of road to the police or some other agency or administrator. Similarly, in the case of stop signs, a legislature may validly delegate the authority to determine where stop signs shall be placed, but not authority to make it a crime to run the sign. To cite another example, a legislature may permit an administrative agency to grant, deny, or revoke licenses, such as medical licenses. But a legislature cannot (if we are to believe the common law in most jurisdictions) delegate to an administrator the power to determine whether or not it is a crime to practice medicine without a license. Only a legislature can assert that it is a crime to practice medicine without a license, or to violate the terms of a permit. However, a legislature may give an administrative agency power to lay down the terms of a permit to practice medicine.

An administrative agency cannot make something a crime if crime is defined as an act punishable by fine, imprisonment, or by some other traditional punishment, although agencies do make certain acts all but criminal by imposing sanctions not technically or traditionally regarded as criminal punishment. It seems narrow and old-fashioned to define punishment primarily in terms of direct fine or imprisonment as the law usually does. There are indirect ways that an administrative agency can deny liberty and money. A state board of medical examiners may revoke the license of a medical doctor, or suspend it for a period. The Federal Communications Commission may revoke a license to broadcast. These are examples of terrible punishments which are not technically within the definition of criminal punishments, but which are (or could be) as painful as direct fine or imprisonment.

Furthermore, some statutes permit imposition of what one might call quasi-fines as civil sanctions, for such things as willful evasion of tax payments. These seem to be upheld by courts as long as they do not look too much like criminal fines or get too big, a vagueness characteristic of many points of common law.

ALTER OR SUSPEND STATUTES: It almost goes without saying that an agency which is created by statute cannot alter or suspend the statute that created it, nor alter or suspend any statute except by permission of the maker of the statute. If the maker of a statute gives that permission by saying, for example, "This law is in effect until such and such an event in which case the agency may suspend or alter the law in such and such a way," that would be legal and is in fact done (reciprocal trade laws, for example, which allow executive adjustment of tariff schedules).

However, the rule about altering statutes is not quite as elementary as I have stated it. Federal courts now seem to give a lot of weight to interpretations which agencies have made of their own enabling acts. The United States Internal Revenue Service, for example, issues regulations interpreting various provisions of the tax laws. "It is the settled rule that the practical interpretation of an ambiguous or doubtful statute that has been acted upon by officials charged with its administration will not be disturbed except for weighty reasons," said the Supreme Court of the United States in *Brewster* v. *Gage,* 280 U.S. 327, 336 (1930). Naturally, these administrative interpretations of their own enabling acts are (also for practical reasons) given great deference by individuals who deal with the agency.

DELEGATION OF UNBOUNDED LEGISLATIVE POWER: It is no longer easy to argue that legislative bodies in America are forbidden to delegate their legislative power even in its most bald-faced unlimited form. There are numerous statutes today which do delegate undefined power. The Federal Trade Commission is told that it may prohibit unfair methods of competition, as though anyone actually knows what is fair and unfair. In effect the FTC is given a kind of carte blanche.

Nevertheless, much lip service is paid to the idea that legislative bodies which give agencies discretionary power must always define the limits of that power. According to that doctrine a legislature which gives power without accompanying standards has in effect abandoned its own authority. The standards are the limits of power. Those limits are like a leash that keeps the dog under control. It is the leash that keeps quasi-legislative power from becoming pure legislative power. In the cases of *Panama Refining Co.* v. *Ryan,* 293 U.S. 388 (1935) and *Schechter Poultry Corporation* v. *United States,* 295 U.S. 495 (1935), certain federal laws were struck down because they granted undefined authority; both cases are eloquent statements of a theory of separation which is not as virile as it once was. Perhaps the doctrines of separation and delegation of power are like guns behind the door available for use whenever it pleases the court to do so. Courts do occasionally strike down acts which are too vague, particularly where administrators are given vague power to limit fundamental liberties such as freedom of speech, press, religion, and assembly. But the fact remains that many vague delegations of quasi-legislative power survive judicial review, particularly in the area of business regulation.

State governments and the federal government have varying judicial rules about the subject of standards.

Judicial Power: Its Definition Is Uncertain:
There is no adequate definition of judicial power and therefore no adequate definition of what power belongs to the judicial branch. If judicial power is defined as the power to decide things, then that is what practically everybody in government is doing. The

U.S. Constitution, Article 3 uses only two words to describe the judicial power: "cases" and "controversies." But what is a case and what is a controversy? If they are simply disputes, surely no one contends that courts must settle all disputes. Disputes are going on everywhere all the time and nearly everyone is involved in trying to settle them. It is outrageous to suggest that only courts settle cases and controversies. But then what is the judicial power? It is the power to settle any case or controversy that *reaches* a court. And what is a court? Is it not anything that some statute or constitution so designates? We are dealing in mere labels.

Judges have from time to time tried their hands at defining judicial power, but all their verbiage begs the question. It has been defined as the "power to decide and pronounce a judgment and carry it into effect between persons and parties who bring a case before court for decision" (87 A.L.R. 701). The U.S. Supreme Court defined it in 1911 as "the right to determine actual controversies arising between adverse litigants, duly instituted in courts of proper jurisdiction" (219 U.S. 346). These definitions seem to say that judicial power is the power to determine controversies, not necessarily all of them but some of them; to be specific, the ones that come before courts. And that is the vaguest of vague definitions. Nor does the Supreme Court's effort in 1926 to define judicial power add anything: it described it as the "power to entertain the suit, consider the merits and render a binding decision thereon" (271 U.S. 228).

If it is true that the judicial power is merely whatever power the judiciary happens at any moment to have, then it is clearly impossible to violate the constitutional command that "The judicial power of the United States shall be vested in one supreme court, and in such inferior courts as the Congress may from time to time ordain and establish" (Article 3, section 1). Anything not so vested is, by definition, not judicial power.

With that, constitutional purists may relax in sweet assurance that the constitutional principle of separation of powers cannot and will not ever be trampled upon so far as judicial power is concerned.

However logical the above line of reasoning may seem, it is a bit too facile in the opinion of quite a few lawyers, and for their chief guild, the American Bar Association. Deep in the hearts of lawyers there is the uneasy feeling that whatever anyone may say, administrative agencies today *are* exercising judicial power and doing it wholesale.

The courts themselves are responsible for some of this wholesale practice of judicial power by agencies. Courts have sought to shield themselves from the onrush of appeals from administrative decisions by closing the courtroom door upon many kinds of controversies and/or upon important aspects of many cases. They have, for example, applied judicial self-restraint to questions of fact, and even to questions of mixed fact and law. Courts delegate judicial power to administrators by default. Administrative decisions thereby become in effect final, and *finality* has long (at least since *Hayburn's Case*, 2 Dall. 409 [1792]) been emphasized by the courts themselves as an essential attribute of judicial power.

American courts have the authority to give the *final* interpretation of laws, whether they be provisions of a constitution, statutes, ordinances, or administrative rules. A legislature probably cannot validly deny the courts this right in a constitutional system of government, for to do so would shatter the pillar upon which constitutionalism rests: rule of law. Legislatures do not give persons in the executive branch the power to make final interpretations of laws, at least not with judicial favor. For example, a legislature will not give to police officers the authority to make a final interpretation of the phrase reckless driving. Naturally the officer has to get it straight in his own mind what he plans to label reckless before he arrests somebody, and in that sense he interprets the law. But the arrested person may challenge the officer's interpretation. Final interpretation will then be made by the court.

A legislature may not delegate power to assess the amount of loss sustained by one person as damages against another. This has been held to be a uniquely judicial power, although the imposition of reparation payments has been allowed some agencies including the Interstate Commerce Commission.

HOW PRECISELY MUST THE LEGISLATURE DEFINE A DELEGATION OF LEGISLATIVE POWER?

Plenary Delegations: Plenary means full, complete, entire, absolute, or unqualified. A delegation of plenary power would be a delegation of power unrestricted by standards. This is the broadest sort of delegation.

ACTIVITIES INIMICAL TO THE PUBLIC WELFARE: In some states the courts have held that the legislature is free to give administrative agencies almost unlimited power to make whatever rules for whatever purpose for the regulation of those businesses, occupations, or activities that are deemed inimical to the public welfare. This is quite contrary to what the courts will often permit when socially acceptable activities are involved. Thus, while it might be proper for the legislature to say to an administrative agency that it may do what it likes when it comes to saloons, secondhand dealers, or soliciting magazine subscriptions, it might not be at all proper for the legislature to give an equally free hand to an agency regulating the practice of medicine. In the latter case the agency is supposed to have from the legislature a clear—or at least what the courts deem to be a clear—delimitation of their authority. The legislature is supposed to draw boundary lines around the authority of the administrator and set standards. It is not supposed to turn him loose to do as he pleases.

LOCAL GOVERNMENT: Local government seems to be in some ways an exception to the rule against delegations of undefined legislative power to agencies. Local governments *are*, in a sense, agencies. The U.S. Constitution does not specifically recognize them as governments, that is, it does not mention them. The federal constitution divides all power between two sovereignties: federal and state. Furthermore, most state constitutions do not grant much power directly to local government. Local governments, like other agencies, ordinarily get their power from the state legislature which passes statutes creating them and conferring power upon them. Local governments, like other agencies, are creatures of the state, and as creatures or agencies of the state they fall under the ban of the Fourteenth Amendment. For instance, the Fourteenth Amendment implies (according to the U.S. Supreme Court) that no state shall segregate the races by law. Local governments are also, therefore, forbidden to enforce segregation laws because they are, like other agencies, instrumentalities of the state. Local governments are also covered by the due process clause of the Fourteenth Amendment for the same reason, a fact of significance to local officials because so much administrative law touching directly on them and dealing with fair procedure stems from the due process clause of the Fourteenth Amendment.

Although local governments have the same constitutional status as state agencies for the most part, courts almost never put local governments in the same class as administrative agencies where the question of delegated legislation is concerned. Outright delegations of power to local governments routinely go unquestioned and unchallenged.

Constitution-Created Agencies: While all state constitutions are color-dyed with the principle of separation of powers, a principle which is sometimes even highlighted by special clauses, it is not uncommon to find provisions in them creating regulatory agencies armed with a union of powers. We find such agencies provided for in the constitutions of Virginia, Nebraska, California, Louisiana, South Carolina, Arizona, and Oklahoma, to mention a few. Some state constitutions directly create the agency and provide for its powers in the manner of Virginia's State Corporation Commission. Others may simply authorize the legislature to do so. In either case, it is uphill work for a court of law to find reasons to declare the acts of these constitution inspired agencies unconstitutional, particularly when the agencies are exercising bountiful power directly bestowed by the highest law.

War Power and Foreign Relations: Congress need not be particularly scrupulous about delegating undefined authority to the president for the purpose of prosecuting a war. As the U.S. Supreme Court said in *Lichter* v. *United States,* 334 U.S. 742 at 780 (1948), "In time of crisis nothing could be more tragic and less expressive of the intent of the people than so to construe their constitution that by its own terms it would substantially hinder rather than help them in defending their national safety." Petitioners in the Lichter case claimed that Congress had unlawfully attempted to delegate legislative power, by authorizing administrative officers to determine whether companies working on defense contracts were making excessive profits and to recover such profits if found. The act did not define excessive profits and therefore left administrators a piece of very wide and undefined authority.

The U.S. Supreme Court in *United States* v. *Curtiss-Wright Corporation*, 299 U.S. 304 (1936) seems to say that the constitutional objections to delegating legislative power do not apply in the field of foreign relations because the power to conduct foreign relations is a cognate power. (Cognate means related by birth, of the same parentage, related in origin.) It is a power that the government holds by virtue of being the government of a sovereign nation and is not a power given to it by the people through the constitution. Therefore, since the government is not an agent in this matter, the power can be subdelegated from Congress to the president, assuming that Congress has *any* authority in foreign relations.

That assumption is necessarily in doubt because it is not clear which branch of government has power over foreign relations. Certainly the president, by virtue of having authority to appoint ambassadors and the power to negotiate treaties, has by implication power to conduct foreign relations. The president's power in this area rests on as clear a constitutional mandate as that of Congress whose functions appear rather secondary. Therefore, it would seem somewhat pointless for the courts to narrowly limit the power of Congress to delegate that which is scarcely that of the Congress to delegate.

Where is the line between foreign relations and foreign commerce? Although Congress is explicitly given authority over foreign commerce by the U.S. Constitution, it seems logical because of the close relationship between foreign relations and foreign commerce that the court would permit Congress to give especially broad delegations of power to the President in areas of interstate or foreign commerce affecting foreign relations.

Granting versus Denial of a Right or License: The authority to grant a right such as to *grant* a license to practice medicine usually requires a far less rigid standard, far less definite guidelines than would be required in a delegation of authority to *deny* property, or to deny a right or a license.

Courts have struck down many laws which give vaguely defined authority to deny rights such as the right to keep a license to practice medicine. For instance, the California legislature in 1901 passed an act for the regulation of the practice of medicine by a Board of Medical Examiners. It gave to this board power to revoke the license of a physician for making grossly improbable statements in advertising. Of course, there were other grounds specified for revocation of a license, but this particular one seemed a bit ambiguous. When the board revoked the license of Mrs. S. J. Bridge for advertising a cure for cancer, Mrs. Bridge took the case to court charging that the legislature had illegally delegated its own power to the board by giving it undefined powers to determine what grossly improbable advertising means. The court concluded that Mrs. Bridge was quite right in her contention, and voided the provisions of the law under which the board had revoked the license, and asserted that the right of a physician to practice medicine cannot be made to depend upon such vague provisions of law (*Hewitt* v. *Board of Medical Examiners,* 148 Cal. 590 [1906]).

Yet vagueness is almost the trademark of statutory provisions defining the powers of administrative agencies which are not involved in revoking licenses or other rights. Indeed, as we have seen, legislative standards for the guidance of some administrative agencies are almost so vague as to be missing altogether. Consider the power of state boards of medical examiners in exercising authority, as so many do, to license persons who have graduated from a reputable medical college. What is a reputable medical college? On the other hand if a board is given authority to revoke the licenses of those who had already been granted licenses but who had not graduated from reputable medical colleges, then the courts might insist that the legislature define precisely what it means by reputable.

First Amendment Situations: Courts tend to require stringent legislative standards where power is granted to an administrative agency to regulate the right to exercise freedom of speech, press, religion, or assembly—the freedoms set forth in the First Amendment to the U.S. Constitution. Guidelines which are definite enough for most purposes are often inadequate when the right to exercise First Amendment freedoms is involved. *In Re Porterfield,* 168 P.2d 706 (1946), illustrates the judicial disposition to require strict standards in laws which give officials power to limit speech. The labor organizer James Porterfield was imprisoned for violating an ordinance of the city of Reading which prohibited soliciting by professional organizers without first obtaining from the city council a license which would be given only if the city council found that the applicant was of good moral character and that he would not resort to force, violence, threat, menace, coercion, intimidation, or corrupt means in his proposed work of solicitation.

Porterfield argued that the ordinance was an unconstitutional limitation on his right to freedom of speech and the court agreed with him saying, "We are of the opinion that on the face of the ordinance the indefinite standards which it enunciates provide a mechanism for the deprival of constitutional rights."

State and local governments have a right to limit exercise of First Amendment freedoms when their exercise would jeopardize the public health, welfare, safety, or morals. A state might have a right to prohibit union solicitation by persons of low moral character or by persons who might be expected to resort to force, violence, threat, menace, coercion, intimidation, or corrupt means. But if it does try to prohibit union solicitation or any other kind of speech for those reasons it ought to try to define precisely what those words mean so that the administrator is held within very narrow and concise boundaries and cannot in the guise of enforcing a city ordinance enforce his own prejudices.

At the federal level, the U.S. Supreme Court has set forth comparable principles requiring clear standards in the exercise of administrative power in the field of First Amendment civil rights.

WHERE DOES ONE LOOK FOR THE BOUNDARY LINES OF DELEGATED LEGISLATIVE POWER?

Courts at all levels of government go out of their way to find an act of the legislature constitutional, and try to avoid declaring laws unconstitutional. If an act of the legislature granting semi-legislative authority to administrators does not clearly set forth the guidelines of that power, the courts will look in some very dark corners to find guidelines. Courts will read the statute as a whole. Taken as a whole, it may contain a system of implied boundary lines nowhere specifically stated. Courts may find that several or a series of legislative acts are related and that the standards for them all are stated in one but not in the others. In their search for guidelines limiting exercise of executive discretion courts may find them in the realm of public knowledge which the court feels the legislature need not explicitly state. Courts may even find standards and boundary lines which have been set outside the legislature, sometimes by expert groups.

TO WHOM, OTHER THAN ADMINISTRATIVE OFFICERS, MAY A LEGISLATURE DELEGATE AUTHORITY?

To Itself: While the state constitutions generally impose separation of powers upon the state government, they do not impose the same thing upon local governments. Therefore, while the state legislature may not delegate administrative power to itself, a *local* legislative body may establish itself or any one or more of its members as executive officers. It may constitute itself a board of tax appeals, for example.

To Private Groups: Legislative bodies are commonly allowed to delegate a kind of legislative power to private groups. A question was once raised whether San Francisco made an unconstitutional delegation of legislative power to its Milk Commission when it gave it the power to prohibit the sale of milk for human consumption which is not certified. The local ordinance defined certified to mean milk which conforms to the rules, regulations, methods, and standards adopted by the American Association of Medical Milk Commissions, a private organization. In effect, San Francisco delegated to a private association the right to determine what milk is qualified to be sold. The court upheld its constitutionality. (*Natu-*

ral Milk Producers Association et al. v. *City and County of San Francisco et al.* 124 P. 2d 25 [1942]) .

To Other Governments: For a government to put itself in the same relationship to another government as the city of San Francisco put itself in relation to the American Association of Medical Milk Commissions (just described) is generally viewed by courts as an abandonment of sovereignty. A government may adopt the *past* rules of another government, but not the *future.*

To Citizens: Citizens themselves are occasionally given a kind of administrative power by legislation making the consent of some percentage of those who will be directly affected by administrative action a condition to the exercise of the authority by the agency. However, laws of this kind are likely to be held unconstitutional when they give citizen groups power to force an agency to act.

SOME VARIETIES OF QUASI-LEGISLATIVE POWER:

Power to Give Effect to Contingent Legislation: If a legislative body permits an administrative officer to enforce, suspend, or modify a statute when and if some particular situation comes to pass it is called contingent legislation. Legislatures are supposed to set standards for the exercise of this power. The standards consist of spelling out *what* is to be done and *when* it is to be done. How hard the courts look for whats and whens in reviewing contingent legislation depends upon their mood on the subject of restricting executive discretion, a mood which in recent decades has been rather permissive.

An example of contingent legislation is the flexible tariff laws which allow the president to adjust U.S. tariffs (the what) if other countries adjust their tariffs (the when) . Another example of contingent legislation is the embargo acts that allow the president to prohibit shipment of certain goods (the what) to certain nations if those nations violate American neutrality or do some other specified thing in international relations (the when) .

Perhaps the first encounter by the U.S. Supreme Court with this sort of legislation was in 1813 when the court upheld its constitutionality in *The Brig Aurora*, 7 Cranch 382. That case concerned a federal law putting restraints on British shipping if and when the president found that certain specific situations occurred. Today an important use of contingent legislation is to provide for activation of statues when and if the president declares the existence of a national emergency. Many of these emergency statutes give additional power to the president himself. There may be seven or eight dozen such statutes waiting like a mothball fleet for activation in time of emergency.

Power to Supplement Statutory Provisions: The power to "fill up the details" of statutes, as Marshall described it in *Wayman* v. *Southard*, 10 Wheat. 1 (1825), is a second general species of quasi-legislative power. The administrative rules or findings which supplement statutes are often referred to as subordinate legislation. Some subordinate legislation is directed to the general public and some is directed to particular persons or parties. The latter, such as rate-making for utilities, smacks of adjudication and is usually required to be done after fair notice and hearing.

Of course, there are thousands of examples of subordinate legislation and I will cite only a few here for illustration. It would be subordinate legislation if, under the Federal Aviation Act, the Administrator of the Federal Aviation Administration, in pursuance of his authority to regulate air commerce in such manner as to best promote its development and safety, makes a rule prohibiting passengers from carrying bombs aboard commercial airliners.

Other examples of subordinate legislation drawn at random include delegation to administrative officials of authority to make rules governing the use of forest reservations; permitting reasonable variations and tolerances in the marking of food packages to disclose their contents; designating tobacco markets at which grading of tobacco would be compulsory; establishing priorities for the transportation of freight during a period of emergency; prescribing price schedules for the distribution of milk, or for other commodities in time of war; regulating wages and prices in the production and distribution of coal; and prescribing methods of accounting for carriers in interstate commerce.

In upholding the constitutionality of this sort of delegation of power, the U.S. Supreme Court through Justice Marshall said in *Wayman* v. *Southard,* that Congress was justified in delegating power over matters of "less interest," but that it would be a violation of separation of powers if Congress delegated power over "important" subjects. To quote Marshall, "The line has not been exactly drawn which separates those important subjects, which must be entirely regulated by the legislature itself, from those of less interest, in which a general provision may be made, and power given to those who are to act under such general provisions, to fill up the details." If the line was difficult to draw in 1825, it is no easier today. And if the line is supposed to be drawn between important and less important matters, it has been drawn by a blind man, for administrative decisions today affect gigantic interests dwarfing many things done directly by Congress.

An interesting variation of subordinate legislation is what might be called classification. From time to time a legislative body will say something like this to an agency, "We want you to decide which drugs are (1) pure and safe, (2) impure and unsafe, (3) doubtful and for experimental use only." The statute then goes on to say how these different categories are to be dealt with. The agency is asked to regulate through the process of classification. The federal Food and Drug Administration is notable for its use of classification as a regulatory device.

Chapter 5

Can Rule-Making Be Made Democratic?

☆ ☆ ☆

FEW RULE-MAKING RULES:

Administrative rule-making is much freer from procedural restrictions than is administrative adjudication. It has far fewer constitutional and statutory "t's" to cross and "i's" to dot. The law is more zealous about protecting people as individuals than people as part of the public. Courts seldom question the *procedure* of a legislature (partly for political reasons) and they seldom try to impose any particular procedure on the rule-making function of agencies except those few procedures required by statutes. This contrasts with the great concern of courts over *adjudicatory* procedure.

There are some statutes which govern quasi-legislative procedure, including state and federal administrative procedure acts. But these are far more skeletal than statutes governing quasi-adjudication. The U.S. Administrative Procedure Act gives only one-tenth of its space to rule-making.

Agencies themselves make some procedural rules governing their own rule-making process, but these are also relatively brief. The "Practice and Procedure" part of the Federal Communications Commission book of rules and regulations (Volume 1, part 1) is about seventy pages long. Less than two of those pages concern rule-making proceedings, while most of the rest concerns adjudication.

WHY ARE RULE-MAKING RULES SO SKELETAL?

For reasons of sheer practicality, the law hardly ever requires legislators or quasi-legislators to give a full hearing to everyone affected by their proposed ordinances. Occasionally, however, legislatures will require by statute that certain rules be made on the record after opportunity for an agency hearing. If so, administrative procedure acts usually require that the hearing be conducted like a regular adjudicatory hearing. But this is rare, and it must be rare for there would not be time for hearings on all legislation.

Congress cannot listen to tens of millions of people, nor can administrative agencies. The direct immediate parties to adjudication, on the other hand, are usually very few and they can be heard, while those immediately and directly affected by legislation are too legion to be heard. (Admittedly, those ultimately affected by adjudication are also legion.)

Common law does not require a lawmaker (by that is meant a statute maker or an ordinance maker or a rule maker) to listen. Nor does the U.S. Constitution. However, the U.S. Administrative Procedure Act does require agencies in most situations to give advanced notice in the *Federal Register* of its intention to make a rule, and after such notice has been given the agency is required by the act to afford interested persons an opportunity to participate in the rule-making by giving their views. (The agency may require these views to be in writing.) The agency is then required by the act to consider those views, but it is not required to be influenced. There is no general doctrine requiring the agency rule, when it is finally made, to rest upon evidence presented as there is in adjudicatory decisions.

The rules which federal agencies adopt to govern their own rule-making procedure generally reiterate the provisions just described of the administrative procedure act, and seldom go further into

96

detail. The Federal Communications Commission rules for rule-making described earlier do not, for example, really add anything significant beyond the brief APA requirements. Nor do state administrative procedure acts go much beyond the federal act, nor does the Uniform Law Commissioners' Revised Model State Administrative Procedure Act of 1961 (although the model act does require the agency to grant an *oral*, and therefore time consuming, hearing if requested by twenty-five or more persons).

A second reason for the brevity of rule-making rules is the fear that if rule-making becomes too encrusted with procedural arthritis and made difficult, it will drive rule-making underground. Examples of underground rule-making are to be seen on college campuses (among many other places) in situations where administrators will enforce their own private rules about various matters (such as the maximum size of classes) rather than suffering the pain and effort of formal establishment of such rules through the ponderous committee machinery of a typical college. Procedure can be its own worst enemy, for when it becomes too mountainous, people begin to tunnel under or skirt around it.

A third reason for brevity of rule-making rules in administrative procedure acts is that the basic purpose of the administrative process is to *simplify* procedure and to make it more *flexible*. Complexity in an administrative procedure act defeats those goals.

Among state administrative procedure acts, the Georgia Act is an example of one which sets forth rule-making procedures more elaborately than usual.

The American Bar Association appears to favor more rule-making procedure, judging by the Association's past legislative proposals for revising the federal APA.

A NOTE ON REFERENCES TO ADMINISTRATIVE PROCEDURE ACTS:

Let us digress here for a moment. I have referred, and will continue to refer to the federal Administrative Procedure Act and to the Revised Model State Administrative Procedure Act. It seems most sensible to cite these acts for illustrative purposes in this book rather than to cite individual state acts, although occasionally some of the peculiarities of various state acts will be pointed out. The federal law is obviously of general interest, and the model act is a prototype state law. Citations could be drawn from the administrative procedure acts of the various states, but that seems less desirable than reference to the model act. Most of the state acts are largely or partly based on the model act.

A majority of the states have administrative procedure acts. The purpose of an administrative procedure act is primarily (1) to produce substantial uniformity among a state's various agencies in their rule-making and adjudicatory procedures, and (2) to improve those procedures. Currently there is progress toward enactment of administrative procedure acts in many states, and where such acts already exist they are under constant study by legal scholars, by committees of the bar, by legislative committees, and by others. Among the states which have administrative procedure acts (acts which go under various titles) are North Dakota, Wisconsin, North Carolina, Ohio, Virginia, California, Pennsylvania, Missouri, Indiana, Michigan, Massachusetts, Oklahoma, Arkansas, Georgia, Maine, Illinois, Colorado, and West Virginia.

The absence of an administrative procedure act in any state does not mean there is no administrative procedure there, nor does it mean that existing procedures are unfair. What it probably means most of all is that state agency procedures conform substantially to accepted principles of fairness and that various groups (including lawyers who specialize in practice before certain agencies, especially those who practice before public utility commissions and workmens' compensation commissions) do not want to upset familiar procedures with reform and change. The agencies themselves have frequently opposed administrative procedure acts for similar reasons.

Local governments seldom have administrative procedure acts. This may seem strange since their administrative procedures are more likely to be informal and imprecise and unfair than those of state agencies. But there is less interest among practicing attorneys in local procedure, possibly because practice before local agencies is so sporadic and temporary: the heavy artillery of legal reform has not considered local procedure a priority target. However, there is an ever-increasing level of attention being paid to local administrative procedure, particularly in the states with heavily urbanized areas.

DEMOCRACY NEEDS RESPONSIVE ADMINISTRATORS:

It is necessary in a democracy for lawmakers (including rule-makers) to be responsive to the public. Formal rule-making rules alone will not produce responsive administrators (who make most of the statutory law in this country).

The problem of administrative responsiveness is particularly serious because administrators are not ordinarily elected. They are appointed. Of course, state and national chief executives are elected, but most of the appointments they make and rules they promulgate are actually made by assistants and advisors. A governor or a president may influence broad policy in a few spheres that interest him or in crisis matters, but one man cannot really control the thousand-and-one things that modern governments do, or the hundreds of thousands of people who do them. There are too many things for any human being to know about and too many people and agencies for any human being to supervise. This means that most decisions are made down the line by people who are not elected or adequately supervised by elected officials. These lower echelon people are made all the more independent by the fact that they are ordinarily tenured and can hardly be fired.

Without doubt the overshadowing question of modern democracy is: How can the public control administrators? The question becomes more critical as administrators are given more and more legislative work to do, and as the work of government becomes so complicated that legislatures and the public are baffled by it. Legislators are too much in the dark to ask intelligent questions about what administrators are doing, and even if they were not in the dark they would not have *time* to ask intelligent questions (or time to receive the answers) about what administrators are doing. This is not intended to be a slur upon elected legislators. Rather, it is a commentary on these times which are technological beyond belief.

HOW CAN ADMINISTRATION BE MADE DEMOCRATIC?

Under the circumstances, if there is to be democratic procedure within the enormous piece of the law-making function which is controlled by administrators it must be for the most part invented, fostered, practiced, championed by the administrators themselves.

Democratic administration is the phrase used to describe that kind of democracy. It is a method of carrying on the administrative process in such a way as to encourage participation or at least the sense of participation in the decision-making process by those affected by the decision. *Consultation* is the heart of democratic administration.

An administrator who wishes to proceed democratically need not call an election every time something is to be done. Administrators are not asked to be impractical, nor to be fools in order to be democratic.

Perhaps the classroom itself is a good place to find a meaningful example of how democratic administration might work if the professor were so minded and had the time. A professor (who, after all, is an administrator of his class) can be very democratic about things without calling elections. Before setting the date of an examination he might encourage discussion of its timing, etc. More significantly, he might try to use the Socratic method in class and allow the principal lessons to emerge or seem to emerge from the students themselves. It may be that this classroom democracy is in some cases only a slick performance by the professor to swindle students into believing they are having something to say about the lessons they are to learn or things to do, but, deception or not, its effect can be good. People respond when they believe they are participating in decision-making that affects them. That belief may be based on fact or fiction (hopefully, fact), but the belief is important. Some professors find it difficult to be democratic owing to a prison warden view of education which enthrones the order-giving, lesson-giving ego of the teacher and squelches the ego of the order-taking student. But autocratic administration of a class or of anything else is likely to be inefficient and expensive, no matter how self-satisfying it may be to the autocrat himself.

Democratic administration does not mean weakness. It is not weakness to solicit people's opinions or to make subordinates feel they are participating. Most students and employees can testify that they work harder under supervision that is encouraging rather than repressive. Nor does democratic administration imply weak enforcement of rules once made.

PROFESSIONALISM:

It is hardly possible to force administrators by statute to be democratic. Democracy in administration depends very much upon the heart of the administrator. He must want to be democratic if there is to be much democracy. There is no statute that can make an autocratic heart democratic, although statutes can tell administrators how to be democratic if they want to be, and can also require them to follow a few democratic routines even if they do not have a democratic heart.

Disregarding statutory requirements for the moment, how can administrators be encouraged down democratic paths? The answer lies partly in professionalization of administration, and by that is meant the development of ethical and professional standards within the profession, a development which is fostered to a very large degree at the institutions of education through which candidates for the profession should pass. Graduate and undergraduate schools of public administration can help create democratic procedures in administration by teaching it and urging it. A professional education should include it perhaps as part of the ethics of administration. That element in a public administrator's education may be the last best hope for the preservation of anything really approaching democracy in a modern technological state.

SOME SPECIFIC TECHNIQUES OF DEMOCRACY IN ADMINISTRATIVE LAW-MAKING:

Notice of Proposed Rule-Making: If the public is to participate in rule-making it needs to know in advance what new rules are under consideration. This is elementary. The requirement of antecedent publicity is absolutely central to democratic administration, and is, in fact, an unparalleled condition precedent to public participation. All administrative procedure acts worthy of the name include something about prior notice of proposed rule-making. The federal APA does require prior notice, but fails to say exactly how much. The Revised Model State APA specifies twenty days.

There are circumstances in which prior notice is not required.

IN EMERGENCIES: Regulations of such urgency that there is no time for notice and hearing are exempt from prior notice and hearing. The federal APA does not require any kind of notice at all in emergency cases. The Revised Model State APA requires an agency issuing an emergency rule to give notice and accord interested parties an opportunity to present views within 120 days after adoption of an emergency rule.

WHERE IMPRACTICAL OR CONTRARY TO THE PUBLIC INTEREST: Various sorts of impracticality may also justify issuance of rules without notice of proposed rule-making. Under the federal APA each agency determines for itself what is impractical or contrary to the public interest. Certainly there are such situations. For example, in the case of Securities and Exchange Commission regulations there is no doubt that advanced notice that a new rule is about to be made might have an impact on the market contrary to the public interest. The Revised Model State APA takes care of this problem under the emergency rule clause, which gives parties an opportunity to present views within 120 days after adoption of the rule. The federal APA does not have any provision for subsequent notice and hearing.

There is room to question whether it is a good idea to have a provision of any sort in an APA allowing exemptions for situations where advanced notice would be impractical or contrary to the public interest. Certainly some agencies in some situations should not have to give prior notice. But these exceptions should perhaps be in the separate statutes that relate to the powers and functions of the various agencies. The APA is supposed to be, or at least should be, a general statement and not one dealing with special situations, and an APA probably should not provide for exemptions available to any agency that wants to take them.

OTHER FORMS OF EXEMPTED RULE-MAKING: Agencies sometimes issue interpretive rules, that is, rules which interpret the statute under which the agency is operating, or which interpret a previous rule. Often APA's (such as the federal) do not require notice of proposed rule-making when an agency is making an interpretive rule. This is an unreasonable exclusion. These interpretations can have sweeping effect, as, for example, when an agency interprets a rule that prohibits bars within one block of a school to mean one block as the crow flies. The interpretation could very well put some people out of business. They have a right to know what interpretation the agency is contemplating. They who are about to be injured might want to present their views on the subject.

Agencies sometimes issue general policy statements which are not technically rules. The federal APA permits these to be issued without general notice of proposed rule-making. These policy statements may have sweeping effect. Why should agencies be permitted to issue policy statements without notice any more than they are permitted to issue rules without notice?

Agencies also issue rules of agency organization, procedure, and practice. Again the federal APA permits these to be issued without notice of proposed rule-making. Yet, why without notice? Why should not an agency let interested parties know how the boat is to be rocked by change? Lawyers, to mention one group, might have good reason to submit views on proposed changes in rules of practice and procedure.

The cause of democracy in rule-making is served by opening the doors of public participation as widely as possible. Where law allows an agency to omit notice of proposed rule-making, it makes more difficult the democratic process in administration. Although agencies are not required by the federal APA to give notice prior to issuance of policy statements, interpretive rules, or rules of agency organization, procedure, or practice, a few agencies give notice anyway. The Federal Power Commission, for example, gives notice on procedural rules; the Interstate Commerce Commission on general statements of policy; the Federal Communications Commission, Federal Trade Commission, Interstate Commerce Commission, and Securities and Exchange Commission on interpretive rules.

The federal APA allows still other exemptions. It says that when agencies make rules concerning their own personnel or management they do not have to tell anybody in advance. Why let agencies keep these things a secret? If an agency wants a rule requiring employees to wear neckties at work, why not give advance notice? There might be some people, including mainly the employees themselves, who would want to try to dissuade the agency from promulgating such a rule. I cannot see much justification for *any* rule-making without antecedent publicity except in emergencies or where advance notice would somehow hurt the public interest. Yet the federal APA goes further and exempts still other things from its rule-making procedures, including any matter relating to public property, loans, grants, benefits, and contracts. There is every reason to believe that members of the public might have some strong views and some useful views on questions relating to those matters. Why encourage arbitrary government by permitting all those vital economic transactions to go without any interested citizen having a chance to offer his view before the deal is closed? I can imagine that some people might be interested in knowing in advance that the Park Service is about to sell Old Faithful to a steam generating company.

The federal APA also exempts any military or naval or foreign affairs function from its rule-making provisions. We seem to be conditioned to think the armed forces can do no wrong and should not be interfered with, and that everything they do should be secret. But in this era when one of the biggest undertakings of the federal government is military, and when one of the biggest departments is Defense, there is reason to believe that democratic procedures should more than ever be insisted upon in all rule-making or policy-making that does not have to be kept secret—namely, most of it. What is so wrong with asking the Navy to let it be known in advance that it intends to let a contract for a bombtesting laboratory next door to a grade school, to conjure up an improbable example?

None of this means there has to be full formal hearings on everything. The APA does not require hearings in rule-making (though occasionally they may be desirable). The federal APA does require advance notice to interested parties to allow participation in the rule-making through submission of written data, views, or arguments. Agencies are not required by the act to hear anything orally, nor are they prohibited from holding oral hearings.

One of the most serious shortcomings of administrative procedure acts today, particularly state acts, is that many *agencies* are exempt from their provisions, often the biggest most important agencies. Michigan is typical. Among the agencies its APA does not cover are the Workmen's Compensation Commission, the Employment Security Commission, the Department of Revenue, and the Public Service Commission.

There is still much room for the improvement of administrative procedure acts where they exist. Progress among the states has been especially laggard, with isolated exceptions, of course. And it is precisely at the state and local level where the administrative process is most likely to be unfair because of the greater intimacy of human relationship in the conduct of business (the impersonality of larger bureaucracies in itself yields a kind of objectivity and unavoidable fairness), and because state and local agency heads are less likely to be lawyers. Parties are also more likely to be represented by nonlawyers. And when you have persons without legal training practicing before judges without legal training, all beneath a blanket of local intimacy you have a situation that cries for the guidance of clear-cut administrative procedure acts.

Opportunity to Present Views:

RIGHT TO PETITION: The federal and the Revised Model State APA's permit (as a general thing) any interested person to petition agencies requesting adoption, amendment, or repeal of a rule. The federal APA says nothing about what the agency must (or even should) do about such petitions. I should think it would be plain enough that anyone may petition any agency without an APA saying so. But I guess it does not do any harm, and may guide some innocents. The really important question is what sort of reception a petition will receive. The California APA says something about that by requiring agencies to answer petitions within thirty days by either denying them in writing or scheduling the matters for public hearing. The Revised Model State APA similarly requires agencies to do something with petitions.

CONSULTATION AND CONFERENCE: Agencies frequently establish committees of interested persons for regular advice and consultation, and/or agencies will confer with interested persons in other ways prior to promulgation of new rules.

Sometimes advisory committees for particular agencies are directly provided for by law, but more often the whole procedure of consultation is left up to the agency.

Of course, we have now touched the core of democratic administration, but consultation is generally defective as a democratic process in one remarkable way: it fails to consult the public and fails to adequately consider the public interest because the public is not organized.

I realize that social scientists bridle when they meet indefinable terms like public interest. I realize that it is hard to trap a definition of public. It is like trying to trap a cloud of gnats. Maybe it is true that the public interest is merely the sum total of the private special organized interests as it is currently popular to contend. But the public I am talking about when I contend that it is not often consulted or that its will is not sufficiently heard is the consumer, to use another inadequate word. The consumer is all of us, even including the producer who helps to consume his own product. I would put my money on a philosopher as the best person to represent the public interest or consumer interest or national interest. I know it is taking a chance. And let us defer the question of how philosopher is defined.

Organization is often a prerequisite to effective participation in politics. The organized interests are not only able to represent themselves, but also are eager and compulsive about doing so. The public, on the other hand, is essentially unorganized, yet its interest should, one would think, tower above all other interests in a democratic country.

Some attempts have been made to correct this deficiency of public representation by appointing persons to advisory boards to speak for the public. This is not especially satisfactory, however, because, to repeat, no one really knows what the public interest is, or can really define it.

According to one view, government officials themselves represent the public and there is therefore little need for public members on advisory boards. This is absolutely correct in theory and almost absolutely false in practice. Administrators respond to pressure much as legislators do, and if the public cannot invoke organized pressure then the public is a lost cause. Frankly, I do not believe the public's cause can be helped much by public members on advisory boards. They do not represent anything or anybody with strong teeth, and teeth are all that count in politics. But a public member might help some by trying to introduce the public's point of view, so to speak, into the conversation. He might in that sense have some baby teeth.

HEARINGS: While sometimes statutes will require administrators to hold hearings before making certain rules, this is not a common requirement.

Sometimes adversary procedure is employed in quasi-legislative hearings, particularly in rate regulation, but usually inquisitorial procedure is used. An adversary proceeding is one having opposing parties. As used here, adversary means the opposite of inquisitory. An inquisitorial proceeding, which is used as the main judicial technique over much of the non-English speaking world, *does* have parties, but the role of the parties in litigation is not emphasized and the role of the judge is stressed. Shorn of its dreadful reputation, an inquisition is simply a judicial inquiry, investigation, or inquest. Where the inquisitorial system prevails in the world it means purely that the judge takes the responsibility for seeing that all relevant facts are brought out during the trial. There *are* parties who have lawyers, but the evidence and information brought forward during the trial is by no means limited to that which the parties and their lawyers produce.

The adversary system, as a system, is not really interested in the "truth, the whole truth and nothing but the truth." It is more interested in truth as seen by two contesting parties, both of whom may be wrong. *Some* rule-making hearings are adversary, with the agency on one side and those hostile to the proposed agency rule on the other. But, to repeat, most rule-making hearings are inquisitorial, as are the hearings of Congress and other legislative bodies.

The federal APA does not require (though it permits) oral hearings in rule-making situations. Often there is no need for *oral* hearings because information on complex issues can often be presented best on the printed page. An oral hearing has little value except in situations where the demeanor of a witness is important in detecting the truth, as in criminal trials and administrative quasi-criminal trials.

The Legislative Veto: Although the administrative process is a way of relieving legislatures (and courts) of a burden they are not equipped to handle, this does not mean that legislatures must abandon their administrative creatures and leave them as orphans in the world. Legislators are the parents of the administrative process and in a democracy everything should be done to maintain reasonable parental authority over them, so long as the parents do not make insufferable nuisances of themselves. Of course, everyone knows that American legislatures try, as they should try under separation of powers, to compete with administrators for control of power. Legislators have been forced by the growing amount and complexity of law-making required in a technological world to surrender much power to administrators. In spite of that, legislatures still have ways of controlling or trying to control administrators. Some of those ways are ancient and some are new and evolving.

The classic techniques of legislative control of administration include: (1) control of executive organization and activities, (2) budgetary control, (3) control through the audit, (4) control through personnel legislation, and (5) control by investigation. Through these a legislature can influence the quasi-legislative activities of administrators along with everything else administrators do. There is no room here to discuss those five.

A sixth (and somewhat newer) technique is the legislative veto. Through it a legislative body may attempt to place itself directly in the production line of rules and regulations between the agency and the public. A legislative body would be establishing a legislative veto if it said to an administrator, "You go ahead and handle a certain problem, but before you may do certain things you must first tell us and if we don't say 'no' within a certain length of time then you may go ahead and do it." Or, in other words, the legislature tells the administrator to do certain things, but reserves the right to veto his action.

To some this may not seem new. Legislatures have always had the right to change or reverse almost anything an administrator does by simply passing a law. Therefore, how is the legislative veto an improvement? It is an improvement because its procedure is easier, quicker, more practical, and more workable than the procedure of passing a new law.

A legislative veto is ordinarily accomplished by *resolution* of some type. Congress employs various kinds of resolutions for various purposes:

Simple Resolution: A simple resolution deals with matters entirely within the prerogatives of one house or the other. It requires neither passage by the other chamber nor approval by the president and does not have the force of law. Most resolutions deal with the rules of one house. They are also used to express the sentiments of a single house, as condolences to the family of a deceased member or to give advice on foreign policy or other executive business.

Concurrent Resolution: A concurrent resolution must be passed by both houses but does not require the signature of the president and does not have the force of law. Concurrent resolutions generally are used to make or amend rules applicable to both houses or to express the sentiment of the two houses. A concurrent resolution, for example, is used to fix the time for adjournment of a Congress. It might also be used to convey the congratulations of Congress to another country on the anniversary of its independence.

Joint Resolution: A joint resolution requires the approval of both houses and the signature of the president, just as a bill does, and has the force of law if approved. There is no real difference between a bill and a joint resolution. The latter is generally used in dealing with limited matters, such as a single appropriation for a specific purpose or the granting of congressional approval for executive actions—for example, international executive agreements.

For purposes of legislative veto, the joint resolution is not used because it requires a presidential signature. Concurrent and simple resolutions do not need presidential signatures, and are therefore ideal for vetoing the president and the executive branch because there is no possibility of a presidential veto of a legislative veto.

In American government the legislative veto is not at present a very commonly employed procedure. Hostility to it at the federal level has come, as might be expected, from the White House, and not alone because it permits legislative escape from the presidential veto, but also because it has been viewed by presidents as an interference with the proper role of the executive.

The legislative veto is of recent origin. Congress experimented with it apparently for the first time in 1932 when it enacted a bill authorizing the president to reorganize departments and agencies. The authority was made subject to the provision that the president's reorganization orders must be submitted to Congress sixty days before going into effect and could be set aside by a *resolution of either house.*

The nature of the veto was altered by Congress in 1939. Rather than vetoing executive orders (a practice alleged to be an unconstitutional invasion of executive power), the Congress would henceforth veto only plans. The president was required to submit reorganization plans instead of executive orders to Congress. These plans could be set aside within sixty days by a concurrent resolution. Presumably the use of a *concurrent resolution,* rather than the 1932 act's *resolution of either house,* was to further strengthen the constitutionality of the whole procedure by making the veto procedure more like the procedure of a regular bill (both houses involved and in agreement).

Since its first use to veto reorganization plans and orders, the legislative veto has been employed with increasing regularity by Congress in other matters.

A new development '(since 1944) is *legislative veto by committee.* It was first employed under a statute passed in 1944 which required the Secretary of the Navy to "come into agreement" with the Naval Affairs Committee of *each* House before entering into certain real estate transactions. Of course, it is not new for legislative committees to have large influence over agencies, but it *is* new for committee action to be made a formal condition precedent to the execution of administrative acts.

A 1949 act required the Armed Services Committees to agree to acquisitions of certain kinds of land before the government could acquire it.

Presidents have fought these "come into agreement with a committee" provisions of statutes, just as they have opposed the legislative veto generally. Eisenhower vetoed several bills with such provisions on grounds of unconstitutionality. One veto message said, "The bill would violate the fundamental principle of separation of powers. . ." (House Document 430, 83d Cong., 2d Sess.). As for the issue of constitutionality, at least two things must be said in defense of the legislative veto. First, while the legislature may be exercising administrative authority contrary to the Constitution, it is no worse in degree or in kind than the wholesale exercise of quasi-legislative authority by administrators. Second, since Congress grants authority to administrative officers, it may impose such conditions on the use of that authority as it wishes. Yet, on the other hand, it can be argued that once Congress has created an executive function, Congress may not violate the Constitution by seeking to formally participate in the exercise of that authority.

As for the veto by committee, it is also open to constitutional objection on grounds that the Constitution does not permit a committee of Congress to make final determinations on behalf of Congress. The simple resolution of each house method is open to constitutional objection on the same grounds, i.e., one house may not act for the whole Congress.

A method of legislative control over administration which approaches but does not quite reach the status of legislative veto is what might be called the requirement of advance reports. An example of this was an act of 1927 which provided that tax refunds of more than $75,000 had to be reported to the Joint Committee on Internal Revenue Taxation sixty days before being paid. This gave the Committee time to refuse to approve payment if it so desired. That provision is still in effect.

The Nuclear Regulatory Commission is a leading example today of an agency whose functions are closely supervised by a congressional committee by the requirement of advance reports.

The legislative veto is easily capable of being misused by being turned into a huge nuisance. However, if used responsibly it can restore to the people's representatives a deft and easy way of putting a stop to offensive administrative actions or rules. Thereby, representative government and democratic safeguards can better survive.

By 1977, thirty-four states had some form of legislative review of administrative regulations. Ohio agencies, for example, must lay proposed regulations before the legislature sixty days before adoption. A joint committee reviews them. If the committee objects to any rule, it forwards its recommendations to the full legislature, which can amend or modify, but must act within the aforesaid sixty days or else the rule becomes effective as proposed by the agency. The South Carolina legislature operates in a similar way, but uses standing committees rather than a joint committee, and allows ninety days for legislative action. In some states the power of the legislature is limited to making comments or observations on proposed rules, although, of course, all legislatures have the power to amend any statute under which an objectionable rule may have been promulgated, whether or not they have power to amend or quash the rule itself. The Revised Model State APA does not provide for legislative review of rules, nor does the federal APA.

Deferred Effectiveness and Publication: To give the public or any affected part of it an opportunity to learn of rules before they are enforced, and to give those affected an opportunity to lodge eleventh hour protests, the federal APA requires publication of rules thirty days before they become effective. The Revised Model State APA has comparable provisions. Federal rules and regulations are first published in the *Federal Register*, a daily publication which is periodically codified into the *Code of Federal Regulations*. Most states have some sort of filing system, many requiring all rules to be filed with the Secretary of State prior to their becoming effective. Courts tend to give very strict construction to these filing requirements.

Lawyers and the public can be exceedingly inconvenienced in their dealings with the multitude of agencies by their various organizational forms and procedural rules. Therefore the federal APA and the Revised Model State APA both require agencies to publish descriptions of their organization and procedure.

It would also help if agencies were required periodically to publish codifications of the policies they develop through adjudication and through other methods whose product is not required to be published.

In 1966 a Freedom of Information Act (5 U.S.C. § 552 [see Appendix A of this book]) was passed and made part of the federal Administrative Procedure Act. It supersedes the old public information section of the federal APA. Like its predecessor, the Freedom of Information Act requires publication in the *Federal Register* of the substantive rules made by each agency and also a description of the agency's organization and procedure, and all final orders in adjudicated cases. The 1966 act is an improvement over its predecessor insofar as it specifies more things to be made public, such as statements of policy and certain staff manuals that affect the public. However, the main contribution of the new act is to make public access to agency records the rule rather than the exception. No longer do persons need to be "properly and directly concerned" as the old act required (60 Stat. 237). Now every agency must make records (with some exceptions) "promptly available to *any person*" (5 U.S.C. § 552 [italics added]) whether he has a proper concern or is just a meddlesome troublemaker. The act also requires agencies to publish an index of their records to help people find out what is available.

The Freedom of Information Act of 1966 fortifies persons requesting information by conferring upon them standing in court to ask for an injunction ordering the agency to cease withholding records improperly withheld from the complainant. Furthermore, the act gives precedence on the docket of the court over everything else and requires the court to expedite the case in every way and to hold a hearing on the suit for an injunction at the earliest practicable date. This rather startling act goes still further and places the burden of proof upon the agency to demonstrate that it legally withheld the requested records. Normally, in court actions the burden of proof is upon the initiator of litigation.

Of course, the act provides some legal excuses for an agency to withhold certain records, and, as a matter of fact, some people think the exceptions almost nullify the grandiose purposes of the act. Whether that be true, certainly governments should not be compelled to reveal *all* their records—defense secrets, medical files, FBI files and the like. It is going to be extremely difficult to administer the Freedom of Information Act of 1966. The colossal importance of opening public business for public inspection in a democracy is balanced by the enormous importance of keeping many kinds of records secret.

Judicial Review: Courts are important in forcing the agencies to do the things required of them. For instance, they will not enforce a rule that has not been published, unless it is one of the exempted variety. Courts are among the pillars supporting the democratic process. They may nullify rules made without adherence to required procedures. The Florida administrative procedure act wisely provides that "only rules adopted by an agency in the manner and form provided . . . shall be valid or effective." And the Revised Model State APA similarly provides that "no rule hereafter adopted is valid unless adopted in substantial compliance with this section." When courts enforce these provisions and any other fair procedure they are supporting the democratic process. Administrative procedure acts should be as clear as possible so that courts can be decisive in upholding them. Judicial review is further discussed in Chapter 7.

Miscellaneous: Democracy in administrative rule-making should be encouraged, even if it cannot always be successfully commanded. There are various techniques already discussed for throwing open the doors for public participation. Other things could also be done. For example, agencies might be encouraged if not required to maintain a public docket showing the status of rule-making proposals. Agencies might be encouraged to use rule-making for policy formulation rather than adjudication, and if adjudication is relied upon let there be periodic codification of the policies enunciated in that way.

Chapter 6

Fairness in Administrative Adjudication

☆ ☆ ☆

DEFINITION:

The definition of the term judicial power is uncertain. When you boil it down, judicial power is the power to do whatever courts do, a court being any agency so designated by statute, ordinance, or constitution. Now, since adjudicate means to exercise judicial authority, perhaps the best definition of administrative adjudication is that it is the power of administrative agencies to do the same species of work courts do.

Primarily, courts settle controversies among named parties and determine legal rights and obligations of the parties on the points in dispute. Many administrative agencies do the same thing. The disputes which administrative agencies settle by formal adjudication are usually disputes between citizens on the one hand and their government (or one of its agencies or officers) on the other.

FORMAL AND INFORMAL ADJUDICATION:

Administrative adjudication may be either formal or informal. Formality implies a hearing which meets the statutory and constitutional requirements of a fair hearing: right to an oral hearing, right to counsel, right to present evidence and to rebut evidence, right to cross-examine witnesses, and right to have the decision based only upon known evidence. Informality implies settlement of disputes in any less ceremonial way satisfactory to the parties, usually by conversation, conference, interview, inspection, and informal correspondence.

INFORMAL ADMINISTRATIVE ADJUDICATION:

The overwhelming mass of administrative adjudication is informal. Most administrative adjudication begins informally and continues that way for a while even if it ends in a formal hearing. The process seldom becomes formal until a private party feels strongly enough to pursue a dispute up the agency hierarchy or until the agency itself initiates formal hearings. Ordinarily (almost always) a private party will not contest the answer given upon his initial contact with the agency and will let matters drop. For example, most income tax payers do not argue very long or hard with the Internal Revenue Service. This reluctance to contest agency decisions or agency contentions has several causes. First, those decisions mostly involve small matters not worth the time, effort, and expense of a full-scale battle. Second, most Americans probably do not know they have a right to a formal hearing or that they have a right to contest agency decisions through processes within the agency and in the courts. Third, most people seem to be too timid to argue with the majesty of a government agency. Fourth, most people rightly feel they do not have the facts or expertise to successfully argue with an agency. No doubt there are other reasons why people do not fight city hall.

It is not easy to get statistics on the amount of informal adjudication going on because, in a sense, it goes on just about every time a bureaucrat answers a question. We can get some hint as to the magnitude of the informal process by simply looking at the volume of people who have reason to communicate with government about their rights and duties. To pick one federal agency at random, the Veterans Administration administers benefits which potentially may be given to over eighty million persons, if both veterans and their families are counted. There are about twenty-two million veterans. The benefits administered are roughly these: compensation for service-connected disability or death; dependency and indemnity compensation; vocational rehabilitation for service-connected disability; education and training; war orphans' educational assistance, guaranty or insurance of home, farm, and business loans, and, under certain conditions, direct home loans; United States government and national service life insurance; insurance indemnity; hospitalization; domiciliary care; outpatient medical and dental care for service-connected disability; prosthetic and other appliances; special housing for certain seriously disabled veterans; automobiles or other conveyances for certain disabled veterans; World War I adjusted service certificates; a guardianship program for the protection of estates derived from Veterans Administration benefits paid to incompetent or minor beneficiaries; burial allowances; and burial flags. In addition, the Veterans Administration administers the insurance section of the Soldiers' and Sailors' Civil Relief Act for persons in active military service.

It requires no soaring imagination to guess at the volume of people who each day contact the Veterans Administration for information relative to their participation in various veterans' benefits. Yearly the VA conducts around eight million interviews with applicants, five million of them in person and three million over the phone. No one knows exactly where supplying information ends and adjudication begins. We can only guess. We know that most people are satisfied with the answers they get from the Veterans Administration contact personnel. For those who are not satisfied and who wish to contest a point there is appellate procedure within the VA, although this too is rather informal. In fact, by way of footnote, formal appellate procedure is not constitutionally required in the VA because there is no constitutional right to any hearing at all where benefits rather than rights are involved. The VA is largely in the benefit business, and to deny a benefit is not to

117

deny a right. Even though there is no constitutional right to a hearing where benefits are granted, there may be a statutory right, or an agency may voluntarily provide for hearings which include some or all of the procedures implicit in constitutional due process.

When someone wants to contest a point originally determined by the contact person the adjudication division of the regional VA office takes over, and through correspondence, obtains the evidence necessary for proper adjudication. The board within the VA (the Rating Board in the case of some claims) determines the issue.

Federal statutes do not require judicial review of these VA decisions (except where claims on insurance contracts are concerned) and there is no currently recognized constitutional right to judicial review in benefit cases.

Of course, the informal process also goes on massively in other government agencies such as, for example, the Bureau of Old Age and Survivors' Insurance within the Social Security Administration. Tens of millions of Americans are covered by social security, and there are, as one can easily imagine, hundreds of thousands of inquiries about such things as whether or not a person is entitled to certain benefits, the amount of the benefit, the month in which benefits begin, etc. As in the Veterans Administration, decision is made by the initial contact person in the agency, and only a tiny handful of applicants are disposed to appeal beyond his determination.

The Internal Revenue Service also does business with tens of millions of Americans. When the IRS disagrees with an individual's income tax return, the individual will be asked to come to an IRS office where the matter is discussed by the initial contact person. Almost all of those cases are settled then and there, and most people are not disposed to argue the case beyond the contact person and indeed, as said before, most Americans do not have the remotest idea that any avenues exist beyond the contact person.

THE PURE ADMINISTRATIVE PROCESS:

The term pure administrative process has been invented as a label for a process of informal administrative adjudication in which there is no argument, so to speak, but only reference to technical data. That is, if someone claims he is entitled to the Veterans Administration's G.I. educational benefit, there really is not much to argue about. The facts usually speak for themselves, and there is little debate over what are facts: either the applicant did or did not serve in the armed forces, etc.

On the other hand, where the facts are not so clear-cut, where adjudication involves an assessment of evidence, as for example where a board of medical examiners is trying to determine whether a certain doctor did or did not engage in unethical advertising, the adjudicator must exercise his talents of judgment and good sense. Evaluation of evidence is not so important in the pure administrative process. The evidence is clear and simple.

Just why the term pure was seized upon to describe that process is not clear, although the term seems to imply that the talents of the administrator as opposed to those of a judge are called primarily into play.

SHORTENED PROCEDURE: UNION OF FORMAL AND INFORMAL ADMINISTRATIVE ADJUDICATION:

Formal administrative adjudication is growing less and less formal in some jurisdictions through the introduction of various systems for shortening the formal process. One of these is the prehearing conference recommended by the President's Conference on Administrative Procedure in 1953.

The administrative prehearing conference is an adaptation of the judicial prehearing conference as set forth in Rule 16 of the *Federal Rules of Civil Procedure* which provides that:

In any action, the court may in its discretion direct the attorneys for the parties to appear before it for a conference to consider:

(1) The simplification of the issues.

(2) The necessity or desirability of amendments to the pleadings.

(3) The possibility of obtaining admissions of fact and of documents which will avoid unnecessary proof.

(4) The limitation of the number of expert witnesses.

(5) The advisability of a preliminary reference of issues to a master for findings to be used as evidence when the trial is to be by jury.

(6) Such other matters as may aid in the disposition of the action.

Of course, the object of prehearing conferences, in a nutshell is "the achievement of smaller records in shorter and less expensive hearings, and thus the gain of quicker and more certain justice for those citizens who toil in the mazes of hearing proceedings," in the words of J. D. Bond, an FCC hearing examiner, writing in 13 *Journal of the Federal Communications Bar Association* 55 (1953).

Some methods of shortening formal proceedings depend upon consent of the parties. For example, formal procedure can be simplified if the parties will agree to forego an *oral* hearing and permit the whole formal proceeding to be conducted in writing.

FORMAL PROCEDURE:

Almost everyone believes that it is fair to listen to an accused before passing sentence, and fair to give the accused adequate advance notice of the time and place of the hearing and of the nature of the charges so that he may prepare his answer. If there is such a thing as *natural law* in the world (i.e., law that appeals to nearly everyone's sense of justice) then surely the law of notice and hearing are a central part of it. Someone's legal rights and/or legal obligations are normally at issue in administrative adjudication. Justice requires that parties be given an opportunity to defend their claims. In formal administrative adjudication that opportunity is afforded by a formal hearing or, in other words, by a hearing which provides the full array of procedure designed to encourage fairness. In many cases the courts have spelled out quite lucidly the basic elements of a fair hearing. The U.S. Constitution, as interpreted by the U.S. Supreme Court, holds that a person ordinarily has a right to a hearing if he wants one (and to a hearing which is fair), before any administrative agency does anything that would adversely and uniquely affect him. The Constitution provides this right to a fair hearing in the due process clauses of the Fifth and Fourteenth Amendments, which say that no government or government agency in the United States may deprive any person of life, liberty, or property without due process of law.

LEGISLATION VERSUS ADJUDICATION:

As previously explained, courts have held that due process of law means a right to a hearing in *judicial* proceedings, but not in *legislative* proceedings. It is therefore important for an administrator to know the difference between quasi-legislative acts and quasi-judicial acts so that he may know when he is constitutionally required to hold a hearing.

Past-Future Theory: What is legislative and what is judicial? How do they differ? According to one theory which at first blush seems correct, but which leaves must be desired on closer observation, is this: legislation concerns *future* behavior (a law says "do something beginning now, or next week, or next month, or . . .") while adjudication concerns *past* behavior (it asks, "was that behavior against the law?").

The flaw in that theory is that a judgment about the legality of past behavior actually determines the legality of future behavior. Our entire system of common law rests upon the doctrine of stare decisis under which the courts will tomorrow follow the precedent of today. Today's decision affects tomorrow's. Today's decision may place a new interpretation upon law which has the same effect as creating new law. This is so true, that one could reasonably argue that the courts are the chief lawmakers of the land. In fact, more than one expert has declared that 90 per cent of American law is common law (judge-made law). An outstanding example of that is the Supreme Court's decision in 1954 declaring racial segregation in the public schools unconstitutional. The future behavior of school boards was affected in a cataclysmic way by a decision which technically concerned only the past behavior of the three or four school boards involved in that case.

Naturally, it is true that judicial decisions direct themselves in their *immediate* application to the *parties* to the case, whose action *was* in the past. In that narrow sense the past-future theory is correct.

The General-Specific Theory: A second theory distinguishes between legislative and judicial this way: Legislation, it says, addresses itself to a general category or class of parties without naming any particular party. Adjudication, by contrast, names the parties, or if they are not named they are a few parties who are readily identifiable by their relation to the property or interests affected by the adjudication. The general-specific theory resolves itself into a many-few theory, and the problem is to determine how few is few and how many is many. (See the cases of *Bi-Metallic Co.* v. *Colorado,* 239 U.S. 441, and *Londoner* v. *Denver,* 210 U.S. 373.) And a serious flaw in the theory is that while the initial impact of adjudication is directly upon *named parties* or upon parties readily identifiable, the impact radiates to a general unspecified group of people.

What is the answer? There is no answer, no clean-cut way of separating legislative from judicial by definition. The past-future theory combined with the general-specific theory serve in their limited way for most occasions. But in the final analysis, notice and hearing are constitutionally required where the courts *think* they should be required, for only the courts are in a position to enforce the constitution. If an administrator wants to know whether to hold a hearing, let him be a good guesser. Even lawyers have to guess what the courts might say. Courts themselves have evidently been unsure which theory to use. They have chosen, for example, to consider rate-making to be legislation even though rate-making initially affects only a *few* public utilities which are readily identifiable. Of course, rate-making also affects a large general group of rate payers, and that no doubt is why courts have come down on the side of legislation. Rate payers are *not* few, even if utilities are. But is it not true that most administrative acts which at first touch directly on a few, ultimately affect many? And if so, could not nearly all administrative action be called legislation?

EXCEPTIONS TO THE REQUIREMENT
OF PRIOR HEARING:

Decisions of Slight Affect: The courts are less inclined to insist upon notice and hearing when the regulation has slight effect upon the income and expenses of regulated firms, even though the number of firms are a named few, or are readily identifiable. The judicial disposition to exact the protection of notice and hearing rises in direct proportion to the extent to which a regulation affects the finances of business establishments covered.

Emergency Situations: Clearly it would not be in the public interest to permit a grave threat to public safety to go unchecked solely in order to take time to hold a public hearing. Courts permit administrators to seize and/or destroy property without a hearing in emergencies. The United States Supreme Court in *North American Cold Storage Co.* v. *Chicago,* 211 U.S. 306 (1908), upheld the validity of an ordinance providing for the summary seizure and destruction of food (putrid chickens) unfit for human consumption.

How serious must an emergency be in order to justify summary action? This is simply a matter of discretion. Courts hold pretty tight reign on use of summary power by administrators. If an affected party feels that a certain summary action was not justified as an emergency measure, the party can ask the courts to reverse the administrator on grounds that he has acted arbitrarily, unfairly, and without due process. But it is not sufficient for the courts merely to declare that a summary act was illegal, for the act may have involved destruction of property or other loss. In that case, the aggrieved party may bring a damage suit against the public official who acted illegally, if, for example, chickens summarily seized and destroyed were not actually putrid and the officials were in error, a remedy for the loss would lie in a civil suit for damages in a court. In other words, the hearing in emergency cases may come in court *after* instead of *before* the emergency act, if the adversely affected party believes he was dealt with unfairly and illegally. Judicial review of legality and civil suit for damages are the two basic remedies available for misuse of summary procedure. The circumstances wherein governments and government officials may be sued for damages are further discussed in Chapter 8.

Courts have permitted summary action in some situations where it is in the public interest. For example, government may if it chooses act first and talk later in tax cases. Nothing must be permitted to seriously interfere with the flow of government revenue and it is long established that governments may summarily seize property for nonpayment of taxes. Taxpayers may sue for the return of their property if they believe the government erroneously calculated the tax. In the case of *Murray's Lessee* v. *Hoboken Land & Improvement Co.*, 18 How. 272 (1856), the court said there "are few governments which do or can permit their claims for public taxes to become subjects of judicial controversy. . . ."

The Right-Privilege Distinction: Courts have also chosen to excuse government from the constitutional obligation of granting a hearing to persons adversely affected by the denial of a privilege. This has impelled the courts to determine what is a privilege and what is a right. Hearings are a required part of due process only where rights are involved, not privileges. But which is which?

INITIAL LICENSING: A party has no constitutional right to a hearing to determine whether he, she, or it may be initially licensed to carry on a business or activity. A medical doctor has no constitutional right to a hearing to determine whether he is entitled to be granted an initial license to practice medicine. Nor does a lawyer, nor does any person seeking a professional license have a right to a hearing. This is because no one has a *right* to a license to enter a profession, and therefore when the licensing agency refuses to grant a license it is not denying a right, but merely withholding a privilege. A medical doctor with all the requisite degrees may not feel in his heart that a license to practice is a mere privilege. But that is what the law says it is *before* it is granted

After a license is granted it may become a right if the activity permitted by the license is considered socially useful. Doctors, lawyers, and nurses, for example, are deemed to have a property right in their licenses and they have therefore a constitutional right to a formal hearing before the license may be revoked. If the activity is one which the legislature might prohibit altogether such as operation of a liquor store or pool hall, there may be no constitutional right to a hearing prior to its revocation. What falls into the category of socially undesirable is a matter of judicial inclusion and exclusion. When an activity is deemed to be a privilege rather than a right, the door is open to summary revocations, and with that weapon the government can keep closer reign and tighter hold upon socially undesirable activities.

The amount of one's investment in the activity licensed also has a bearing on whether the courts will see the license, once granted, as a property right. Thus, even a license to carry on a socially *unde*sirable activity may be viewed as a right if the holder of the license has invested a great deal of money in his business. Of course, all these things vary from state to state and all we can do here is paint the prevailing picture.

The question might be asked whether it is fair to deny constitutional rights to parties on the basis of yardsticks so dependent in their application upon the subjective judgment of judges about the meaning of right, privilege, socially desirable and undesirable, big investment and little investment. Nothing is ironclad, nothing is absolutely clear. If things were clear and certain we would not need judges. Judges are for judging, and this sort of decision we are talking about is not by any means the most difficult or subjective which judges have to make.

Still it seems rather senseless and unfair to say that the owner of a pool hall does not have as much right to the money and effort that he sinks into *his* business as does a doctor to the money and effort he sinks into *his* business. Revocation of a liquor license does in effect take property, and the U.S. Constitution says that no person shall be denied property without due process of law. It is a shabby fiction that the liquor business is less a property than the medical business. Furthermore, it is shabby reasoning to argue that misuse of a liquor license is any more a threat to society than misuse of a medical license. Surely it is less dangerous for a bar to serve drinks to an eighteen-year old than it is for a drunken doctor to attempt brain surgery. Why is summary action against a bar proprietor more appropriate than summary action against a malpracticing doctor?

As for the amount-invested doctrine, this is a sordid thing upon which to hang constitutional rights. What seems to one man a small amount, may be a fortune to a poor and marginal businessman.

Beggarly as these doctrines may be, they are, nevertheless, practical as a means of controlling certain kinds of problem activities. Yet, perhaps other practical means could be found to do the job, such as summary revocation with right to a hearing within 120 days or something of that sort.

Although there is no constitutional right to a hearing before revocation of certain licenses, there may be, as said before, a statutory right to a hearing. Thus, in some states the department of alcoholic beverage control or other agency must by statute hold hearings before revocation of liquor licenses. As a matter of fact, a large proportion of all the formal hearings held in California, for instance, concern liquor licenses.

DISCHARGE FROM GOVERNMENT EMPLOYMENT: Occasionally it is argued that the Constitution forbids all governmental arbitrariness, even arbitrary denial of a government job. But the due process clauses do *not* make *all* arbitrary government action unconstitutional; only arbitrary denials of life, liberty, and property are forbidden. Can it be argued that bureaucrats own their jobs or have a property right in them?

In the case of *Bailey* v. *Richardson*, 182 F. 2d 46, 341 U.S. 918 (1951), the United States Supreme Court held that no one has a right to a government job, and therefore no one has a constitutional right to a hearing prior to dismissal, although there may be a statutory right to a hearing. Mrs. Bailey, who had been fired because a Loyalty Review Board found reason to question her loyalty, had a hearing but she claimed it was not a fair one as required by the due process clause of the Constitution. She was not told of the specific evidence against her, nor told who testified against her, nor told who evaluated such testimony and evidence. The court concluded that she was not constitutionally entitled to any hearing at all, and that Congress could if it wished (and as it had done), provide for a hearing of a character below the constitutional standards of fairness. Government employment is not a right protected by the due process clause, said the court.

However, since *Bailey* v. *Richardson*, the Court has modified its stand somewhat. Its position now seems to be that if someone, once hired, acquires tenure or other entitlement to the job, that entitlement is a form of property which cannot be denied without due process of law. Such a person, therefore, has a constitutional right to at least some kind of hearing before dismissal. The extent of that hearing may, however, be limited by statute. That at least is what the Court seems to say in *Board of Regents* v. *Roth*, 408 U.S. 564 (1972), and in *Arnett* v. *Kennedy*, 416 U.S. 134 (1974). However, in 1976 the Court in *Bishop* v. *Wood*, upheld dismissal without a hearing of a policeman who had become a permanent employee of the city—no hearing had been provided for in the city personnel rules.

In recent years the United States Supreme Court has also been wrestling with the question of whether government has a right to limit the First Amendment freedoms of its employees, and to make those limitations a condition of employment. See *Civil Service Commission* v. *National Association of Letter Carriers*, 413 U.S. 548 (1973).

ALIENS SEEKING ENTRY INTO THE COUNTRY: Although the Constitution covers aliens once they are admitted, it does not cover them as they stand at the door waiting for admission. They can be dealt with arbitrarily and summarily by officials and without hearing at the door.

Banking and Finance: The courts seem to hold that it is fair procedure for agencies regulating financial institutions to hold hearings after, rather than before, action. Obviously, a prior hearing could ruin a bank even if the decision after a hearing favored the bank. Depositors would have fled with their money at the mere hint of difficulty.

STATUTORY PRECLUSION OF NOTICE AND HEARING:

Occasionally a government (national, state, or local) will assert that notice and hearing are not to be afforded prior to certain denials of liberty or property. These statutory preclusions of hearings have no effect whatever upon the constitutional rights of parties to have hearings. No legislative body may legally deny a constitutional right. Nor, of course, does the mere failure of a statute to mention that there is a right to a hearing preclude that right. Legislatures, however, do in practice almost always provide for notice and hearing by statute wherever judicial power is delegated to administrative agencies.

NOTICE:

Fairness obviously requires that a party whose rights or obligations are directly affected by the results of a hearing be given an opportunity to *participate* in the hearing, be given *time* to prepare arguments, and be told what issues are to be decided at the hearing. Fairness of notice, therefore, revolves around the questions (1) Who is to be notified? (2) How long before the hearing must notice be given? and (3) What information must the notice contain? For the most part these questions are settled by common sense, for it is difficult to answer them except in the most general way. For example, to say that five days notice is adequate disregards the distance which some parties may have to travel and the complexity of the issues. In some situations five days is sufficient notice and in others it is not. The federal Administrative Procedure Act merely says that notice shall be timely. The California APA allows at least fifteen days advance notice of the accusations and issues. But the constitutional requirement of due process demands that the parties be fairly notified no matter what the statutes may say about time limits or about anything else. Fairness is, to repeat, measured by reason and it is a requirement that stands above statutes. The Revised Model State APA spells out the rule of reason in its notice provision which says, "In a contested case, all parties shall be afforded an opportunity for hearing after *reasonable* notice."

The question, which parties are interested parties that have a right to be notified is also answered by reason, and can hardly be touched sensibly by statute.

How much information must the notice contain? This too is a matter of pure judgment as to how much is necessary to prevent the parties from being surprised by accusations and issues. The object is to enable the parties to prepare their arguments. In cases where the hearing is to determine whether a right, authority, license, or privilege should be revoked, suspended, limited, or conditioned, the notice should specify what statutes and rules the accused (respondent is the word preferred in administrative law) is alleged to have violated. The essential facts which led to the hearing should also be included. What did the accused do that motivated the agency to hold the hearing? These are called ultimate facts, as distinguished from evidentiary facts. The notice need not, and probably could not, state all of the facts. After all, one function of the hearing is to bring out facts through cross examination, etc. But where is the line between ultimate and evidentiary facts? The line is set by the purpose of the notice, the purpose being to prevent the accused from being surprised by any central issue at the hearing. If the hearing is to determine whether a barber is to have his license revoked, he needs to be told more than that the hearing is to determine whether his license is to be revoked. He should be told essentially why he is accused.

Not all administrative adjudication arises from accusations. A hearing may be for the purpose of determining whether a right, authority, license, or privilege should be granted, issued, or renewed. In that case the notice should tell what rules the respondent must show compliance with, and must tell any other matter which would authorize a denial of the agency action sought.

Suppose the notice is insufficient? Does inadequacy of notice invalidate the hearing? The law is not consistent on this point (nor upon very many other points, for that matter). But agency lawyers probably do not need to worry very much about whether the notice is perfect because it is always possible during or before the actual hearing to have a continuance (a delay) for the purpose of notifying the parties of anything left out of the original notice. Furthermore, if the hearing is conducted slowly enough it is possible to assume that the parties get the drift of what is going on and therefore cannot be surprised, and therefore cannot charge denial of due process for lack of notice. (This is not meant to be a recommendation for slowness.) If the hearing has already closed, it can be reopened to deal with any issues forgotten in the notice. At least it seems probable that courts will permit amendments of the issues during the course of the hearing, providing no one is unfairly disadvantaged thereby.

Of course, the notice must also indicate the time and place of the hearing.

THE RECORD:

One of the guarantees of fairness enforced by courts under the due process clauses of the U.S. Constitution is the guarantee that adjudicatory decisions shall rest upon the known record. The record should include:

1. All pleadings, motions, and intermediate ruling. One reason for their inclusion is to compel decision on each point raised by the parties. If these points are not plainly laid out, they may be forgotten or slurred over.

2. Evidence received or considered.

3. A statement of matters officially noticed.

4. Questions and offers of proof, objections, and rulings thereon.

5. Proposed findings and exceptions.

6. Any decision, opinion, or report by the officer presiding at the hearing.

7. All staff memoranda or data submitted to the hearing officer or members of the agency in connection with their consideration of the case. This is the most controversial item. Sometimes the staff of an agency will supply information to agency heads or to hearing officers to help them arrive at a decision. Should these staff memoranda also be a part of the record and available to all parties? The Revised Model State APA (in the phraseology of point seven above) says yes. Yet one wonders where the record properly ends. If staff memoranda are included, why not include the text of every law review article ever read by the deciders and everything else that affected their thinking about the case? But, of course, staff memoranda have a direct and unique bearing on the case and should probably be a part of the record.

Records can be voluminous and expensive. To shorten the record, parties involved in an appeal are allowed to stipulate (i.e., agree) to omit from the record superfluous matter.

EVIDENCE:

Burden of Proof: Burden of proof in the law of evidence is the necessity or duty of affirmatively proving facts in dispute and of establishing the truth of a claim by preponderance of the evidence. The burden of proof is upon the proponent of a rule or order. (Naturally, we are talking about adjudication, and not about legislation. When an agency is legislating it does not ordinarily need to prove anything.)

If a state board of barber examiners wishes to deprive a barber of his license, the board must prove that the barber did something wrong. The barber himself does not need to prove that he is innocent. He can sit back in secure possession of his license until the board establishes the truth of its charges. If the board fails nothing happens. Of course, the barber himself will surely want to rebut the board's evidence, and as a matter of fact this rebuttal may be extremely difficult and a great burden. The charge may, in fact, be harder to rebut than to make. To say that the burden of proof is upon the board is not necessarily to say that the board's case is more difficult than the respondent's. Perhaps the phrase responsibility for proof would be more accurate than burden of proof. The bigger burden may be that of the respondent who may be hard put to *prevent* the agency from proving its case. But the term burden is clearly intended to mean responsibility or onus (onus probandi is the Latin for burden of proof) no matter whose case is more burdensome.

The criminal law doctrine that an accused is innocent until proven guilty carries over into license revocation and similar cases in administrative law. It is broadened and widened into the doctrine that the party initiating a proceeding has the general burden of coming forward not merely with a prima facie case, but with evidence that will suffice even in the face of rebuttal, cross-examination, and contradictory evidence.

The burden of proof is always upon any applicant for any license, unless by statute the burden of proof is shifted. In short, the burden of proof is upon the party undertaking an affirmative action of any sort through an adjudicatory proceeding, except where statutes provide otherwise.

Normally and naturally, the party with the burden of proof is first to present its case in an administrative hearing (as in a court) and will try to present at least a prima facie case which is a case that will suffice until contradicted and overcome by other evidence.

The Exclusionary Rules: Generally speaking, there are no specific rules governing admission of evidence in administrative adjudication. Any evidence may be admitted. The exclusionary rules of evidence which limit admissibility in judicial proceedings do not necessarily apply to administrative adjudication (although they may be and are often more or less observed). The mere admission of incompetent, irrelevant, or immaterial evidence into the record of a judicial proceeding can be sufficient in and of itself to vitiate the proceeding. This is not so in administrative proceedings. There is more danger from the *ex*clusion of competent, relevant, and material evidence than from *in*clusion of the opposite. In fact, there is no danger of vitiating proceedings by *in*clusion of anything, but every danger from *ex*clusion.

Insofar as evidence is concerned, courts ask fundamentally only one question when they are called upon to judge the fairness of the administrative order. Is the evidence sufficient to support the finding? In assessing the sufficiency of evidence, the court, when reviewing administrative action, will, of course, weigh the quality of the evidence presented, and it may very well discount or give less weight to evidence which in a regular court would have been excluded. But the mere presence of such evidence in the record does not invalidate the administrative proceeding.

Competency of evidence is not the same thing as credibility of evidence. Evidence may be incompetent yet credible. Incompetent evidence is merely that which may not be legally admitted under the rules of evidence. Incompetent evidence may actually be true and useful.

Why Is Incompetent Evidence Excluded from a Court Trial? If incompetent evidence may be true and useful, why is it generally excluded from a court of law? The reason for its exclusion has partly to do with the jury system. Juries normally are composed of people who are far from expert in the scientific handling of information. Ordinary people dragged off the streets to sit on juries are seldom educated people. An educated person is one who is trained to weigh evidence. That is largely what formal education is or should be all about. Colleges (and the whole educational system) try to exercise students in the scientific method as well as try to transmit information. Education should, and often does, revolve around the question "Why?" In answering the question "why" the processes of proof, of weighing arguments, of weighing the value and credibility of evidence, are central. This is the scientific method. It means no conclusions without substantial evidence.

The uneducated think more often with their blood. They tend more often to base great conclusions on the sand of inadequate evidence. For this reason juries are protected as much as possible from unreliable and prejudicial evidence likely to mislead untrained minds.

In some states the rules of evidence are more lenient in trials before a judge sitting without jury. This makes sense because a judge, if he is expert in anything, should be an expert in weighing the significance of information. He does not need to be led by the hand with rules of evidence, nor do the appellate court judges who normally sit without jury. The Revised Model State APA therefore provides that "the rules of evidence as applied in [non-jury] civil cases in the District Courts of this State shall be followed." The word non-jury is bracketed according to the authors of that act so that the term can be left out of the act in those states where there is no significant difference between the rules followed in jury and non-jury cases.

I think the Revised Model State APA goes too far toward judicialization of the rules of evidence in this provision. Even where non-jury rules of evidence are more lenient they are still too formalized for administrative procedure, in my present judgment.

Why Is Incompetent Evidence Admitted in an Administrative Hearing?

Presumably administrators with quasi-judicial power do not need to be protected. Their adjudicatory authority is often within the narrow boundaries of their field of expertise. They are alleged to be better able than ordinary jurymen to judge the significance of various pieces of evidence for the same reason that a medical doctor is better able to judge the significance of various signs and symptoms of disease than a layman. Furthermore, administrators are ordinarily more educated and more skilled at evaluating information than the average juryman.

These presumptions about administrators are, however, open to serious question in some cases. Some administrators never learned the scientific method very well; some are not expert in the subject matter of their agencies, although they may have expert staffs to advise them.

HEARSAY EVIDENCE: Hearsay evidence is an example of the kind of evidence which is incompetent under the common law rules of evidence, but which is freely admitted in administrative hearings. Hearsay is what a witness says he heard another person say. It is evidence not proceeding from the personal knowledge of the witness, but from the mere repetition of what he has heard others say. It is second-hand evidence, as distinguished from original evidence; it is the repetition at second-hand of what would be original evidence if given by the person who originally made the statement. In a sense, every statement introduced into evidence made by someone who is not present as a witness is hearsay.

Hearsay has several weaknesses. First, it is likely to be erroneous because people are notoriously poor at reporting accurately what other people say. A teacher learns *that* very quickly as he reads on examination papers renditions of what students thought they heard him say. People do not hear exactly alike, perhaps because we often hear what we want to hear. Each report we make is colored and often hugely distorted by our own viewpoint. The reports we make of what we ourselves see, hear, feel, smell, or taste are sufficiently distorted without adding hearsay which is distortion compounded. Still, there is the argument that experts can pretty well judge the value of hearsay evidence *within* their field of competence, just as a football expert can see the flaw in a report that Babe Ruth said he scored a touchdown in the sixth down of the fifth inning of the fourteenth quarter of the game between the Los Angeles Yankees and the San Diego Chargers.

A second fault of hearsay is that the absent person whose statements are reported is not present to be cross-examined. One of the fundamental elements of a fair hearing is the right to cross-examine, a right which cannot be accorded when hearsay is admitted.

Of course, even in a court of law certain hearsay is permitted.

Any document is hearsay insofar as it represents a statement made by persons not present to be cross-examined, but when the statement is made by a public officer authorized by law to make it, the statement may be admitted into the record because it comes within the official statements exception to the hearsay rule.

The right of cross-examination in administrative hearings seems to be limited to examination of those who give their testimony in person, for not only is hearsay evidence permitted on the witness stand, but also a great many statements not subject to cross-examination are received in writing from officials and from private citizens.

OPINION EVIDENCE: Another form of evidence usually excluded from a court trial but freely admitted in administrative adjudication is opinion testimony. A witness in a court trial may not ordinarily draw conclusions. He may only state what he has seen, heard, felt, smelled, or tasted. He may not testify to his conclusions because it is the business of the court and of the jury to draw conclusions. A witness may testify that he saw an ax raised, heard a thud, and later saw a dead man, but he may not testify that in his opinion the dead man was murdered or that he was struck with the ax, etc. Nor may lawyers in a court trial ask witnesses leading questions which involve an answer bearing immediately upon the merits of the fundamental issues in the trial.

However, experts may be permitted to give their conclusions. Psychiatrists are, for example, frequently called upon to testify as to what they observed in a patient, *and* as to what they conclude from those observations. They may say whether in their opinion someone is insane. Many other kinds of experts may also be permitted to supply the court with their expert conclusions and judgments.

To What Degree May an Administrative Order Rest on Incompetent Evidence?

Although the exclusionary rules of evidence do not apply to administrative adjudication, this does not mean that a decision may rest *entirely* upon incompetent evidence. For example, if a worker afflicted with delirium tremens dies, and his wife testifies that her husband told her that his trouble came from a block of ice falling on him at work, the agency in a workmens' compensation case probably would not be permitted to award workmens' compensation to the dead man's estate solely on the basis of the wife's hearsay in the absence of any other witnesses. However, if there had been a witness who said he heard a block of ice fall about that time, or who supplied some sort of corroborative evidence, the award might have been made. An adjudicatory decision may not as a general rule rest entirely upon evidence which in a court of law would be incompetent, but incompetent evidence may be used to reinforce a decision resting primarily upon competent evidence. There ordinarily must be at least a residuum of competent evidence not counting the incompetent evidence.

The federal Administrative Procedure Act does not explicitly say that incompetent evidence may be introduced in federal administrative hearings, but on the other hand it does not forbid it. It merely says that the decision must be "supported by and in accordance with the reliable, probative and substantial evidence." The California APA is far clearer:

The hearing need not be conducted according to technical rules relating to evidence and witnesses. Any relevant evidence shall be admitted if it is the sort of evidence on which responsible persons are accustomed to rely in the conduct of serious affairs, regardless of the existence of any common law or statutory rule which might make improper the admission of such evidence over objection in civil actions. Heresay evidence may be used for the purpose of supplementing or· explaining any direct evidence but shall not be sufficient in itself to support a finding unless it would be admissible over objection in civil actions. The rules of privilege shall be effective to the same extent that they are now or hereafter may be recognized in civil actions and irrelevant and unduly repetitious evidence shall be excluded.

Saying that incompetent evidence *may be* admitted into an administrative hearing does not mean hearing officers or agencies have to admit it. It may be excluded. In other words, the hearing officer may permit the inclusion of incompetent evidence, but he may also elect not to permit it if in his judgment it is unreliable, or if it is not "the sort of evidence upon which responsible persons are accustomed to rely in the conduct of serious affairs," to use the words of the California APA.

The real tests of admissibility of evidence in administrative hearings are the tests of reliability and relevancy, not competency. Of course, a hearing officer does not have to permit the parties to pile up repetitious evidence even if it is reliable and relevant. Careless admission of evidence "for what it's worth" is expensive to the parties, dissipates their energies, distracts them from the main issues, and unnecessarily swells the record.

Other Arguments for Admission of Incompetent Evidence:

There are other arguments against strict enforcement of the exclusionary rules of evidence in administrative hearings besides the argument that rules of evidence are not needed in absence of a jury.

First, enforcement of the common law rules of evidence vastly complicates litigation and delays and formalizes it. This clashes with the objectives of dispatch, elasticity, and simplicity which the administrative process is designed to promote.

Second, it means that every litigant needs a lawyer who is expert in the rules of evidence. The legal profession has been accused of wanting to complicate the conduct of trials as much as possible in order to increase the demand for lawyers. True or not, the law of evidence is difficult to understand and difficult to apply without trained counsel and trained judges. As things now stand, a barber defending himself against license revocation can take the stand and tell his story without the expense of lawyers and without an opposing lawyer interrupting his story with objections. Freedom to testify simply, naturally, and directly without undue interruption is usually more important than strict adherence to rules of relevance, materiality, and competency.

It is said that most of the rules of evidence are merely rules of caution. But caution can be taken into account equally well at the stage of weighing the evidence in the record. A trained hearing officer can do that.

A third objection to the rules of evidence is that they close the door to some relevant evidence. Incompetent evidence, though possibly in error, may also possibly (or even probably) be true.

DISCOVERY: One might think that a trial would be fairer if prior to the trial all parties had a means of discovering all the evidence available to the opposition. After all, trials are not supposed to be sporting contests. Their only purpose is justice, and justice is not always served by surprise evidence. The Federal Rules of Civil Procedure provide a procedure commonly called discovery (28 U.S.C. Rules 26–35) under which the parties in civil cases before federal district courts can extract pre-trial information from each other or from anyone else for the purpose of preparing a case for trial. Parties have a right under those rules to issue written interrogatories, take written and oral depositions, copy documents, and so forth.

Generally it is argued that discovery not only advances the cause of justice by eliminating surprise, but also speeds up the trial and improves its quality by eliminating irrelevancies at the outset and getting promptly to the main issues.

Congress has not specifically provided discovery procedure for use in administrative adjudication except insofar as the Freedom of Information Act of 1966 (5 U.S.C. 552) does so indirectly. But there has been much discussion whether administrative agencies should be required to follow discovery procedure. Of course, they already do so in a voluntary way through pre-hearing conferences in which parties are urged to decide before the hearing just what they agree upon and do not agree upon. Discovery is also freely practiced by agencies against respondents and applicants inasmuch as agencies can use their subpoena power and their inspection and general investigatory power to find out nearly everything they need to know from the respondent before the hearing. That form of discovery is monstrously one sided.

Apparently most administrative agencies do not want respondents to exercise an equal power of discovery. Part of their opposition arises no doubt from a simple desire to retain an advantage in litigation. Their selfishness may be reinforced by the belief that they (the agencies) are devoted to the public interest while respondents seek only a private interest. Also there may be some tendency for agencies to view litigation as a kind of fox hunt in which respondents are viewed as foxes to be endowed with only enough resources to make the chase thrilling for the hunters. Opposition by agencies to granting respondents a power of discovery is probably also rooted in legal conservatism.

It must be conceded that arming respondents with discovery power against government agencies would raise some pretty serious problems, not unlike the problems raised by the Freedom of Information Act of 1966 (see Chapter 5 of this book). Much depends upon what is meant by the term discovery. If it means giving to respondents the authority to freely quiz government officials and romp through government files seeking anything that might be broadly relevant to the respondents' case, that would be intolerable despite the fact that the government can do that to the respondent. If a narrower view of discovery is taken, if it is defined simply as the right of all parties to have timely advance notice of evidence to be presented at the hearing, then there is less reason for denying respondents in an administrative hearing that right—it is a right.

OFFICIAL NOTICE:

Official notice has nothing to do with notifying anybody about anything. It is not at all related to the notice required before hearing. Official notice is the same thing as judicial notice, except that judicial notice is a term used in a court proceeding, while official notice is a term used in administrative adjudicatory proceedings.

Then what is judicial notice? A court exercises judicial notice when it assumes certain facts bearing on the issues to be true without proof. Judicial notice of *notorious* facts is permitted without the production of evidence or argument. It covers matters so notorious that a production of evidence would be unnecessary. A notorious fact is one which is generally known and talked of, well or widely known, forming a part of common knowledge or universally recognized. Judicial notice saves the court a vast amount of time because if everything bearing on the issues of a trial had to be proved, there would be no end to the trial. One might have to prove that a day is twenty-four hours long or that there are such things as ocean tides, and so forth. There is no definite rule as to what matters are deemed notorious other than the rule of reason which governs so much of the law. It is not likely that a judicial decision would be successfully appealed on grounds that the judge took judicial notice of the fact that "A" comes before "B" in the alphabet.

When judges (or hearing officers) take notice of facts which are notorious to experts in some specialized field but not notorious to the general public or known to the parties, then judicial (or official) notice presents an obvious challenge to the theory that parties have a right to judicial (or quasi-judicial) decisions based only upon known evidence.

This problem is particularly sticky in the field of administrative adjudication, because there is great temptation on the part of agencies which are expert in some specialty to make use of their expert knowledge in deciding cases without going to all the bother of trying to prove that their knowledge is true over and over again in successive cases. There is a temptation to use official notice as a way of getting all this knowledge into the record, so to speak, without actually doing so in black and white, and thus to speed and simplify things. An important reason why administrative agencies have been permitted to exercise adjudicatory power is because they possess expert knowledge which judges in ordinary courts lack. But how can this expert knowledge be used unless the specialized knowledge of the administrator is *assumed* to be in the record by virtue of official notice? To prove everything would be too much. Rating boards in the Veterans Administration passing upon veterans' claims learn about injuries and diseases and their disabling effects; the Bureau of Marine Inspection acquires knowledge of the behavior of ships and tides, and so on. Is it necessary to prove over and over again the same facts?

How can the need for the application of expert knowledge in administrative adjudication be squared with the constitutional requirement that everything be in the record unless it is notorious? Should administrators be allowed to take official notice of facts which are notorious to the expert deciders, but not notorious to the public at large or to the parties to the case?

Apparently most courts are now willing to allow an agency to officially notice technical and scientific data within the agency's scope of expertise if the data is generally accepted as true and factual. To that extent agencies may notice things beyond the limits of what a court may ordinarily notice. However, in administrative procedure (unlike judicial) great stress is laid on notifying the parties in advance of decision what basic data is to be noticed rather than proved. This gives parties time to bring in rebutting evidence.

The federal Administrative Procedure Act takes the position that the parties must be given an opportunity to rebut all material facts. That means that if an agency takes official notice of a material fact (one which is essential to the case and without which it could not be supported) the parties have to be told what is being officially noticed, and this must, apparently, be done in the record itself. Thus if the agency takes official notice of the trend of land values over certain years, it must cite the *source* of its statistics (it need not include the actual statistics which may be ten volumes long) so that the parties may if they choose challenge their accuracy.

The Revised Model State APA spells out the matter of official notice rather concretely:

> Notice may be taken of judicially cognizable facts. In addition, notice may be taken of generally recognized technical or scientific facts within the agency's specialized knowledge. Parties shall be notified either before or during the hearing, or by reference in preliminary reports or otherwise, of the material noticed, including any staff memoranda or data, and they shall be afforded an opportunity to contest the material so noticed.

USE OF EXPERT KNOWLEDGE TO JUDGE THE EVIDENCE: LIMITS OF THE RECORD

Closely related to the problem raised by official notice is the problem raised by the use of expert knowledge to *judge* witnesses and evidence. A judicial record cannot ever contain all the information upon which judgment is made, not in an administrative proceeding and not in a court. The record has its limits; it cannot contain the mind of the judge. His attitudes, experiences, and knowledge will affect his decision and this cannot be helped. But it can be minimized, and that is what is meant by the doctrine that parties have a right to a decision based upon the *known* evidence. Known as far as *possible* and practical is what that doctrine means. Actually, the mind of the judge cannot really be known, and the doctrine is, therefore, an unattainable ideal. But the ideal can be strived after, and courts will reverse a decision in which the unrecorded mind of the judge appears to play an *unreasonably* central role in the face of evidence spread on the record. The rule of reason, or the reasonable man doctrine, is the only yardstick we have to measure how much is too much, and similar questions.

It would be senseless and wasteful to ask agencies to ignore their experience, technical competence, and specialized knowledge in deciding cases. An important reason for the development of quasi-judicial power in the agencies had been to capitalize on their experience, competence, and knowledge. The Revised Model State APA acknowledges this by explicitly providing that agencies may utilize their expertise in the evaluation of evidence.

JURY VIEW:

There is another kind of information that cannot be put in the record. It is closely related to the inability to insert the mind of the judge into the record. It is what is known in court procedure as a jury view. When, in a criminal case for instance, the jury goes out to the scene of the crime to take a look for itself, there is no way of indicating in the record what impressions they take with them and subsequently employ in judging the case. Administrators are constantly taking what might be considered a kind of jury view in the process of carrying on their daily routine as administrators of the very matters over which they sit in judgment in adjudications.

CROSS-EXAMINATION:

The right of cross-examination is one of the basic elements of a fair hearing. However, in a great number of instances cross-examination serves no useful purpose, particularly where issues are technical, as are many issues presented for adjudication before administrative agencies. The examination of a witness in a trial or hearing by the party opposed to the one who produced him serves several purposes. It serves (1) to bring out matters left untouched by direct examination, (2) to test the veracity of a witness; (3) to test the accuracy of a witness's perception of the matters to which he testifies, and the extent of his observation, (4) to test the accuracy of his memory, (5) to test the accuracy of his narration, and (6) where expert testimony is given, to test the basis of the expert's opinion.

The accuracy of technical information can often be determined far more efficiently by other means in most situations. If engineering information, for example, is sought, the best way to receive it may be in writing. Many things that can be said orally can be said better in writing. Why waste much time cross-examining an engineer if he can submit everything more completely in writing? The primary value of oral testimony and of cross-examination is to test the human failings (veracity and accuracy) of witnesses whose observations are of key importance. But, in the sort of technical matters dealt with in many administrative adjudications, the issues do not turn upon whether someone is telling the truth (veracity) or upon whether someone tells a straight story or remembers accurately. The issues often turn upon technical data. Of course, technical data may be wrong, but frequently it is best challenged by submission of contrary technical data in writing, not by clumsy, time-consuming, and expensive cross-examination.

There are, of course, administrative hearings (license revocations, for example) where the veracity and accuracy of witnesses may be of extreme importance. When a state board of alcoholic beverage control seeks to revoke the liquor license of a night club owner because he allegedly served liquor to minors, the veracity and accuracy of witnesses is critical.

In an administrative hearing the right to cross-examine appears to be limited by the free admissibility of hearsay evidence. How can one cross-examine someone not in court who is rumored to have said thus and so? Even in a court of law there can be no cross-examination under the recognized exceptions to the hearsay rule (the official statements exception, for example).

Furthermore, it is not really possible to fully cross-examine a witness who testifies by deposition. It is true that these written declarations are made in the presence of representatives of both parties, who may cross-examine, but since such cross-examination is not in the presence of judge or jury, the demeanor of the witness cannot be judged by them.

RIGHT TO COUNSEL:

Right to counsel in administrative adjudication does not mean one has to have counsel, nor does it mean that one's counsel must be an attorney. It is true that in most courts of law it is required that counsel be licensed attorneys. But generally in administrative hearings anyone may serve as counsel. In some a party may be counseled only by specific kinds of counsel such as, for example, accountants in some tax litigation. In most hearings a party may, if he chooses, plead his own case. This flexibility in use of counsel is consistent with the purposes of speed, simplicity, and inexpensiveness. Administrative adjudication was born partly out of a desire to dejudicialize certain kinds of litigation by sweeping away much of the formal procedure in which lawyers are such experts. Lawyers breed procedure, procedure breeds lawyers, and both breed sluggish and high-priced justice.

However, where there is a constitutional right to be heard whether in court or in the agencies there is also a constitutional right to have counsel of some type if one wishes. Attorneys and their associations have for many decades sought to encourage the use of licensed attorneys as counsel in administrative proceedings. Lawyers' associations have fostered statutes discouraging the use of other kinds of counsel and restoring procedure and judicialization to administrative proceedings.

WEIGHT OF HEARING OFFICER REPORTS:

Hearing officers do not finally decide cases. They merely recommend a decision to the agency in whose behalf they hold the hearing. It is the agency head (board or individual) which makes the final decision and the head may accept or reject the hearing officer's recommendation.

The federal APA talks of initial decision rather than hearing officer report, and no doubt initial decision is a better term because the decision is after all merely initial. It becomes the decision of the agency only if it is not appealed to the agency by a party or not reversed by the agency itself within a certain time.

The Revised Model State APA employs the term proposed finding.

A hearing officer's report is not comparable to a lower court decision which is binding unless and until overthrown for legal error (often error in procedure) in an appeals court. An agency can reject the hearing officer's recommendation (1) for reasons other than legal error, and (2) simply because it sees things differently from the hearing officer. An appeals court, on the contrary, is not supposed to reverse a lower court decision simply to substitute its own judgment.

This is not to say that the agency can by any means disregard the hearing officer's report. Nor can it disregard, of course, the record of the hearing. The agency must base its decision on known evidence, and that means it must base its decision on the record of the hearing of which the hearing officer's report is a part. (The agency may reopen the hearing and add new evidence to the record.) The hearing officer's report must be made available to the parties and the agency must permit the parties to rebut and controvert the hearing officer's report before final decision is made.

The entire hearing may have been held before the agency itself, in which case there is no hearing officer report, although a hearing officer may be present to preside over the hearing or to offer legal and procedural advice to the agency as they conduct the hearing. His advice may also be asked in that situation as to how the case should be decided.

Occasionally the question is asked why hearing officer reports must be shown to the parties. In England these reports are viewed as private communications between the hearing officer and the agency. In the United States this is not at all the case, for, as pointed out a few paragraphs above, the report is a part of the total record of the case and it simply cannot be kept secret from the parties under our principle that every adjudicatory decision must be based on the known evidence. It is absolutely fundamental in American practice that ex parte evidence (evidence made known to one party but not to the other) may not be considered in arriving at a decision. This is part of a larger principle often called the principle of exclusiveness of the record. The hearing officer's report could not be a part of the record if it were secret. If secret it would be ex parte. If considered by the agency without being shown to other parties, the agency would not be basing its decision exclusively on the known record.

MUST A DECISION INCLUDE AN OPINION?

A decision may, and often does, include a statement of findings and an opinion. The decision itself, which in a court of law is perhaps more correctly referred to as a judgment, is the official decision of the court or agency upon the claims of the parties in litigation. A decision is not the same thing as an opinion. An opinion is the reasons given for a decision and is an expression of views by the judge. Sometimes the words opinion and decision are used interchangeably, but a decision need not be accompanied by an opinion. A decision with an opinion is sometimes referred to as a reasoned decision.

American courts strongly encourage administrative agencies to give opinions, but there is no recognized necessity to do so, apart from express statutory requirements that may possibly exist. The federal Administrative Procedure Act does not require opinions. That is, the word is not used. But it does provide that all decisions shall include in addition to findings and conclusions, "the reasons or basis therefore." This may mean that the relationship of the findings and conclusions to the evidence in the record should be pointed out by the agency so that the parties and/or a reviewing court can see how (and whether) the decision rests upon the known evidence. Statements of reasons, however, may be long or short. The federal APA does not impose upon agencies the duty of formulating elaborate opinions.

There are strong reasons why decisions should be reasoned. Judicial review of an administrative decision is more difficult when courts are not shown how the decision relates to the evidence. Second, the necessity of writing reasoned decisions evokes care and fairness on the part of deciders. Third, a reasoned decision serves to convince those who are subject to decisions that they are fair. It is important that decisions *seem* fair as well as *be* fair. Respect for judicial processes rests as much upon the appearance of fairness as upon the reality of it. A reasoned decision is not only fair; it has the appearance of fairness.

Finally, reasoned decisions also greatly facilitate administrative agencies in their effort to follow their own precedents. It is true that the principle of stare decisis is not binding upon administrative agencies in quite the same way it is supposed to bind courts. After all, one reason for the rise of administrative adjudication was to liberate some kinds of judicial activity from the inflexibility of stare decisis. Nevertheless, administrators, like judges, are strongly motivated to follow their own precedents, partly because it seems fair to treat similar cases similarly and partly because it simplifies the job of deciding in each case. So impelling and attractive is the habit of following precedent that it threatens to give cadaveric rigidity to the whole administrative process. Be that as it may, it is easier to follow precedent by setting down in the decision of each case why and how the decision was arrived at.

FINDINGS:

The decision of the agency should include findings of fact and law which support the decision. Among the findings should be one showing that the agency has jurisdiction over the case. If, for example, the Interstate Commerce Commission wishes to allow a railroad to abandon a commuter line, it should show in its decision that the line was actually in interstate (as opposed to *intra*state) commerce and therefore under the regulatory jurisdiction of the commission. The jurisdictional finding should be made even if the issue of jurisdiction is not brought up as an issue in the hearing.

Perhaps it might be argued that the question of jurisdiction is a legal question more appropriately decided by courts than by agencies. But agencies are not precluded from making findings and decisions on legal issues involved in a case, and in truth they have no alternative but to decide all relevant issues in a case directly or by implication. Therefore if the findings are going to support the decision, there must be findings as to each and every issue, both factual and legal. Only in that manner are parties protected and assured that the case has been fully and completely determined. And only if each issue is supported by findings which support the decision can parties know what they must show to successfully appeal the decision. Accordingly, the federal Administrative Procedure Act provides that all decisions shall include findings and conclusions, as well as the reasons or basis therefore, upon all the material issues of fact, law, or discretion presented on the record.

The decision should also include findings to support the type of sanction imposed. A sanction is not justified which deprives a party of more than is necessary to correct the evil where property or other rights are involved. Thus, if a firm produces a product which bears a misleading trade name (in which, of course, the firm has a property interest) the decision may not forbid use of the name altogether if the evil of mislabeling can be corrected by addition of explanatory words to the trade name.

THE MORGAN PROBLEM:

Several years ago in *Morgan v. United States*, 298 U.S. 468 (1936), the U.S. Supreme Court held that in administrative adjudication "the one who decides must hear." This would seem to threaten the administrative process because it is manifestly impossible for the heads of most agencies to actually sit as hearing officers in all the cases they decide. But the *Morgan* decision hastened to add that the heads of agencies were not expected to act as hearing officers, but only to address their minds to the evidence and to actually make the decision in each case. They were permitted by the decision to employ examiners to take evidence and to employ competent subordinates to sift and analyze the evidence. But the officer who makes the determination must, said the court, consider and appraise the evidence which justifies those determinations. Almost always the head (board or individual) of the agency is responsible for making such determinations. In many situations it is not really possible for an agency head to seriously consider the evidence even after subordinates sift and analyze it for him. The *Morgan* case itself began as an administrative hearing in which the transcript of the oral testimony filled 13,000 pages and another 1,000 pages of exhibits. A meaningful analysis of all that evidence by subordinates would surely have to be as long as a book itself. The Secretary of Agriculture (who in the *Morgan* case was alleged to have issued a decision without hearing or reading any of the evidence) would have had to spend, one would imagine, at *least* a full day and probably a full week or longer reading and considering even a summary of the evidence. And the *Morgan* case is only one of many cases being decided by the secretary. In fact, when the *Morgan* case reached the courts it was consolidated with forty-nine other suits against the Secretary of Agriculture for the same failure to consider the evidence, and these fifty suits concerned only one of about forty or more statutes the secretary enforces. It is clear that the secretary does not have time to consider even in the most offhand way the cases which are decided in his name. As a very high political officer of the government, he *should not* divert himself from important policy questions or permit himself to be swallowed up in the minutia of a thousand cases of adjudication.

Who does really decide? His staff, his technical experts, his lawyers, and other subordinates in the department actually do the deciding. It is difficult to know specifically who makes the decision within the department. Different aspects of a case may be decided by different persons. The Department of Agriculture as an institution collectively decides cases. And so it is in many if not all the departments and agencies of the federal government and in the independent agencies; and so it is in many state and local agencies. These decisions by faceless bureaucrats delivered in the name of the head of the agency are known as institutional decisions. Lawyers have long bitterly complained about that mode of decision-making, a mode which is far from the judicial practice wherein decisions are made personally by the trier of the facts.

Despite the Morgan decision of 1936 (known as the *first* Morgan case), the evil therein condemned continues, and the reason it continues is twofold: first, without institutional decisions the administrative process could not survive, and second, the Supreme Court in the *second Morgan* case (*Morgan* v. *United States,* 304 U.S. 1) in 1938 graciously came to terms with that reality by holding that parties may not in a lawsuit raise the question of how *thoroughly* the head of the agency considered the evidence. Courts will not attempt the impossible. It is no more practical to inquire into the mental processes of an administrative judge than it is to probe the mind of a court judge, and the latter is never done. If courts waded into the morass of that kind of inquiry it would take even more of the agency head's time on the witness stand undergoing psychological and judicial investigation, and that would leave him even less time than at present to read and consider the evidence of cases.

The severity of the "he who decides must hear" problem is somewhat lessened by Par. 557(b) of the federal APA, which makes the initial decision of the administrative law judge the final decision of the agency unless there is an appeal to the agency or unless the agency itself acts to review the initial decision. Agency heads may also set up intermediate appellate boards to help them review the administrative law judge's initial decision.

HOW ARE ADMINISTRATIVE ORDERS ENFORCED?

A sanction is a penalty provided as a means of enforcing obedience to law. The sanction, of course, lies at the end of the enforcement trail. There are various routes along which enforcement of an administrative order may travel (i.e., there are various kinds of enforcement proceedings), and a penalty or sanction is what may ultimately result.

Criminal Enforcement and Criminal Sanctions: One of the enforcement routes is criminal prosecution and the penalty or sanction at the end of that route is usually fine or imprisonment. A criminal proceeding is the method of enforcing the decisions of draft boards, for example. The registrant who violates the orders of a local draft board commits a felony. Other examples of criminal sanctions are those which back up certain cease and desist orders of the Interstate Commerce Commission regarding water carriers and freight forwarders, and of the Secretary of Agriculture regarding packers.

There is some judicial disposition to question the validity of a statute which requires a person to walk into the open jaws of criminal prosecution as the only means of litigating the validity of an administrative order. Courts seem loath to close their doors to those who wish to challenge the legality of an administrative order but who do not wish to risk jail to do it.

150

While criminal sanctions may *back up* administrative orders, criminal sanctions may not be *directly imposed* by the agency. A court must always (except for certain temporary confinements) stand between the agency and the jail house. A court must determine whether the agency order was in fact violated and impose the penalty. Of course, the police may temporarily confine criminal suspects, but this is done subject to and surrounded by the protections of criminal procedure. By tradition and long practice administrative offices may also, it appears, temporarily confine persons in immigration cases.

Fines: Although the basic rule is that only a court (not an agency) may impose a criminal sanction, the rule *seems* to be violated in the administrative imposition of fines. Administrative agencies do directly impose fines and these fines look like criminal penalties, but technically they are not criminal penalties and cannot be for various reasons including the reason that the Sixth Amendment guarantees the right of jury trial in all criminal prosecutions. Agencies have no juries. Yet some administrative agencies such as the Internal Revenue Service are by statute authorized to levy fines. In Chapter 4 it was asserted that when a statute provides for punishment by fine or imprisonment, it is a criminal statute. How, if that is true, can a statute provide for a fine without being a criminal statute? The answer is found in a semantic trick: fines imposed by administrative agencies are classified as civil fines, rather than as criminal fines.

A great many monetary penalties are provided for by statutes which ordinarily employ the terms fine, penalty, or forfeiture. Usually the administrator does not have to determine what the fine shall be but only the question of guilt. Usually the amount of the fine is fixed by statute. Occasionally, however, the fine is flexible. For example, the Federal Power Commission's power to impose a flexible forfeiture up to $1,000 on a public utility which deliberately does not provide required reports. An example of a fixed penalty is the $50 fine which the Secretary of the Department in which the Coast Guard is operating may inflict for each violation of the Federal Boating Act.

THE CEASE AND DESIST ORDER:

One of the commonest and most significant methods of enforcement is the cease and desist order. This is comparable to an injunction in almost every way except one: an injunction is enforced by the court which issues it, while a cease and desist order cannot be enforced by the agency which issues it. A cease and desist order is, in reality, a warning of impending judicial enforcement. If the warning is not heeded, a court may be asked to enforce the cease and desist order by injunction or other appropriate decree.

Many agencies are permitted to issue cease and desist orders. For example, the Federal Communications Commission may order a radio station to cease and desist using obscenities or profanity in broadcasts. Or the National Labor Relations Board may order labor unions to cease and desist from certain unfair labor practices, and so on.

Statutes vary as to who is responsible for getting the ball rolling toward judicial enforcement of a cease and desist order. The statute may authorize the agency which issued the order to initiate enforcement. Or, any party aggrieved by another party's failure to comply with the order may be permitted to institute enforcement proceedings. Or the Attorney General or the U.S. Attorneys may be permitted to start enforcement proceedings. Each statute provides a method. These suits for enforcement of federal cease and desist orders go first to the United States District Court, with possible appeal to the U.S. Courts of Appeals and to the Supreme Court.

A party does not ordinarily become liable to punishment for violation of a cease and desist order, but he does for violation of the court's enforcement order. This means a party may ordinarily commit a wrong at least three times to be punished for it, at least once to cause issuance of the cease and desist order, a second time to cause a suit for enforcement, and a third time in order to be found guilty of contempt of court for violation of the court injunction or other enforcement order.

OTHER KINDS OF ORDERS:

Agencies give many different kinds of orders, but none of these orders can force anybody to do anything without the assistance of a court, nor can they stop anybody from doing anything without assistance of a court. This is because the ultimate sanctions are criminal penalties and only a court can impose them. It is true that an agency may revoke a person's license to, let us say, practice medicine without going to court. But only a court can make the person stop practicing medicine if he persists. In fact there are many sanctions that an agency can impose directly without resort to court. Official clearance, for example, may be withheld from a ship which must have it to depart legally from a port. But, still, only a court can punish illegal departures by imposition of the ultimate sanctions.

In his book, *Administrative Agencies of the U.S.A.* (Detroit, 1964), Dalmas H. Nelson discusses many different kinds of agency orders under the following headings: (1) *Assessment Orders* under the internal revenue and customs laws, (2) *Penalty Orders* (monetary and non-monetary), (3) *Social-Stigma Orders* (Internal-Security-Act cases, the Attorney General's List, the Loyalty-Security Program affecting public and private employees), (4) *Censorship Orders*, (5) *Corporal Orders* (confinement orders, prison administration orders, selective-service orders, alien entry orders, deportation orders), (6) *Cease and Desist Orders*, (7) *Declaratory Orders and Related Orders* (closing agreements, opinions of the Attorney General, orders concerning Indians, valuation orders), (8) *Workmen's Compensation,* (9) *Liquidation and Receivership Orders*, (10) *Reparations Orders*, (11) *Orders Deciding Private Disputes* (certification of collective bargaining representatives), (2) *Benefactory Orders* (entries and patents on public lands, grazing permits, veterans' benefits, second class mailing permits, benefactory orders in agriculture, air carrier and ship subsidies), (13) *Orders Granting Legal Protection* (patents, trademarks, copyrights), (14) *Remissive Orders* (the remission of penalties, remissive orders regarding federal prisoners, suspension of deportation of aliens, remissive orders regarding claims of the United States), (15) *Orders Deciding Claims against the United States* (personal injury or death or property loss or damage, government contracts, property taken by the government, particular groups of persons, the settlement of public accounts, rewards to informers, refunds of fees, penalties, and other charges), (16) *Orders Deciding Claims of the United States*, (17) *Miscellaneous Type of Orders* (obstruction-removal orders, vesting orders, orders deciding contracts disputes, orders removing federal employees) .

INFORMAL SANCTIONS:

In addition to these formal orders, there are many informal pressures which an agency can bring to bear. Most people who have regular dealings with a government agency, for example, wish to maintain the good will of that agency, and fear of its loss is sufficient sanction in many circumstances.

INVESTIGATORY POWER:

Any regulatory agency needs to find out what is going on among those subject to its regulation, otherwise, obviously it could not do its job. Regulatory agencies do some of their investigating by means of subpoenas and subpoenas duces tecum. The former commands a witness to appear and give testimony, and the latter commands a witness to produce a document or paper he has in his control. We will use the word subpoena to include both varieties of subpoena. Administrative agencies are commonly permitted by law to issue subpoenas. However, at the federal level and in most states only a court can enforce a subpoena by fine or imprisonment. Therefore, most administrative subpoenas are not directly coercive, but do, nevertheless, have a somewhat coercive affect on people since the probability is high that a court will order the administrative subpoena enforced.

Official curiosity is a necessary part of the regulatory process. Yet, freedom from unreasonable official curiosity is one of the guarantees of the Fourth Amendment which says, "The right of the people to be secure in their persons, houses, papers, and effects, against unreasonable searches and seizures, shall not be violated, and no warrants shall issue, but upon probable cause, supported by oath or affirmation, and particularly describing the place to be searched, and the persons or things to be seized."

That amendment would seem to condemn subpoenas which do not aim at some particular item of information. But a regulatory agency may not know what particular item of information it wants.

The agency may simply be curious or perhaps suspicious—mildly or intensely. A regulatory agency may need to subpoena a hoard of documents, not knowing precisely what it is looking for, perhaps only wanting to see if anything needs further prying into. Is such a practice unconstitutional owing to its lack of particularity?

In 1924 the United States Supreme Court said that "anyone who respects the spirit as well as the letter of the Fourth Amendment would be loath to believe that Congress intended to authorize one of its subordinate agencies . . . to direct fishing expeditions into private papers" (*Federal Trade Commission* v. *American Tobacco Company*, 264 U.S. 298).

It is difficult to see how the regulatory process could go on without fishing expeditions. In recent years the United States Supreme Court has seen the truth of this, and has apparently abandoned its 1924 doctrine, influenced no doubt by the practical necessity for agencies to conduct broad investigations. The Supreme Court does not now require much particularity in describing the documents to be produced by subpoena. Courts are interested in the *relevancy* of the subpoenaed materials to the investigation only to the extent of wanting to know whether the investigation is authorized by Congress, whether it is for a purpose Congress *can* authorize, and whether the documents sought are relevant to the inquiry.

Courts are not much interested in entertaining suits alleging that the subpoenaed materials are not relevant to the jurisdiction of the agency. This judicial reluctance to discuss the jurisdiction of the agency is for two reasons. First, an agency often cannot know whether certain documents or materials concern the subject of the agency's jurisdiction until the agency gets hold of them and looks. Second, if the courts start entertaining suits challenging jurisdiction the entire regulatory process would be stalled and disrupted with litigation because a jurisdictional question can always be invented.

The power of administrative agencies to conduct fishing expeditions has been likened, by the United States Supreme Court, to the power of grand juries to conduct general investigations. In comparing agencies to grand juries a whole host of questions is opened up as to the rights of witnesses. If a grand jury can conduct secret hearings, can deny witnesses the right to counsel, can prohibit cross-examination, can listen to only one side of the story—then so can administrative agencies if indeed agencies are comparable to grand juries. And if they are comparable, then agency investigations can become inquisitions in the worst sense of the word.

If a regulatory agency could not send inspectors out to search for violations of the law it is supposed to enforce, its regulatory job would simply not be possible. Yet the 4th Amendment to the United States Constitution says that people do not have to consent to a search of their persons, houses, papers, and effects by officers who do not have a proper search warrant. According to one view, the protection of the 4th Amendment against warrantless searches applies only where the purpose of the search is to acquire information pertaining to a crime. If so, no warrant would be necessary where the purpose of the search is merely to uncover evidence of a civil (as opposed to criminal) wrong such as violations of housing, health, or building codes. Such was the majority opinion in *Frank* v. *Maryland*, 359 U.S. 360 (1959), upholding warrantless inspections by health officers.

But in 1967 the United States Supreme Court all but reversed itself in *Camara* v. *Municipal Court*, 387 U.S. 523. That decision upheld the right of the manager of an apartment building to refuse entry by San Francisco city officials who demanded to inspect the building for possible violations of the city's housing code, without a warrant. Simultaneously, the court upheld the right of a Seattle businessman to refuse admittance of fire inspectors to his warehouse without a warrant. (*See* v. *Seattle*, 387 U.S. 541.)

But in 1971 the Court seemed on the verge of again reversing itself by upholding the right of welfare inspectors to make warrantless searches of homes of persons receiving Aid to Families with Dependent Children (AFDC) (*Wyman* v. *James*, 400 U.S. 309). Acceptance of the aid was deemed to constitute implied consent for home inspections—recipients could bar inspectors only at the risk of termination of AFDC support. And in 1972 the Supreme Court took a further step toward warrantless searches by upholding the right of gun control officers to make unannounced searches without a warrant. Enforcement of the gun control law would be impossible, said the Court, if officers had to get a warrant before each inspection (*U.S.* v. *Biswell*, 406 U.S. 311).

At present the Court seems to favor application of the 4th Amendment to administrative searches for evidence of civil wrongs, but at the same time the Court is willing to make exceptions where warrantless searches are absolutely essential to the regulatory process.

Chapter 7

How Do Courts
Review Administrative Action?

☆ ☆ ☆

WHAT IS JUDICIAL REVIEW?

Political science students often acquire the false notion that judicial review means only the power of the *U.S. Supreme Court* to declare an act of *Congress unconstitutional.* That definition is much too narrow. Judicial review is the broad power of *any* court (federal, state, local—supreme, appellate, or inferior) to judge not only constitutionality but *all legal issues* affecting not only acts of Congress but of *any government official, agency, or legislative body.* When a justice of the peace passes on the validity of a marriage license, that is judicial review as much as a decision by the U.S. Supreme Court declaring an act of Congress unconstitutional.

Lawyers are keenly interested in the details of judicial review. They need to know a lot about how to get into court with their case, when to go to court, what sorts of parties, and what sorts of issues courts will listen to, and so forth. However, the picture of judicial review will be painted here in broad strokes for nonlawyers. Actually, the case law of judicial review (touching on the basic questions of judicial review, namely: whether courts will review, who has standing in court, how to get judicial review, and how much of a decision will be reviewed) is so conflicting that even lawyers are driven to think in broad shaky generalities. Many policies governing judicial review are inconsistent within the fifty states and also between them.

Courts act differently from case to case. They, however, do certain things fairly regularly. They generally keep out of certain kinds of cases and keep away from certain aspects of controversies, generally keep their power in abeyance until a certain stage of events, and generally require certain forms of procedure for those seeking judicial relief. Their habits in those regards are what we call principles of judicial review, and whenever a court wishes to open or shut its door in some way it usually does so in the name of one or more of those principles.

If one tried to sum up the entire law of judicial review of administrative acts in one sentence, it might be stated: when a party has a controversy with a government agency (or within its purview), courts will not touch the case until the agency itself has been given an opportunity to adjudicate it, nor until the other party has carried his case as far as he can within the agency, nor unless the other party has been adversely affected by the agency in interests which courts are willing or allowed to protect, nor unless the proper form of relief is asked for by the plaintiff. All these, of course, are wrapped up on a cloud of ifs, ands, and howevers.

May Congress Limit the Power of Courts to Review Administrative Acts?: It could be argued that federal courts have authority to hear any case they want to within the broad scope of power expressly delegated to them by the Constitution. Except insofar as express delegations also imply limitations, nothing is said in the U.S. Constitution about the jurisdiction of courts being limited in any way, nor does the Constitution give Congress power to limit jurisdiction except insofar as it permits Congress to regulate some of the appellate jurisdiction of the U.S. Supreme Court. Nothing at all is said about congressional power over the jurisdiction of lower federal courts. On the contrary, the U.S. Constitution in its characteristically free manner vests broad, ill-defined power in the federal courts by saying simply, "the judicial power of the United States shall be vested in" federal courts.

Nevertheless, it is often taught in political science classes that Congress has power to regulate the jurisdiction of federal courts. In fact, both Congress and the federal courts have, since the beginning of the Republic, generally assumed that Congress had power to confer and deny jurisdiction.

Congressional power over jurisdiction is mainly a "political truth," to use the words of Justice Chase. The First Congress *assumed* that it had power not only to "constitute tribunals inferior to the Supreme Court," but also to determine their jurisdiction. The Judiciary Act of 1789 (a contemporaneous interpretation of the U.S. Constitution by Congress) did both: It established courts and determined their jurisdiction. In a sense, courts have generally regarded the question of jurisdiction as a political question, one which courts would leave for political settlement no matter what the constitution says. The Supreme Court has found that the power to "constitute tribunals" and "ordain and establish" courts implies also the power to determine their jurisdiction (*Turner* v. *Bank of North America*, 4 Dall. 8, 1799). And, as the Supreme Court reiterated in *United States* v. *Hudson and Goodwin*, 7 Cr. 32, (1812), the power of Congress to create inferior courts necessarily implies "the power to limit the jurisdiction of those courts to particular objects."

It appears that a difference has been drawn between judicial power which the U.S. Constitution gives to the federal judiciary, and jurisdiction which, under current interpretation of the Constitution, is simply the subject matter over which courts are by law permitted to exercise judicial power.

May Congress Make Administrative Decisions Final?: The array of precedent supporting the idea that Congress may determine all of the jurisdiction of lower federal courts and some of the jurisdiction of the Supreme Court is impressive, but there is also an impressive (or at least intriguing) spearhead of judicial precedent contradicting that idea. These are cases in which federal courts proceed to review administrative decisions which Congress has said shall be

159

final. Statutes giving administrative agencies their authority are sometimes completely silent concerning judicial review or may say that certain administrative action shall not be reviewed or shall be final.

STATUTORY RIGHT TO REVIEW: With one hand Congress gives courts broad power to do such things as issue writs of mandamus and injunction, and with the other hand sometimes denies courts power to review certain kinds of administrative decisions. As a result, courts can usually find somewhere in their broad statutory powers the power to review even that which other statutes say shall not be reviewed. The broad statutes saying yes, more or less clash with the narrow ones saying no. Thus, while Congress determines most federal court jurisdiction (in theory at least), courts themselves determine their own jurisdiction when they really want to by picking and choosing among statutes, and in other ways.

Consistency is not one of the virtues (or vices) of a legislative body. The *intent* of Congress, which courts so often look for, is almost bound to be temporary and fleeting. At one moment Congress may lean toward closing the doors of judicial review in some regard. Congress may not have thought too long or too deeply about it. In another moment Congress may enact sweeping assertions throwing open the doors of judicial review so wide that even the courts are embarrassed. Congress was in just such an expansive mood in 1940 when it passed the Walter-Logan Bill which would have given practically everybody affected by an administrative order a right to appeal it to courts. Probably even the judges were trembling in fear of a deluge. The bill was vetoed.

Congress was in another expansive mood in 1946 when it passed the Administrative Procedure Act although its generosity was tinged with caution. The temper of the act, that is, of its chief advocates, suggests that the intent of Section 10 was to increase the availability of judicial review. As restated by Public Law 89-554 in 1966, Title 5, Section 704 reads, "Agency action made reviewable by statute and final agency action for which there is no other adequate remedy in a court are subject to judicial review."

No matter how clear the statutory language prohibiting review, courts experience little difficulty interpreting that language to allow review. Likewise no matter how clearly the statute seems to throw open the doors of review, courts are still able to shut them.

CONSTITUTIONAL RIGHT TO REVIEW: When statutory authority to review runs thin, there remain armies and battalions of constitutional authority to review—reserve forces circumspectly mentioned by judges from time to time.

In the case of *Estep* v. *United States*, 327 U.S. 114 (1946), the U.S. Supreme Court gave a striking demonstration how to open the door of judicial review by invocation of the constitutional right to review. The *Estep* case involved the selective service act which gave local draft boards authority to classify registrants, and made that authority final. Estep was classified 1-A by the local board. He claimed that he was entitled to a classification of 4-D under Section 5 (d) of the Selective Training and Service Act, which exempted regular or duly ordained ministers of religion from service. He claimed status as a minister by virtue of his membership in Jehovah's Witnesses which views all of its members as ministers. The local board did not interpret the word minister to include all the members of Jehovah's Witnesses. Estep refused to be inducted, and was indicted under Section 11 of the act, found guilty, and sentenced to a term of five to ten years. He appealed his conviction on grounds that the local board had erroneously classified him in the first place. The question immediately before the court was whether it had any authority to hear this particular case in view of the fact that the selective service statute made no provision at all for judicial review of local board decisions, and, in fact, declared local board decisions to be final.

The court disposed of the finality problem by simply asserting that Congress intended the board's decision to be final only if it is legal. Legal means, among other things, staying within statutory authorization. When an agency goes beyond what the statute authorizes, it is beyond its jurisdiction and acting illegally. The question whether an agency is acting beyond its jurisdiction is a judicial question, said the court in the *Estep* case. The purpose of courts is to judge legality. Since the question whether a person is or is not an ordained minister within the meaning of the statute is a legal question, any affected party who wants to appeal the decision of a local board on legal grounds can do so despite the fact that the statute says local board orders shall be final. Congress, said the court, has from the beginning conferred upon federal courts the power to judge legality. It is not necessary for Congress to provide for judicial review in every statute. Its silence is not to be construed as a prohibition of judicial review, nor does Congress intend to prohibit courts from judging legality when it enacts statutes saying that the decisions of administrative agencies shall be final. The Court said in *Estep,*

> We start with a statute which makes no provision for judicial review of the actions of the local boards. . . . That alone, of course, is not decisive. For the silence of Congress as to judicial review is not necessarily to be construed as a denial of the power of the federal courts to grant relief in the exercise of the general jurisdiction which Congress has conferred upon them. Judicial review may indeed be required by the constitution.

The Court then said, "It is only orders 'within their respective jurisdiction' that are made final." By jurisdictions the court apparently meant legal authority.

While the authors of *Estep* paid ceaseless homage to the intent of Congress (for, after all, they were interpreting an act of Congress) there was in that decision a persistent drumbeat suggesting that no matter what Congress intended, courts had a constitutional right to review certain excesses of jurisdiction. While the court used the rhetoric of congressional intent (it said Congress did not really mean to do this and that) the court was, I suspect, asserting a constitutional right to judicial review. This erupted at one point when the court said, "judicial review may indeed be required by the constitution." The court constantly referred to the constitutional right of fair procedure and to the gross violation of fairness that could result if courts were barred from even looking to see whether fairness were being exercised. "If," said the court, "the intention of Congress was to preclude courts from looking into the validity of an induction order . . . the Act is unconstitutional." Saying otherwise would mean that an administrative agency asserting powers wildly beyond anything intended by its enabling act could in effect cause people to be arrested, tried, and sent to jail for violating its outrageous orders, and no court could judge the validity of the agency's soaring claims of power.

Therefore the court said in *Estep*, "Before a person may be punished for violating an administrative order due process of law requires that that order be within the authority of the administrative agency."

The court in *Estep* conceded that Congress could tell courts not to substitute their judgment for that of an agency just because the court weighs the evidence differently than the agency (which is the meaning of the finality clause of the selective service act in the view of the court). But that is a far cry from an attempt by Congress to tell the courts they cannot even look to see whether there is any shred of fact justifying the agency's holding. "Can a person," asks the court, "be criminally punished without ever being accorded an opportunity to prove that the prosecution is based upon an improper administrative order?" And in a highly significant commentary on the unassailable power of courts under the U.S. Constitution to inquire into any alleged denial of liberty or other constitutional right, the court said, "Under our system there is no warrant for the view that the judicial power of a competent court can be circumscribed by any legislative arrangement designed to give effect to administrative action going beyond the limits of constitutional authority."

This point had also been made by the Supreme Court in *Stark* v. *Wickard*, 321 U.S. 288 (1944) in which the court held that statutory authority granted by Congress is a valid matter for the court to review even though the statute makes no provision for judicial review.

> When Congress [said the Court] passes an act empowering administrative agencies to carry on governmental activities, the power of those agencies is circumscribed by the authority granted. This permits the courts to participate in law enforcement entrusted to administrative bodies only to the extent necessary to protect justiciable individual rights against administrative action fairly beyond the granted powers. The responsibility of determining the limits of statutory grants of authority in such instances is a judicial function entrusted to the courts by Congress by the statutes establishing courts and making their jurisdiction.

No matter what Congress says about finality of administrative decisions, a plaintiff has only to raise a jurisdictional question to approach the court providing he is qualified to do so in other respects. If rule of law is to prevail, it is difficult to see how it could be otherwise, for, if courts had no power to quash ultra vires administrative actions, what would prevent the Civil Aeronautics Board from regulating the price of milk? And surely no one would want to depend on Congress to pass new laws every day explaining what its statutes really mean. There are too many statutes, too many words, too many agencies, and Congress is too slow. In *United States ex rel. Knauff* v. *Shaughnessy*, 338 U.S. 548, Justice Frankfurter said, ". . . in enacting legislation Congress is not engaged in a scientific process which takes account of every contingency. Its laws are not to be read as though every 'i' has to be dotted and every 't' crossed." Although agencies themselves have to supply some of the dots left out of the statutes, courts must stand ready to quash any dots or other interpretations too grossly beyond legislative intent as the court views that intent.

Provisions for finality have been made in miscellaneous statutes over the years. Three leading situations in which Congress has attempted to give administrative finality are selective service, government contracts, and deportations of aliens. The Immigration Act provides that administrative decisions in deportation cases shall be final. As for government procurement contracts, they ordinarily include some fine print making "final and conclusive upon the parties" the government contracting officer's decision in all disputes arising under the contract.

Habeas corpus is a means that should not be overlooked for getting judicial review other than by suit challenging jurisdiction. A person who finds himself in the armed forces and who thinks the draft board was beyond its authority, can, despite the alleged finality of the decisions of the Selective Service agency ask for a writ of habeas corpus after he is inducted.

To determine whether a man was illegally drafted and is being illegally detained in uniform, a court would, in a habeas corpus proceeding, have to review the legality of the local board's classification of the man in the first place, and that constitutes judicial review of the board's supposedly final determination. A person in custody for deportation might also use this technique for securing judicial review of final deportation orders.

There is yet another (but somewhat risky) way of securing judicial review of laws and administrative orders, and that is by simply violating them and then, in the course of defending against whatever enforcement action is brought to bear, one can raise the question of the validity of the law or order. This is what Estep did. He challenged the local board's action in classifying him 1-A by committing the crime of refusing to be inducted. He was found guilty and sentenced to a term of five to ten years, but appealed his conviction and won. The general position of the Supreme Court seems to be that one should not be forced to pursue that course to obtain judicial review. There should be a means of obtaining review of such a classification other than by having to commit what could turn out to have been a crime.

But, to return to the central point of this discussion, courts themselves are basically the architects of judicial review, both as to its availability and scope. Congress in this, as in so many things, reigns but does not rule.

The discussion so far might lead one to suspect that courts strive to get into every controversy. This is miles from the truth. Courts *do* strive for the freedom to get into everything, but they do not for a moment want to exercise that freedom all the time, for they strive no less vehemently for the freedom to keep out of controversies. It has perhaps been harder for them to find excuses to keep out of cases, or out of certain aspects of cases, than excuses for getting in. Naturally, they are helped in their search for an arsenal of reasons for keeping out of things by the presence of finality clauses previously discussed. Courts are inconsistent in their interpretation of those clauses and will as freely cite them as a reason for keeping out as they will scorn them when they want to get in, depending on circumstances.

Benefits: Courts will frequently (perhaps even usually) shut the door to judicial review when a statute gives administrative finality to an agency dispensing grants, benefits, and privileges to individuals. Veterans' benefits are an example. Congress has provided that the decisions of the Veterans Administration upon all claims for benefits which it administers "shall be final and conclusive and no other official or any court of the United States shall have power or jurisdiction to review any such decisions." The sheer volume of benefits now distributed by government and the resulting volume of disputes about claims for such benefits has perhaps driven courts to erect a doctrine upon which to base denials of review in benefit cases. The U.S. Supreme Court has occasionally justified its denials by saying, in effect, that a government ought to be able to give something away without people feeling they have a legal right to it. Or, as the Supreme Court put it in *Dismuke* v. *United States*, 297 U.S. 167 at 171 in 1936, "The United States is not, by the creation of claims against itself, bound to provide a remedy in the courts. It may withhold all remedy or it may provide an administrative remedy and make it exclusive, however mistaken its exercise." However, in the lay mind, when people qualify for a government benefit they have a right to it. Thus, the post World War II statute which authorized benefits to veterans of that war was known by everyone as the G.I. Bill of Rights. It would be plainly unfair if a person entitled to those benefits were denied them by an administrative agency, and it would not be difficult or unreasonable for courts to find some rationale for declaring that kind of discrimination unconstitutional.

Perhaps in response to this feeling, the United States Supreme Court, in 1970, held that welfare recipients have a constitutional right to a due process hearing before termination of their benefits (*Goldberg* v. *Kelly*, 397 U.S. 254). That, and subsequent similar decisions, have now all but abolished the right-privilege distinction in the area of benefits, and opened a wider door to judicial review.

Contracting with the federal government is also considered a privilege, and courts are occasionally disposed toward upholding administrative finality where terms of the contract are under dispute. This helps make legally possible the renegotiation of contracts (a kind of unilateral rewriting of contracts by the government when the government feels a contractor is making excess profits).

Privileges, Socially Undesirable Business, Rule-Making, Executive Decisions: Courts tend not to listen to cases involving the initial grant (or denial) of a privilege such as a license to practice medicine. Courts assume that no one has a property right in a privilege *before* it is granted and therefore the constitutional guarantees of due process do not govern the administrative process of granting the privilege. Government is free to allow or withhold a privilege at its discretion and courts hesitate to interfere.

Courts also hesitate to review administrative adjudications involving certain types of business activity thought to be socially undesirable (saloons) which the state can prohibit altogether. Courts often assume that persons holding licenses to engage in that kind of business have less (or no) property right in their licenses, and are therefore less protected by due process and have less standing in court. On the other hand, persons who hold licenses to operate desirable businesses or professions are generally considered by courts to have a property right in their license *after* the license is granted. If statutes require due process in the process of granting or denying or revoking a privilege, then, of course, affected parties will have greater standing in court.

Courts hesitate to review administrative acts (such as the designation of a bus route) which are essentially matters for executive decision-making and which in their basic elements smack more of quasi-legislation than of quasi-adjudication.

WHO HAS STANDING TO ASK FOR JUDICIAL REVIEW?

Courts have erected various rules about who may come into court and ask for a judicial remedy. To have locus standi (a place of standing or right of appearance in a court of justice) one must among other things be claiming a *legal right* that the court is prepared to enforce. Section 10 (now 5 U.S.C. § 702) of the federal Administrative Procedure Act gives standing to "any person suffering *legal wrong*. . . ." Not every wrong is a legal wrong. A legal wrong is one which deprives a party of a legal right. One has a legal right only against those wrongs which courts and/or legislatures consider to be legal wrongs.

If an individual is hurt only by being a member of a larger group which is collectively hurt, courts are prone to declare that he has no standing. A person suing as a taxpayer or as a consumer is liable to be tossed out of court for lack of standing. In some states, however, taxpayers are considered by courts to be beneficially interested persons who may sue to compel public officials to conduct governmental business in accordance with law. But many other courts would consider a taxpayer's interest to be too impersonal to warrant standing. "A petitioner does not have standing to sue unless he is 'interested in and affected adversely by the decision' of which he seeks review. His 'interest must be of personal . . . nature,'" said Justice Frankfurter in *Joint Anti-Fascist Refugee Committee* v. *McGrath*, 341 U.S. 123 (1951).

It is rather difficult to say anything very definite about standing, because the policy of state and federal courts is liberalizing and changing. Furthermore, the courts of different states have varying policies and courts including federal courts are in conflict with themselves about standing. Where standing has been denied to persons as members of a collectivity, it has been done perhaps largely to protect the courts from the annoyance of suits by persons with relatively small interests, and perhaps also to protect public utilities from having to slap down endless suits by consumers and to protect the government from the same bedevilment by taxpayers. Should a person who paid ten cents tax be allowed to tie up the government with suits challenging the legality of anything and everything that crosses his mind? Yet, on the other hand, some taxpayers pay very large amounts, and some consumers are greatly affected by changes in public utility rates, etc. Perhaps, as Kenneth C. Davis seems to contend, courts would be fairer if they gave standing to everyone with a substantial injury (see *Administrative Law Text* [St. Paul, 1959], Chapter 22). No doubt there would also be inconsistencies in the definition of what is substantial, but those inconsistencies might be less offensive to logic than the other rule inasmuch as rules denying standing to a plaintiff as a member of a collectivity are already applied inconsistently within and between jurisdictions.

WHEN WILL COURTS REVIEW? (TIMING):

Courts have some rules of the road about the timing of judicial review. One of the objects of judicial rules about timing is to give a right of way to agency action in order to assure that the courts will come onto the road only after the agency has finished its part of the job and not before. Agencies do a vast amount of judicial work and this is well appreciated by courts which as a general thing happily let a dispute run its course through the decision-making and adjudicatory procedures of the agencies.

Priority of Jurisdiction: A doctrine called the primary jurisdiction doctrine deals with the question whether the agency or the courts shall first decide a controversy. Many cases first decided by the agency are subsequently carried to the courts where they are finally decided. The question of *when* cases may be carried from agency to court for judicial review is covered by another doctrine: the doctrine of exhaustion of remedies, to be discussed later.

The primary jurisdiction doctrine, to repeat, answers the question *who* gets *first* crack at deciding. It gives priority to agencies in cases where there are disputes about fact in technical matters concerning which the agency is supposed to be expert. One of the most important reasons why legislatures have vested agencies with quasi-judicial power and why courts have acquiesced, is that the agencies are believed to have expertise not possessed by judges of the regular courts. A proper coordination of the work of courts with the work of agencies would naturally give initial decision to the experts so that when and if a controversy ever reaches a court the court may have the benefit of the agency's judgment. Consider, for example, the voluminous and technical evidence which the Interstate Commerce Commission must weigh in determining railroad rates. It would be foolhardy for courts to take initial jurisdiction of a case in which a railroad company is contending that the Commission's rate is unreasonable. As Justice Brandeis said in *Great Northern R. Co.* v. *Merchants Elevator Co.,* 259 U.S. 285 (1922),

> Whenever a rate, rule or practice is attacked as unreasonable or as unjustly discriminatory, there must be preliminary resort to the Commission . . . because the enquiry is essentially one of fact and of discretion in technical matters. . . . Moreover, that determination is reached ordinarily upon voluminous and conflicting evidence, for the adequate appreciation of which acquain-

tance with many intricate facts of transportation is indispensable; and such acquaintance is commonly to be found only in a body of experts.

If there is no question of fact to be decided but only one of law, then courts have priority of jurisdiction. It is not always easy to separate fact questions from legal questions. It is for the court to decide whether an issue is exclusively legal. If it concludes there is nothing but a legal question at issue there is no reason why the court should not promptly take jurisdiction.

Legal questions often revolve around the meaning of words in a statute. Courts often settle cases by defining words. Thus, there may be a dispute about whether a statute authorizing some agency to regulate the price of haircuts includes power to regulate the price of trimming beards. Does trimming a beard constitute a haircut? Such a question is *both* factual and legal. If a case depends upon the definition of haircut, courts will have to decide whether the rendering of such a definition is sufficiently technical to warrant lodging primary jurisdiction in the hands of the agency. Courts, to repeat, generally welcome an opportunity to give agencies primary jurisdiction, and, of course, agencies usually wish to have a chance to initially decide because this helps them do their regulatory job. Ordinarily disputes involving the subject matter of an agency go automatically to that agency for initial decision without reference to courts.

Exhaustion of Administrative Remedies. Ripeness for Review: Once it is conceded that the agency has primary jurisdiction of a controversy, when may a plaintiff appeal his case from the agency to a court for review? Agencies frequently have within them an entire hierarchy of appeals procedures similar to that of the courts themselves. A federal income taxpayer in disagreement with the Bureau of Internal Revenue about the amount of his tax, may have his case heard both informally and formally at several stages before he has exhausted his opportunities for satisfaction within the agency. The doctrine of exhaustion of remedies is a judicial policy which holds that a party may not transfer his appeal to a court of law until he has pursued every opportunity for remedy within the agency itself. Exhaustion does not *always* require a plaintiff to go through each and every step of the appeals procedure within an agency; a case may become ripe for review before then, just as a banana may become ripe for eating before it reaches market. If a party will be irreparably hurt in ways which a court wishes to prevent by the delay of administrative procedures, a court will deem it ripe for review. Parties are, of course, hurt in a sense by having to suffer the pain and expense of going through any procedures at all, and this is true of judicial as well as administrative procedures. But procedure, and its associated pain and expense, are part of the cost of living in civilization. The administrative procedure must threaten some harm over and above the cost of procedure itself to warrant its premature interruption by judicial review. For example, a student who has been promised a job if he graduates in June and who is expelled one month prior to that, may justly feel that he does not have time to go through the appeals procedure of the college and must go straight to court to avoid irreparable harm. Courts may possibly view his case as ripe for review.

It very often happens that a question of jurisdiction will be raised in the controversy. A party will claim that the agency is acting outside of its authority. A company may claim, as did the Bethlehem Shipbuilding Corporation in 1938, that it is not subject to federal regulation because it is not in interstate commerce. Why, asked Bethlehem, should it be forced to exhaust its remedies and go up and down the ladder of agency procedure when the jurisdiction of the agency is questionable in the first place? The answer of the Supreme Court in the case of *Myers* v. *Bethlehem Shipbuilding Corporation*, 303 U.S. 41 (1938) was simply a reassertion of the doctrine of exhaustion. While the issue of jurisdiction is a legal one, it is also a factual one. Indeed, the question whether Bethlehem was or was not in interstate commerce was a highly technical factual problem, the sort of factual problem that the agency was expert at untangling and that courts like to leave to agencies. In situations where the issue of jurisdiction is simply and clearly legal requiring no specialized factual knowledge in a realm supervised by an agency, the courts are more likely to accept jurisdiction. But even then they hesitate because, for one thing, judicial intervention interrupts orderly conduct of an agency's business. Courts are inclined to intervene only when the agency is clearly and grossly beyond its jurisdiction. This was not the case in Bethlehem where certain aspects of the company's business were such that might warrant its being classified as interstate.

Another very important reason courts hesitate to enter every dispute at the drop of the hat when a jurisdictional question is raised, is that a jurisdictional question can be raised in nearly every case. Neither the doctrine of primary jurisdiction nor the doctrine of exhaustion of remedies would be workable at all if any party could promptly get into court by simply asserting that the agency lacks jurisdiction.

FORMS OF PROCEEDING:

Courts have different forms of proceedings to accomplish different things. A form of proceeding is like a road and each leads to a separate destination. The particular form of proceeding which a plaintiff elects to use depends on where he wants to go and what he wants the court to do.

Prerogative Writs: After a court hears a case it will generally order something to be done or not done, and these orders are called writs. Some are called prerogative writs because in English law they were intended to correct by special exercise of the power (prerogative) of the crown (which controlled the courts) certain wrongs which could not be corrected by the courts exercising the power they already had for routine cases. A court exercising prerogatives of that sort was called a court of equity. This terminology carried over to many of our courts in the United States which for no good reason still say they are acting as a court of equity when they hear a petition for one of the prerogative writs.

There are various kinds of prerogative writs and a plaintiff in many jurisdictions must beware of asking for the wrong writ. Each writ is by tradition designed to correct a certain species of wrong, and by tradition courts will not issue a prerogative writ unless it is the only remedy available. It is not difficult to ask for the wrong writ because it is sometimes confusing just which writ is appropriate to the object sought. For example, a plaintiff might mistakenly ask for mandamus rather than injunction. A writ of mandamus is a court order saying *do* something, while a writ of injunction says *do not do* something. You can tell a party to do something by saying "do not refrain from doing" (injunctive phraseology). Conceivably, therefore, one could reach the same result (court willing) by either injunction or mandamus. But courts are not always willing; they may be strongly biased in favor of a traditional way of asking for something. By tradition mandamus is used only to compel an officer (or agency) to perform a purely administrative act which it is his (or its) clear duty to perform (for example, to compel issuance of a building permit to an applicant who is clearly qualified to have it).

Besides injunction and mandamus there are other prerogative writs. Prohibition is issued when an agency, in performing its judicial functions unlawfully, assumes a power it cannot legally exercise because that power is beyond its jurisdiction. It is not easy to define judicial power or function (is a Secretary of State exercising it when he decides which names to put on a ballot?) and there will be delay and expense if the court holds that the administrative act was not judicial and that another writ should have been asked for.

Among the prerogative writs are certiorari and procedendo. Certiorari is a court order in which a superior court orders an inferior court to turn a case over to the superior court for decision. In some jurisdictions judges will not issue a writ of certiorari to review an administrative adjudication, giving as their reason that an administrative agency is not a court nor are its cases really cases nor are its decisions really judicial. The writ of procedendo sends a case back to the same court from whence it was improperly taken by certiorari.

Quo warranto is another prerogative writ. Its traditional purpose is to prevent continued exercise of authority unlawfully asserted. For example, the exercise of authority by an alleged county sheriff who was elected by an allegedly illegal or invalid process. The immediate object of the writ is to summon the alleged usurper and command him to show by what authority or by what warrant he exercises his authority.

One of the most important prerogative writs in our system of justice is the writ of habeas corpus. In Latin, habeas corpus means "You have the body." Habeas corpus is possibly the most celebrated writ in Anglo-American law. It has been called the "great writ of liberty." It is a remedy for illegal confinement, addressed to the person detaining another, and commands him to produce the body of the prisoner or person detained and to state the reason for his detention. If, in the opinion of the court, the reason shows that the detention is illegal, the court will order release.

In the United States the writ of habeas corpus is a constitutional guarantee of great importance. "The privilege of the writ of habeas corpus shall not be suspended, unless when in cases of rebellion or invasion the public safety may require it," says Article 1, Section 9 of the U.S. Constitution.

Any or all of these prerogative writs may be changed from the status of common law remedies to the status of statutory remedies, as was habeas corpus just noted.

With all these different ways of saying *no* or *stop it*, it is easy to see how a lawyer might pick the wrong form of proceeding which, if he did, would in many jurisdictions involve at least delay, expense, and frustration.

One might ask why courts bother with form. Why not let anyone who can show a right to some relief come into court and show it and let the court grant the appropriate relief if it sees fit without reference to form? Why not dispense with these various remedies and their confusing boundaries (boundaries made all the more confusing by inconsistent and contradictory court decisions regarding them)? There is a trend toward allowing fewer forms to serve more causes. These writs were developed long ago and the special conditions of judicial organization and procedure that gave rise to them no longer prevail. Some state court systems are moving toward the practice of granting whatever relief is appropriate regardless of the form of proceeding brought by the aggrieved party.

In federal practice, injunction and declaratory judgment have become the main forms of proceeding for review of administrative action. They are available when no other specific remedy has been provided by statute for reviewing the actions of a particular agency. The wider use of injunction by federal courts has caused them to readjust their policies about the uses of that writ because traditionally injunction was used only when there was a threat of irreparable injury to a party who had no other remedy at law than injunction.

Statutory Remedies: It should be evident from this discussion so far that there are two kinds of judicial review: statutory forms provided by legislation, and non-statutory forms developed by courts. The non-statutory forms include the prerogative writs discussed above.

As for statutory remedies, legislatures frequently provide specific methods for reviewing the orders of specific agencies. Statutes often provide either (1) that parties affected by administrative orders may petition for judicial review, or (2) that the agency has to sue in court for enforcement of its own orders (naturally the court will enforce the order only after determining that the order was properly made within the scope of the agency's legal authority).

As time passes and new agencies are created, legislative bodies tend to provide separate variations of review procedure for the different agencies. Consequently, in the course of time a lush jungle of statutory remedies grows up to confuse lawyer and layman. Ideally they should all be swept aside together with all the prerogative writs and the whole business replaced by a single, statutory, all-purpose form of review. Progress along those lines has been made in some states (California, for instance) and at the federal level.

One rather intriguing statutory remedy is the declaratory judgment. It does not order anybody to do anything. One who asks for a declaratory judgment is merely asking the court for its opinion. However, courts do not like to be burdened with idle questions; to ask for a declaratory judgment it is necessary to be in a situation where real damages are threatening and there is uncertainty as to whether those damages can be legally avoided. For example, an insurance company may not be sure whether, in a certain situation, it is obligated to defend a party who holds a policy. By asking the court for its opinion as to the insurer's liability, the insurance company can either relax and go about its other business if found non-liable, or get busy with the defense if it is liable. And all this is before anybody has sued for damages, although it is necessary that someone have made a claim.

The mere allegation of a claim is enough to make a case. Does a certain administrative regulation apply to you, is it a valid regulation, etc.? Before complying, it may be well to ask for a declaratory judgment as to your legal obligations. Someone has defined declaratory judgment as a remedy designed to enable one to turn on the light before descending the dark and cluttered basement stairs. Generally the parties to the dispute, knowing in advance how the court would decide, simply comply without further difficulty.

This form of proceeding is available in federal practice for review of administrative action. A Federal Declaratory Judgments Act was first adopted in 1934. Most states also have declaratory judgment acts.

When an administrative agency gives its opinion in circumstances similar to those in which courts give their's in declaratory judgments, the administrative counterpart is called a declaratory order rather than judgment. While administrative agencies are commonly permitted by law to give declaratory orders (sometimes derisively referred to as good housekeeping seals of approval), agencies do not seem to like to give such orders. This is perhaps understandable because agencies are supposed to be more fluid and flexible in their policies than courts, and it is difficult for an agency to have a flexible policy if it is going to commit itself in advance.

WHAT ASPECTS OF AN ADMINISTRATIVE DECISION ARE SUBJECT TO JUDICIAL REVIEW?

Up to this point the discussion of judicial review has centered on the question of its *availability:* upon the administrative acts reviewable in a suit, who may sue, when will a court take jurisdiction, and what form of proceeding must be used. Now, finally, we address the question what is the *scope* of judicial review: what aspects of an administrative decision will a court review if and when it does review? And what yardsticks will the court use to determine what to review?

Law-Fact Distinction: Briefly, the answer to the scope question (much oversimplified) is this: A court will review questions of law but will not review questions of fact except as to the question of the reasonableness of the administrator's finding of fact. A law question is often a jurisdictional question. It is the question whether an official was or was not authorized to do what he did. The question of vires (authority) is the central legal question. For example, if the Civil Aeronautics Board made a rule governing the price of haircuts in Des Moines, Iowa, someone would probably challenge the CAB's authority and any court would probably view the problem as a legal one. If, on the other hand, the CAB in a hearing to determine whether a pilot should have his license revoked determined that the pilot landed his plane in a reckless manner, that determination would no doubt be considered a factual one by courts because the definition of reckless is mainly factual.

The relationship between agency findings and the subsequent review of those findings by a court, is more or less comparable to the relationship between a lower court finding and the review of that finding by an appellate court. Purely factual decisions by lower courts are not ordinarily reviewed by appellate courts; the appellate court reserves itself for review of the legality of proceedings below as well as for review of questions of law raised in the case. Thus, Caryl Chessman spent a decade on death row appealing his conviction. His guilt or innocence was not primarily at issue in those appeals. Guilt is a factual question which appellate courts generally assume to be settled below. Chessman's appeals revolved mainly around the legality of the trial. He claimed the trial was illegal because the court reporter died leaving questions about the accuracy of the record of the trial.

Now we must hasten to observe that there is *one* legal question at the heart of every finding of *fact* which courts do review, namely the question of the sufficiency of the evidence upon which the finding of fact was based. If the CAB finds that a pilot was flying recklessly, and bases its finding on inadequate evidence, the result is an *unreasonable* finding. Whatever is unreasonable is illegal (if it results in a denial of life, liberty, or property). The Constitution of the United States forbids both the federal government and the states (and through the states, all local governments) to act unfairly with regard to life, liberty, or property. That is the meaning of the due process clauses of the Fifth and Fourteenth Amendments.

Mixed Questions of Law and Fact: The discussion thus far assumes an easy distinction between law and fact. Frequently, however, the distinction is extremely foggy. If, for example, the law gives power to the National Labor Relations Board to regulate certain aspects of companies engaged in producing coal, the meaning of the word producer is a legal question governing the jurisdiction of the NLRB, and it is also a factual question, which in this context cries for the judgment of the agency which is expert in the subject. These foggy law-fact situations are called mixed questions of law and fact (when the court wishes to call them that). When they are designated mixed, the court will not rely on agency opinion as it would rely on that opinion in solely fact questions. The court might treat the mixed question as though it were solely legal; the court might decide both the legal and the factual elements de novo.

It is, of course, a matter for judicial decision whether it wishes to classify a question a mixed question. When it makes that decision, it is also deciding whether to review the fact element with the same completeness employed by courts in reviewing legal questions.

Substantial Evidence Rule: Courts follow the substantial evidence rule as a yardstick for determining the reasonableness of an administrative finding of fact. A finding not backed up by substantial evidence is illegal. But what is meant by substantial? How much and what kind of evidence is substantial? That is a matter for judicial judgment. Prior to 1946, substantial meant to many courts just enough evidence to make the finding of fact appear reasonable to a reasonable man looking only at the evidence *supporting* that finding. In other words, prior to 1946, judges in many courts did not look at the *whole record,* but only at that part of the record supporting the finding. This was to save time and effort. Courts were usually eager to assume that an administrative agency is a better judge of its own subject matter than a court, and that while courts had to check on the reasonableness of agency findings they did not want to delve into it very deeply. A cursory glance at *supporting* evidence was considered enough.

However, many elements of the bar did not feel that that was enough, and in 1946 the federal Administrative Procedure Act provided in section 10 (now 5 U.S.C. § 706) that substantial evidence shall be determined by reference to the whole record. Today federal judges extend their cursory glance both to the evidence in the record *supporting* a finding and to evidence in the record *opposing* that finding. If in the light of both a finding still seems reasonable, courts will let it alone.

The substantial evidence rule has not been a perfectly clear and lucid guide to how much judicial deference should be given to administrative findings of fact. The rule itself is perhaps symbolic of judicial confusion and split personality on the subject of administrative adjudication. Judges are not sure whether to view their administrative cousins as usurpers or as respectable, reliable, and worthy people. Sometimes both attitudes see-saw for control producing widely varying judicial attitudes about how much review is appropriate under the substantial evidence rule. At different times and places courts employ different standards of substantiality. What is substantial enough for one judge is not for another. No one really knows what substantial means. Its very definition is insubstantial.

Courts employ what is known as the clear error test for review of lower court decisions, and it has occasionally been suggested that substantial evidence should be abandoned altogether in favor of clear error for review of administrative decisions. The word clear is presumably clearer than the word substantial. It has been said that a finding is clearly erroneous when the judge is "left with a definite and firm conviction that a mistake has been committed" (333 U.S. 364). Judges seem to agree on what they mean by clear error. They know, for example, that they are not supposed to substitute their assessment of the evidence for that of the lower court if the lower court's assessment is one which a reasonable man could have made. They know that it is clear error they are looking for, not just a difference of opinion.

179

Chapter 8

Should Governments and Officers Be Liable for Tort?

☆ ☆ ☆

If the driver of a post office truck wrongfully crashes into someone, the victim probably would not be content with a court decree that merely declares, "His collision with you was illegal." A declaration of illegality does not always right the wrong and certainly does not repay the victim. Victims want damages.

In Chapter 7 it was explained how courts can nullify and/or stop the illegal acts of governments and government officials. The purpose of this chapter is to explore to what degree officers and governments may be made to pay damages for their wrongful acts. In other words, what is their tort liability?

WHAT IS A TORT?

A tort (from Latin *tortus,* meaning twisted) is a *civil* (private) wrong or injury which means that the victim can sue the tortfeasor (wrongdoer). A civil wrong may at the same time be a criminal wrong (crime) if there was wrongful *intent,* as when a post office driver intentionally runs someone down. In that situation there is both a crime and a tort committed, and the possibility of both a criminal prosecution and a civil suit is present. Violation of a duty owed under contract, by the way, is not considered a tort. A tort is a private wrong independent of contract.

It is not true that every act that hurts someone is a tort. It is no tort for a businessman to harm another by being an efficient competitor, though, of course, some forms of competition are tortious (throwing a bomb, for example). It is no tort for a professor to harm a student by giving him an "F" for failing work. It is not a tort when the state harms people by relocating a highway. People and governments are free to harm each other so long as their harms are not tortious. Some harms are considered by courts and legislatures to be tortious and some are not, just as some are considered criminal and some are not. We are discussing the liability of government and of the officers of government for those wrongs considered to be torts, and we will also inquire into what ought to be considered a tort.

SOVEREIGN IMMUNITY OF GOVERNMENT:

The basic rule about the tort liability of government is that one cannot sue the government without its consent. One might ask, "Why, then, would a government voluntarily open itself to a law suit if it did not have to?" The answer is that it is *fair* to do so. Accordingly, the federal government and many states with a democratic interest in fairness have passed laws permitting themselves to be sued for damages in certain circumstances, such as auto accidents.

Justification for Sovereign Immunity: To many people the curious thing about sovereign immunity is that it exists at all. *Why,* they may ask, should anyone have to get permission to sue? If a government unfairly hurts someone, why should it not be just as liable to a damage suit as any other wrongdoer?

One answer sometimes given is that the American doctrine of

sovereign immunity is simply an inheritance from the British doctrine that the king can do no wrong. The king ruled by divine right and could no more do wrong under that theory than God himself. Furthermore, since the king created the courts it was assumed that he himself could not be sued in them. Justice Frankfurter described our doctrine of sovereign immunity as "an anachronistic survival of monarchical privilege" (327 U.S. 573).

It would seem that the United States would be the last place in the world where monarchical privilege and divine right should survive.

But the doctrine of sovereign immunity rests upon a very sound logical basis that has nothing to do with anachronistic survivals. The irrefutable argument for sovereign immunity is that a supreme authority cannot be forced to do anything. The supreme authority in the United States is the people. They made the Constitution (in theory) and only they can change it (in theory). Nothing in the Constitution authorizes the courts to assess damages against the government, and even if it were in the Constitution the people would have to retain authority to take it out of the Constitution. Otherwise, how could they be sovereign?

Furthermore, the Constitution makes it quite clear that only Congress may authorize expenditures of money. Control of the purse is a cornerstone of legislative power in all democratic countries and nowhere is that power more rigorously exercised than in the United States where the Constitution begins its enumeration of congressional power with the words, "The *Congress* shall have power to lay and collect taxes, duties, and excises; to *pay the debts* and provide for the common defense and general welfare . . ." (Article 1, Section 8, clause 1—emphasis mine). Congressional control of the purse strings is totally inconsistent with judicial control of the purse strings. It is true that legislatures have permitted the courts to assess damages against the government in certain kinds of cases, but this power is revocable and must be if Congress is to retain its ultimate control of the purse.

Justice Holmes saw this quite correctly in 1926. He said, " . . . I can't understand how anyone should think that an instrumentality established by the United States to carry out its will . . . should undertake to enforce something that ex hypothesi is against its will. It seems to me like shaking one's fist at the sky, when the sky furnishes the energy that enables one to raise the fist" (*Holmes-Laski Letters* [Cambridge, 1953], Vol. 2, p. 822). In other words, the principle of sovereign immunity is merely a manifestation of power. But Frankfurter answers, "Whether this immunity is an absolute survival of monarchical privilege, or is a manifestation merely of power, or rests on abstract legal grounds . . . it undoubtedly runs counter to modern democratic notions of the moral responsibility of the State" (322 U.S. 47).

Sovereign immunity may, it is true, run counter to morality, but this does not detract at all from the basic truth that a sovereign must (if it chooses) be immune in order to be sovereign. Sovereign immunity as the starting point of the law of governmental tort liability is a logical imperative that simply cannot be helped or avoided. Many things that cannot be helped run counter to modern democratic notions of the moral responsibility of the state —war for example. The mere process of governing hurts some and helps others.

There is a school that holds that the courts are independent architects of justice within our constitutional system, and that they should feel free to abolish sovereign immunity when and where it pleases them. This view overestimates the freedom which courts actually have in our constitutional system. Congress is given clear authority over money matters and it, not the judiciary, is the main architect in that area, at least formally. Furthermore, Congress is widely assumed to have authority to regulate most of the jurisdiction of federal courts.

Nevertheless, courts do on their own authority commonly hold governments liable for tort in their proprietary functions (those of a business character, like publicly-owned utilities). The distinction between governmental and proprietary functions is a judicial invention, and is a doctrine of governmental liability flatly at odds with the doctrine of sovereign immunity ordinarily sustained by the courts. If courts without statutory authorization can hold governments liable for torts committed in their proprietary functions, why not in all their other functions?

But this practice of holding governments liable in their proprietary functions is not a refutation of sovereign immunity, for the sovereign, by acquiescing in those judicial holdings, gives implied approval of them. Undoubtedly, legislative bodies could sweep away all such judicial erosions of sovereign immunity.

Tort Claims Acts: Naturally, a government can and probably should voluntarily permit itself to be sued for some varieties of tort. The federal Tort Claims Act is a step in that direction. Various states have similar acts.

The federal Tort Claims Act begins by saying that the United States shall be liable for tort claims "in the same manner and to the same extent as a private individual under like circumstances" (28 U.S.C.A., § 2674) and then proceeds to unsay much of what it just said by adding a sweeping array of exceptions found primarily in 28 U.S.C.A. § 2680.

These exceptions include so many of the things anyone would ordinarily think of as a tort except auto accidents, that the act has been jocularly referred to as the federal Negligent Operation of Motor Vehicles Act. Some of the exceptions are:

(a) Any claim based upon an act or omission of an employee of the government, exercising due care, in the execution of a statute or regulation, whether or not such statute or regulation be valid, or based upon the exercise or performance or the failure to exercise or perform a discretionary function or duty on the part of a federal agency, or an employee of the government, whether or not the discretion involved be abused.

(b) Any claim arising out of the loss, miscarriage, or negligent transmission of letters or postal matter.

(c) Any claim arising in respect of the assessment or collection of any tax or customs duty, or the detention of any goods or merchandise by any officer of customs or excise or any other law enforcement officer.

(d) Claims or suits in admiralty.

(e) Any claim arising out of an act or omission of any employee of the government in administering the provisions of sections 1–31 of Title 50, Appendix.

(f) Any claim for damages caused by the imposition or establishment of a quarantine by the United States.

(g) Repealed.

(h) Any claim arising out of assault, battery, false imprisonment, false arrest, malicious prosecution, abuse of process, libel, slander, misrepresentation, deceit, or interference with contract rights (except for certain acts of law enforcement officers).

(i) Any claim for damages caused by the fiscal operations of the Treasury or by the regulation of the monetary system.

(j) Any claim arising out of the combatant activities of the military or naval forces, or the Coast Guard, during time of war.

(k) Any claim arising in a foreign country.

(l) Activities of the Tennessee Valley Authority.

(m) Any claim arising from the activities of the Panama Canal Company.

(n) Activities of a federal land bank.

DISCRETIONARY FUNCTIONS: The case of *Dalehite* v. *United States*, 346 U.S. 15 (1953) illustrates how much wrong can be committed by the United States government without the government being held liable in any way under the Tort Claims Act. The Dalehite case grew out of a titanic explosion in Texas City, Texas, in 1947. The explosion was caused by a fire that started in the hold of the S.S. Grandcamp which was loaded with ammonium nitrate. It touched off more fire and explosions in the adjacent dock area of Texas City. Five hundred and sixty persons died and about 3,000 were injured in the holocaust. The fertilizer which exploded had been manufactured by the United States government. Over 300 suits were brought against the government under the Tort Claims Act charging negligence on the part of the entire body of federal officials and employees involved in manufacturing, supervising, storage, etc. Claims added up to about 200 million dollars. The government should have known, argued the plaintiffs, that special care should have been taken in bagging fertilizer because it cools very slowly inside. The bags should not have been made of paper and should have carried warning of the explosive character of the contents, the granules of fertilizer should have been covered with a coating of paraffin, rosin, and petrolatum.

The Supreme Court held that the government was *not* liable under the Tort Claims Act for damage caused by the explosion. The reasoning of the court spotlights the exceptions to the act. The act says that when the exercise of discretion hurts someone, the government is not liable for damages even if the discretion was an exhibition of bad judgment. The act says in plain words that the government is immune from liability "whether or not the discretion involved be abused." The Supreme Court asserted in the Dalehite decision that the fault was a fault of judgment and an error of discretion by high level officials who originally made the decision not to experiment further with the combustability of materials and who also made the decision to proceed with actual manufacture and storage. The whole operation was initiated by a high level policy decision. It was not the fault of persons at the operating level who merely executed the policy. "Acts of subordinates in carrying out the operations of government in accordance with official directions cannot be actionable . . . ," concluded the court. If the damage had been caused purely by the negligence of workers whose job was to do what they were told, then the government *would* have been liable because that is precisely the kind of thing the Tort Claims Act says government is liable for.

A ministerial act (non-discretionary) done without *due care* is the main thing for which the government is liable under the federal law. But what is a ministerial act? Is there *any* act that does not require some discretion? Surely the driver of an automobile exercises discretion, yet driving is exactly the sort of thing that is most likely to be called ministerial. The ministerial-discretionary line is an important line to find because the federal government under the Tort Claims Act is liable for faulty ministerial acts but not for faulty discretionary acts. The Dalehite court offered this theory about where the line between discretion and non-discretion should be, "Where there is room for policy judgment and decision there is discretion." The court seems to have in mind high cabinet-level policy making.

In a later case, *Indian Towing Company* v. *United States,* 350 U.S. 61 (1957), the U.S. Supreme Court held the federal government liable for damages resulting from negligent maintenance of a lighthouse by the Coast Guard. In the court's view, discretion was exercised by the Coast Guard in *deciding to operate* a lighthouse, but in this case (unlike Dalehite) there was negligence in actual carrying out the policy decision. When the officials at the operating level (i.e., the officers and men of the Coast Guard who were supposed to keep the light actually operating) failed to exercise due care to keep the light operating, the government became liable when a barge loaded with phosphate went aground owing to the extinguished light, causing $62,659.70 in water damage to the cargo.

Wherever courts draw the line between discretionary and non-discretionary, the exemption of torts arising from discretionary acts constitutes a very large gap in governmental tort liability.

DUE CARE: A second gap of huge dimensions in the federal tort liability act is the due care exception. The government is not liable for any tort committed by an official acting with due care. This means there must be fault. Many torts are committed by officials exercising due care: a police officer's bullet may accidentally ricochet into someone; a fireman may unavoidably spray water into an adjacent building; a legislative decision to tax candy may hurt the candy industry. Indeed, almost any decision by government is bound to hurt someone. There must be *fault* at the *operational* level to justify a claim under the federal act. Fault implies want of care or intention to hurt (although intention to hurt is also an exempted form of tort).

WILLFUL TORTS: As just mentioned, a third large gap in the federal government's liability for tort is that which exempts willful torts (except for certain wrongs committed by law enforcement officers). The tort liability act prohibits any claim arising out of assault, battery, false imprisonment, false arrest, malicious prosecution, abuse of process, libel, slander, misrepresentation, deceit, or interference with contract rights. Thus the federal act closes the door to liability for most torts intentionally committed. It is difficult to think of many intentional torts that would not fall into one of the exceptions just listed, although there are some, such as trespass and conversion.

SOME EXAMPLES OF SUCCESSFUL SUITS UNDER THE FEDERAL TORT CLAIM ACT: The federal Tort Claims Act restricts suits almost exclusively to torts committed through negligence in exercise of an operational function. Here are some examples of successful suits under the act, offered purely for illustration.

Brown v. *United States,* 99 F. Supp. 685 (1951): A sailor was partially sucked into the drain pipe and drowned while a pool was being drained. No warning of danger was posted and no screen was over the drain. The court found negligence on the part of the government. Where a swimming pool was provided and maintained by the U.S. at a naval station for the benefit of service men, their guests and families, there was duty on the U.S. and its agents to use reasonable care in maintenance, operation, and drainage of the pool for safety of those persons authorized to use same.

Dishman v. *United States,* 93 F. Supp. 567 (1950): The United States was liable under the federal Tort Claims Act for personal injuries suffered by the plaintiff while an employee of the Veterans Administration Hospital when a medical officer of the same hospital mistakenly poured carbolic acid in the plaintiff's ear during treatment.

Blaine v. *United States,* 102 F. Supp. 161 (1952): The United States was liable under the Tort Claims Act for injuries sustained by an invitee in a fall on a defective sidewalk constituting part of post office property. One slab of the sidewalk had sunk approximately three-fourths of an inch below the level of adjacent slabs due to negligent maintenance by agents of the United States.

Other Ways Governments Pay for Their Torts: Some writers argue that all governments in the United States could and should open wider the doors of governmental tort liability. They argue that in reality governments already pay for many of their torts by the following circuitous techniques:

PROPRIETARY FUNCTIONS: In most states the law of municipal tort liability makes municipal governments liable for their torts committed in the exercise of proprietary functions. That liability is comparable to the tort liability of an ordinary private business concern. Under this rule, if the front steps of the municipal water works were negligently maintained in a dangerous condition causing someone to fall down them, the city would be liable inasmuch as a water works is a business-type activity which is classified as non-governmental and proprietary. But if the same thing happened on the front steps of the police station the city would be immune from liability (unless made liable by statute) owing to the sovereign immunity of the state in exercise of governmental functions.

This distinction at the municipal level of government is based on the theory that a municipal government is in some ways like a private corporation in that it is set up to meet the special needs and wants of a particular group of people. A municipal government is a corporation in the eyes of the law, and is therefore designated a municipal corporation. It differs from a private corporation in three ways: (1) It has geographical boundaries, (2) Its members are anybody living within those boundaries (a private corporation is composed of specific individuals without regard to geographic boundaries), and (3) Some of its functions are those of the state (governmental).

But insofar as a municipal corporation carries on private, non-governmental, proprietary activities it is legally almost exactly like a private corporation that might carry on the same functions for the private benefit of its members. One of the characteristics of a private corporation is that it can be sued, and so the courts have entertained suits against cities for torts committed in the exercise of proprietary functions while denying suits for governmental torts.

Some courts even hold state governments, counties, and other governmental units liable for proprietary torts, ignoring the fact that these governments are not corporations in the sense that a municipal corporation is a corporation.

Courts of the various states flounder about terribly trying to decide which activities are governmental and which are proprietary. It is simply a process of inclusion and exclusion as each situation comes up. When the lady who, in our illustration above, fell down the front steps of the police station brought suit, the court had to decide first of all whether the police function was or was not governmental. Of course, police functions have universally been declared governmental and therefore covered by sovereign immunity except where immunity is waived by statute. In our illustration we had the police department and the water department in separate buildings, but suppose they had been housed in the same building

—city hall. Suppose she fell down the front steps of city hall and then sued the city for negligent maintenance of the stairs? Since city hall is used to house both governmental and proprietary functions, is operation of the building itself a governmental activity or is it a proprietary activity? In some states the liability of the city in that case would depend on whether the lady who fell was in city hall on police business or on water business.

So difficult is it to accurately define the words governmental and proprietary that courts of the various states often disagree as to which is which. In one state a swimming pool may be governmental, in another proprietary.

The judicial knife slides deftly and circuitously through the maze of municipal functions, separating each into governmental or proprietary category. In California some of the activities which have been declared proprietary are: operation of a bridge, road, wharf, dock, harbor, water works, street car, auditorium, community theater, oil well, airport, and operation of parking lots serving proprietary functions. California courts have held the following functions to be governmental: operation of a hospital, art gallery, police department, jail, park, zoo, fire department, school, summer camp, childrens' playground, merry-go-round, swimming pool, and carrying on activities such as burning weeds in a vacant lot to abate a fire hazard, improvement of highways within the municipality, piloting ships in a harbor, and care of the aged. These lists are far from complete and are merely illustrative.

Occasionally a court will hold that governmental activities are only those which are *traditionally* carried on by government. But how long does it take to make a tradition? Cities have for decades owned water works. Some courts hold that a governmental act is one which promotes health and safety. But practically everything any government does promotes health and/or safety. Surely a water works promotes health. A community theater may even promote mental health.

Some courts hold that business enterprises carried on by government are proprietary. But what is a business enterprise? Surely a municipal hospital has to pay some attention to income and outgo of money, to profit and loss; yet a hospital is often held to be governmental.

The U.S. Supreme Court in 1955 spoke of "the 'non-governmental'—'proprietary' quagmire that has long plagued the law of municipal corporations. A comparative study," continued the court, "of the cases in the forty-eight States will disclose an irreconcilable conflict. More than that, the decisions in each of the States are dis-harmonious and disclose the inevitable chaos when courts try to apply a rule of law that is inherently unsound" (350 U.S. 61).

We must consider the liability of governments for torts in their proprietary functions to be an evasion or erosion of sovereign immunity wrought by the courts. Though this liability is not often provided for in tort claims acts, it is approved by legislatures through default and acquiescence.

PRIVATE LAWS: A second way in which governments pay for their wrongs, despite sovereign immunity and despite the narrowness of tort liability acts, is by means of private laws.

One fourth the laws passed by Congress are private. A bill introduced into Congress may be either private or public. A private bill is for the benefit of a particular person, place, or institution; a public bill deals with situations by classes.

Private bills almost always concern either (1) claims against the government, or (2) the immigration and naturalization of particular individuals. Almost all private bills are handled by the judiciary committees of each house. The House Judiciary Committee and the Senate Judiciary Committee each have two subcommittees to deal with private bills; one to handle claims, the other to handle immigration and naturalization.

Each subcommittee on claims is something of a court in the sense that it judges the worthiness of the claims. A congressman or senator who introduces a private bill to pay a money claim is expected to supply the claims subcommittee of his house with supporting evidence, and the department of government involved in the act that gave rise to the claim is expected to file a report. Upon this documentation the subcommittee judges the claim and then passes its findings on to the full judiciary committee which then makes its finding and passes it along to a special group of official objectors appointed by the presiding officer of the house to review the committee's findings. If the bill survives those hurdles it is then passed upon by the house and sent to the other house for comparable procedure, and then to the president for signature.

Hundreds of claims are paid each year through the private bill procedure. People go to Congress with their claims when they discover that their claim is one which the Tort Claims Act does not permit them to press in court. For example, many of those who unsuccessfully sued the federal government in the Dalehite case, later collected from the government by prevailing upon Congress to vote them the money by private bill procedure.

One wonders why Congress, busy as it is, continues to process swarms of tort claims. No doubt the answer is largely political: congressmen and senators win friends and influence people with private bills. Yet Congress *has* surrendered much of its burden by passing the Tort Claims Act. One wonders whether it will eventually pass on even more of its burden to the courts by widening the liability of the government under the Tort Claims Act.

Here are some examples of claims paid in 1964 by private law during the 2nd session of the 88th Congress:

1) Claimant paid various sums to cover severe injuries sustained when shot in the neck by a psychotic patient at a public service hospital (Private Law 88-212, 78 Stat. 1139).

2) Claimants paid $250 for damage sustained when a National Guard aircraft crashed into their fishing boat (Private Law 88-246, 78 Stat. 1153).

3) Claimants paid $7,500 for the death of their minor son who was killed by the explosion of an anti-tank rocket which the boy had found adjacent to Fort Leonard Wood (Private Law 88-258, 78 Stat. 1158).

4) Claimant paid $1,000 for the inconvenience and disruption incident to the crash of a B-47 aircraft of the U.S.A.F. on her farm (Private Law 88-260, 78 Stat. 1159).

5) Claimant paid $483.12 for loss through theft of his personally owned hand tools stored on government quarters (Private Law 88-265, 78 Stat. 1161).

6) Payment of $1,091.18 to a member of the airport police to reimburse him for a judgment against him for false arrest (Private Law 88-236, 78 Stat. 1149).

7) Reimbursement of a government employee for paying out of his own funds judgments rendered against him as a result of an accident while operating a government vehicle (Private Law 88–240, 78 Stat. 1151).

Congress passed 141 private laws during the 2nd session of the 94th Congress in 1976, and during the same session passed 588 public laws.

Frequently claims are paid even when the government is not at fault, which is a far more generous operating principle than the one upon which the Tort Claims Act rests. The act, as explained above, makes the government liable "in the same manner and to the same extent as a private individual under like circumstances" (except for the exceptions). The private law of tort is based on *fault*, either intentional or unintentional. Passage of private bills holding the government (in effect) liable even where there is *no fault* (known as absolute liability), lends aid and comfort to those who advocate that governments abandon their immunity from suit under the doctrine of sovereign immunity and that the government pay everyone who is in any way hurt by governmental action.

However, the payment of claims by Congress in situations where the government has not been at fault does not appear to have gone so far as to include payment of the claims of persons whose only hurt is the hurt caused by legislation which adversely affects them. Tort liability to that extreme degree is apparently practiced in France where damages were paid to a manufacturer of cream substitutes when a law was passed outlawing the manufacture of cream substitutes.

INSURANCE: A third way in which governments pay for their wrongs other than through suits under tort liability acts, is by means of insurance policies which insure the government against certain kinds of claims which it really would not have to pay at all if it stuck to its rights under sovereign immunity. Actually, such a policy is a circuitous kind of tort liability act. When a government takes out an insurance policy to cover certain of its torts it is in effect saying, "We acknowledge liability for these torts." Courts in most cases have required the insured government to waive its immunity to the extent of the insurance coverage, and forbade it to set up sovereign immunity as a defense.

INDEMNIFYING OFFICERS AND EMPLOYEES: Sometimes persons hurt by governmental action will try to collect damages from the officer or employee involved rather than from the government. The common law doctrine of officer liability is that an officer is as liable for his torts committed in public employment as he would be if he were not in public employment, even those committed within the scope of his duties. Where the doctrine of sovereign immunity is waived, both the government and the employee may be liable. But where the government has not waived its immunity from tort liability, the officer stands as the only remaining target of a damage suit. Some governments have volunteered to pay their employees the amount of any damages assessed against them by a court, and have in that way indirectly waived their sovereign immunity. This sort of thing is permitted, for example, by California law which provides that,

> If an employee . . . of a public entity requests the public entity to defend him against any claim or action against him for an injury arising out of an act or omission occurring within the scope of his employment as an employee of the public entity and such request is made in writing not less than ten days before the day of trial, the public entity shall pay any judgment based thereon or any compromise or settlement of the claim or action to which the public entity has agreed.

CONSTITUTIONAL PROVISIONS THAT PROPERTY MAY NOT BE TAKEN WITHOUT JUST COMPENSATION: The doctrine of sovereign immunity collides with a doctrine enshrined two places in the Constitution (Fifth and Fourteenth Amendments) that a government may not deprive any person of "life, liberty or *property* without due process of law (italics added) ." If a government *does* take property without due process (meaning without fairness) , then it can be sued and it will acquiesce in spite of sovereign immunity.

Property is sometimes taken under the sovereign's power of eminent domain. States or the federal government may take any property (the federal government may even take the state's property) provided it pays a fair price. The question sometimes is raised as to just what constitutes a taking of property. Obviously, direct appropriations of property for public use do constitute a *taking*. But what about *consequential injuries* resulting from the exercise of lawful power? For example, what if the noise and glaring lights of planes flying below the navigable air space and landing at or leaving an airport leased to the United States, interfere with the normal use of a neighboring chicken farm? What if a railway tunnel operated by a corporation chartered by Congress emits so much smoke that it injures an individual's property? What if the government imposes a servitude on land adjoining a fort by repeatedly firing guns across the land? In each of these situations the U.S. Supreme Court has declared a taking of property to have occurred. The Supreme Court set forth its doctrine of consequential taking in *United States* v. *Dickinson,* 331 U.S. 745 (1947) wherein the court held that property is taken within the meaning of the Constitution "when inroads are made upon the owner's use of it to an extent that, as between private parties, a servitude has been acquired either by an agreement or in course of time."

Sovereign immunity or not, suits are regularly entertained against the government under the due process clauses for unfair denial of property and under the just compensation clause.

To What Degree Should Governments Waive their Sovereign Immunity?: We live in an imperfect world. Perfect justice may not be possible this side of heaven. Perfect justice is one of the rewards of the next world and perhaps it would be greedy to insist on it here and now. It is, of course, true that we can keep on *trying* to perfect our justice, or at least trying to improve upon it. Yet, sometimes a cure can be worse than the disease. Every case, for example, could theoretically be tried over and over to assure justice. But then the cost would itself loom as an injustice, and the delay of repeated trials would also subvert justice, for it is said that justice delayed is justice denied.

INJURIES CAUSED BY LEGISLATIVE ACTS OF THE LEGISLATIVE BRANCH: There are some questions which cannot be submitted to adjudication at all simply because it would be pointless or impractical. Many of the alleged wrongs of governments are in that category. Among these are the hurts, harms, and wrongs which arise from acts of legislatures. Every policy decision (and that is what a legislative act often is) must hurt some and help others. It would be impractical to allow everyone who is wronged by a law forbidding the use of narcotics (addicts denied their pleasure) to sue the government for damages, or everyone harmed by failure of Congress to pass a bill raising the salaries of government employees. Governments cannot correct these wrongs without inflicting new and worse wrongs upon those who would have to pay the bill. There is often no fair way on this planet to remedy that sort of wrong. And to submit questions of that sort to a court would not cure the injustice. A re-judgment by courts might result in a greater injustice than the original judgment of the legislature.

INJURIES CAUSED BY ADJUDICATORY ACTS OF THE JUDICIAL BRANCH: Nearly everyone who loses a case at law might contend that he was wronged, for in every case both parties contend that they are right. Surely, no one would argue that every loser in court be paid damages by the government. But suppose the judge were motivated by malice, or suppose he were careless in his consideration of factual and legal issues (in other words, suppose he used poor judgment)? A government could hardly open itself to law suits on those grounds for there would then be no end of litigation. Practically every loser in court is ready to contend that the judge was either a poor judge or malicious. Every trial might be followed by another trial to inquire into the validity of the first trial, which might be followed by another trial into the validity of the second trial, which might be followed by another trial, and another trial, and another trial. The mind of the judge has never been recognized as a fit subject of judicial inquiry in determining the validity of a judgment.

Here again the evils of opening government to tort liability for injuries caused by the judgments of judges far outweigh the evils of not doing so. Clearly, some innocents will be hurt by judicial negligence in handling a case, but that is the price of living in an imperfect world.

INJURIES CAUSED BY ADMINISTRATIVE EXERCISE OF FORMAL QUASI-LEGISLATIVE AND FORMAL QUASI-JUDICIAL POWER: All the reasons for not opening a government to tort liability for the acts of legislatures and courts applies equally to the quasi-judicial and quasi-legislative acts of administrators.

INJURIES CAUSED BY OTHER ADMINISTRATIVE EXERCISES OF DISCRETION: Any act of administrative discretion has legislative and judicial overtones, and the reasons which justify excusing governments from liability for wrongs committed in formal exercise of those powers might conceivably be used also to justify excusing governments from liability for discretionary acts.

But there are some acts of discretion which cause wrongs for which governments may wish to make themselves liable. For example, the damage caused people who are hurt by a dangerous or defective condition of public property which the government knew about (or should have known about) but failed to repair: icy city hall steps, let us say, which could have been sanded but because they were not caused a person to fall. Clearly there was a wrongful failure of some kind on the part of the city to sand the steps. It may have been a failure of discretion, and probably was because nearly all actions involve some discretion.

It is difficult to find a formula for determining what the government should be liable for and what it should not. It would be futile to draw the line between discretion and non-discretion, for no one knows where that line would be. Every act, to repeat, involves some discretion. If the government wants to make itself liable for some torts, the best way to do it is to specify *what kind* of torts, rather than talking about discretionary versus operational acts. It is best to *specify* wrongs, such as injuries caused by negligent operation of motor vehicles, injuries caused by a dangerous and defective condition of public property, etc. The discretionary–operational dichotomy can become as ludicrous and as unsatisfactory as the governmental–proprietary dichotomy. Fuzzy words like these have no more meaning than the bark of a dog, and this throws much of the burden of deciding what the government shall be liable for upon the courts.

NONFEASANCE: Nonfeasance means nonperformance of some act which ought to be performed, such as failure of a fire department to respond to a call. The word is not generally used to describe breach of contract. And it is also quite distinct from misfeasance which means the improper doing of an act, and distinct from malfeasance which is doing an act which one ought not do at all. Nonfeasance means, to repeat, the total omission or failure of an agent to enter upon the performance of some distinct duty or undertaking which he has agreed to.

For the most part, governments should be wary of allowing themselves to become liable for nonfeasance without explicitly defining certain kinds. Otherwise, every time the fire department goes to put out a fire the allegation can be made afterward that they could have done a better job, that there were things they did not do that they should have done at the scene of the fire, and so on. The same applies to the work of the police or of any agency or officer of government.

A government may wish to specify some kinds of nonfeasance for which it will be liable. The State of California has made itself liable for injuries caused by the failure of the state or any of its local governments to maintain public property in a safe and effective condition, providing the government knew or should have known of the dangerous and defective condition and failed to remedy it.

INJURIES CAUSED BY OFFICERS ACTING IN GOOD FAITH UNDER AN INVALID STATUTE OR REGULATION: Courts from time to time hold a statute or regulation unconstitutional or invalid. Meanwhile, before being so declared, the law or regulation may have been enforced to the harm and disadvantage of some parties. Let us say, for example, the U.S. Supreme Court holds invalid a law which required segregation of the public schools, as it did in the famous case of *Brown* v. *Board of Education* in 1954. That law worked a disadvantage to Blacks while it was being enforced. Should those Blacks be permitted to go to court and sue the government that had unconstitutionally made and enforced the law?

There are several reasons why a government should not open itself to liability for that kind of wrong. First, for reasons explained above, a government should not be liable for the damage done to persons disadvantaged by statutes. Somebody is always disadvantaged, and it is simply not practical for the government to bare itself to damage suits by everyone opposed to every statute. Second, very often validity is a matter of judgment. The Constitution means different things to different generations and is reinterpreted from time to time to meet changing situations. For many years the Supreme Court upheld the validity of school segregation. Should a government be held liable because times have changed and the court's interpretation of the Constitution has changed with the times? Furthermore, a court's view of the Constitution changes with its changing membership.

GOVERNMENTAL TORT LIABILITY IN CALIFORNIA:

California is one of the nation's more progressive states in things governmental. This surely is true of that state's development of administrative procedure. California has also systematically overhauled its law of governmental tort liability. This was done recently at the insistence of the state's very activist supreme court which, with a startling decision in 1961, plunged the legislature into a crash effort to redefine sovereign immunity. That decision was in the case of *Muskopf* v. *Corning Hospital District*, 55 Cal. 2d 211. The plaintiff was a paying patient at the Corning Memorial Hospital. She alleged that because of the negligence of the hospital staff she fell and further injured the broken hip for which she was being treated. At issue was the question whether the hospital district was liable for the negligence of its agent in operation of the hospital, a function heretofore classified as governmental and under the state's cloak of sovereign immunity. The California Supreme Court held the hospital district liable and in the process went on to say that after a reevaluation of the rule of governmental immunity from tort liability, the court had concluded that the rule must be discarded as mistaken and unjust.

Knowing full well that its *Muskopf* decision threw wide open the doors of governmental liability (wider than anyone would want), the court suspended the effect of its decision for two years to give the legislature time to enact laws redefining the scope of governmental liability. During those two years a study of governmental tort liability was made by the California Law Revision Commission, and many of the recommendations of that Commission were enacted in 1963.

The new California law began by declaring the immunity of public entities, except as otherwise provided by statute. Thus the California law reestablished by statute the broad immunity of public entities which previously had been a construction of the common law. As if that opening declaration were not firm or clear enough, the act went on to describe some specific things for which a public entity shall not be liable, and it did so to preclude some possible implications of other sections of the act which imposed liability on the state: (1) sections making it a mandatory duty to protect against certain injury, and (2) sections making the state vicariously liable for the tortious acts of its employees. Following are some of the things the state asserted that it is specifically not liable for:

1) Punitive damages imposed for the sake of example or for punishing.

2) Failure to adopt an enactment.

3) Failure to enforce any law.

4) Failure to make an inspection; also, making inadequate or negligent inspection of any property except its own.

5) Actions on licenses: not liable for an injury caused by the issuance, denial, suspension or revocation of, or by the failure or refusal to issue, deny, suspend, or revoke any permit, license, certificate, approval, order, or similar authorization.

6) Police and correctional activities: not liable for an injury proximately caused by any prisoner or an injury to any prisoner;

not for failure to provide sufficient police protection; nor for failure to provide an adequate prison, jail, penal, or correctional facility; nor for injuries caused by an escaping or escaped prisoner; nor for injuries caused by failure to make an arrest or by failure to retain an arrested person in custody.

7) Fire protection: a public entity is not liable for failure to provide fire protection service; nor for transportation of any person injured by a fire or by a fire protection operation.

8) Medical, hospital, and public health activities: not liable for an injury proximately caused by any person committed or admitted to a mental institution; nor for an injury to any person committed or admitted to a mental institution, nor for an injury resulting from the decision to perform or not to perform any act to promote the public health; nor for diagnosing or failure to diagnose mental illness.

Rather than saying what it will not be liable for, it might seem easier for a state to list the wrongs for which the state is liable, if the state is operating on the principle that it is not liable for anything not provided for by statute. But it is not easier because, to repeat, statutes imposing liability are a little vague and might be construed to impose liability broader than intended. For example, the California tort liability act has sections making public entities liable for an undefined world of wrongs which an employee himself would be liable for. A public entity is made to stand up and accept liability side by side with the employee in California. Since the basic common law rule of employee liability is that employees are liable for all their wrongs, even for those committed on the job, any law making government liable to the same degree as an employee would greatly widen the portals of governmental liability. Hence, California law hastened to narrow that wide opening by declaring many wrongs for which *neither* the public entity *nor* the employee shall be liable, roughly those listed above. The list of things a public entity in California shall not be liable for reveals to a trained eye that the state legislature prohibited governmental liability for many of the same things that courts had previously shut the door upon under their interpretation of the doctrine of sovereign immunity. Clearly the scope of immunity remained very broad when one considers that the California act, like the federal act, also precluded govermental liability for most discretionary acts (even when discretion is abused) and for almost any other act (or omission) done with due care.

When would a public entity be liable under the California act? Here are some general areas of liability:

1) Injury from negligent non-discretionary acts, such as auto accidents and the like.

2) Injury from dangerous conditions of public property. Under the act dangerous condition means a condition of property that creates a substantial (as distinguished from a minor, trivial, or insignificant) risk of injury when such property is used with due care in a manner in which it is reasonably foreseeable that it will be used. But by statute a number of dangerous conditions are excluded such as, for example, streets made dangerous by failure to provide traffic signals, signs, and markings; dangerous conditions of hunting trails; and unimproved public property.

In order for a public entity to be liable for a dangerous condition of public property, the danger must have been reasonably foreseeable, and the public entity must have had actual or constructive notice of the dangerous condition and a sufficient time prior to the injury to have taken corrective measures.

3) Injury arising from operation of medical facilities subject to regulation by the State Department of Public Health or the State Department of Mental Hygiene, caused by failure to provide the equipment, personnel, and facilities required by statute or by the regulations of those agencies.

4) Injury caused by an intentional or unjustifiable interference with the right of an inmate of a medical facility operated by a public entity or of a prisoner in a jail, prison, penal, or correctional facility to obtain judicial determination of the legality of his confinement.

5) Injury arising from a negligent or wrongful act in prescribing for mental illness or addiction, or in administering treatments prescribing for the same.

6) Injury caused by willful misconduct in transporting a person injured by a fire or fire protection operation to a physician, surgeon, or hospital.

7) Injury caused by medical malpractice.

8) Injury that arises if the employee of a public entity knows or has reason to know that a prisoner is in need of immediate medical care and he fails to take reasonable action to summon such medical care.

9) Injury caused by misrepresentations which are made by an employee of a public entity who is guilty of fraud, corruption, or malice.

10) Injury caused by negligent and wrongful acts or omissions (with certain exceptions), subject to the defenses that would be available to the public entity if it were a private person.

MORE ON THE LIABILITY OF OFFICERS:

Perhaps *the* central problem of all government—if not of all life—is that every good thing is pregnant with evil, and evil is pregnant with good. Perhaps there is even a Newtonian law of political science that every good force generates an equal and opposite force of evil. There is clearly a see-saw of good and evil in the meddling done with the law of tort liability of public officers. The central evil to be avoided is the evil of irresponsible, malicious, and autocratic exercise of governmental power. But good laws designed to prevent such evils encourage other evils. If, in order to make an officer careful and responsible, you say to him that he will henceforth be liable for damage and injury done by his mistakes, his negligence, or his maliciousness, this will surely make him careful and that is good. But he will be *so* careful and fearful that a new evil will rear itself, the evil of public officers unwilling to take risks or to exercise judgment and discretion lest it be erroneous. Officers would be slow or unwilling to act where there is possibility of error.

Until fairly recently courts have applied the theory that individuals must be liable for their wrongs, even public officials committing wrongs in the process of carrying out their official functions. Albert V. Dicey, writing in 1915, said that in England the same law applies to everyone. "With us," he said, "every official, from the Prime Minister down to a constable or a collector of taxes, is under the same responsibility for every act done without legal justification as any other citizen" (*Introduction to the Study of the Law of the Constitution*, 8th ed. [London, 1915], p. 189). When someone wrongfully causes an automobile accident, it would make no difference under that theory whether the negligent driver was in a government vehicle on official business or in a private vehicle on private business. Public employment confers no immunity from damage suit.

The case of *Miller v. Horton*, 152 Mass. 540 (1891) is often cited as a classic example of a public official paying for his official wrongs. In that case the owner of a dead horse sued the members of the Board of Health which had ordered the horse killed. The Board, armed with power under the statutes to destroy all animals diseased with glanders, inspected the horse, diagnosed glanders, and prescribed death. Later the court found that the horse did not have glanders and ordered the members of the Board to pay for the horse out of their own pockets.

The *Miller v. Horton* decision is all the more significant as an extreme statement of officer liability because the Board's error (assuming it was an error) was one of judgment and discretion on a technical matter.

Federal and state law has retreated from the doctrine of *Miller v. Horton* today. In fact, there has been a very interesting general retreat from old doctrines of tort liability, both governmental and officer. The absolute immunity of governments is retreating toward (but has not reached) absolute liability at the opposite pole. On the other hand, liability of public officers at common law is retreating toward (but has not reached) absolute immunity.

In recent decades federal courts have abandoned the practice of holding federal officers personally liable for wrongs committed in the exercise of their discretionary functions. This has been done for reasons well stated by the United States Supreme Court in 1959. Such immunity, said the court, is necessary so that public officers may

be free to exercise their duties unembarrassed by the fear of damage suits in respect of acts done in the course of those duties—suits which would consume time and energies which would otherwise be devoted to governmental service and the threat of which might appreciably inhibit the fearless, vigorous and effective administration of policies of government (*Barr* v. *Matteo*, 360 U.S. 564 at 571).

All federal officials are now largely immune from tort liability while exercising a discretionary duty so long as they are within the scope of their authority. Nor is scope of authority narrowly defined. The shield of immunity covers acts on the outermost perimeter of what might be viewed as an officer's scope of authority, as the decision in *Barr* v. *Matteo* attests. Furthermore, the line between discretionary authority and ministerial authority is not drawn on the hierarchical ladder as it is when the question of governmental liability under the federal Tort Claims Act is at issue. For purposes of governmental liability, only high ranking cabinet level officials are said to hold discretionary authority; but where, on the other hand, officer liability is concerned there is no hierarchical concept. The line is drawn on a different basis and officials at all levels may exercise discretionary authority, and may be immune from liability. The pendulum has swung to a position which allows liability only for negligence in ministerial functions.

Perhaps it should be reemphasized that this trend toward granting immunity to officers in exercise of discretion is only an extension of immunity which has always covered judges in the law courts. Even the common law which made public employees liable for their official wrongs gave immunity to judges. "It is a general principle of the highest importance to the proper administration of justice," said the United States Supreme Court,

> that a judicial officer, in exercising the authority vested in him shall be free to act upon his own convictions, without apprehension of personal consequences to himself. Liability to answer to every one who might feel himself aggrieved by the action of the judge, would be inconsistent with the possession of this freedom, and would destroy the independence without which no judiciary can be either respectable or useful (*Bradley* v. *Fisher*, 80 U.S. 335 [1871]).

Some writers believe that the early common law of officer tort liability was more appropriate for a former era than for today.

Formerly administrative officers were well-to-do upper class people in a position to pay for their wrongs, and therefore the law which made them do so was understandable. Today government officials are a mass of people in very ordinary financial circumstances. One worker in seven in the United States is employed by government and there is no more reason why they should be held personally liable for the errors they inevitably will make in the course of their duties, than for employees of private companies to be held liable.

Perhaps the wrongs which government officials commit in the course of their employment should be considered merely as a cost of government, using the principle of respondeat superior (let the master answer) which prevails in private employment. That principle holds that the master is responsible for want of care on the servant's part toward those to whom the master owes a duty to use care, provided failure of the servant to use such care occurred in the course of his employment.

Unfortunately the doctrine of let the master answer when applied to government runs squarely into the doctrine of sovereign immunity which says the governmental master does not have to answer for anything unless it gives its consent.

But should the government give its consent to be sued in lieu of the tortious employee? This brings us again around to the issue of governmental liability, and to all the pros and cons previously discussed, including the endless suits by all manner of people for all manner of real or imagined wrongs committed by legislators, judges, and the millions of other employees in the executive branch. Furthermore, it brings us around once again to the value which personal liability has as a device for motivating each officer of government to be careful. Should we completely abandon personal liability for official wrong? Which is better: careful but fearful officers, on the one hand, or careless but bold and energetic officers on the other? (There is one of our dilemmas.) Is it possible to have the best of both conditions? Or must we wait until another time for that, too?

Chapter 9

Conclusion

☆ ☆ ☆

In conclusion I would like to draw attention to two ideas now current that promise to serve the cause of fairness and democracy in the administrative process. I refer to the administrative court and to the ombudsman ideas.

ADMINISTRATIVE COURT:

About one dozen separate plans for an administrative court have been introduced into Congress, and all of them have died there without much flourish. But there was a time when even the American Bar Association officially sponsored administrative court bills. That was the mid-thirties. Through recent decades, even to this one, the idea has still been alive though not too vigorous. Nevertheless, I believe I see on the American legal horizon the development of an administrative court. The function of such a court should, in my opinion, be to judicialize the formal adjudications of administrative agencies, not by making the procedure of those agencies more like the procedure of courts, but rather by making the decisions of administrative hearing officers final and appealable only to an appellate court. Now, this is by no means what administrative court bills introduced into Congress have always proposed. On the contrary, those bills have for the most part proposed an administrative court which would more or less take over the role of appellate courts in reviewing administrative acts. Bills introduced into Congress have not really sought to change administrative quasi-adjudication, but rather to change the courts. The bills have dealt with judicial review of administrative acts. Theirs has been a review concept. My concept, on the other hand, is an administrative court composed of administrative hearing officers who would continue pretty much as they are now, except that they would become tantamount to regular judges in the sense that their decisions would not be mere recommendations, but would become as final as the decisions of a federal district court. Hearing officers (or examiners as they are called in federal jargon) should cease to be hearing officers and become administrative judges. In 1972, federal hearing examiners were given the lofty title "administrative law judge," but there are some fundamental changes that need to be made in the status of hearing officers before they really become worthy of the title judge. They need to be more independent and their decisions need to be more final.

Federal hearing officers are somewhat independent; they are partly out from under the thumb of the agency whose cases they hear. Their pay, promotion, and job tenure are partly determined by the Office of Personnel Management rather than by the agency to which they are assigned and whose cases they hear. In most states, on the other hand, hearing officers are simply hired by each separate agency to hear that agency's cases. However, in California some categories of hearing officers are completely removed from the agency and are employed by a special office where they take cases in rotation from a variety of agencies.

For a hearing officer to become a judge in the true sense he should be as independent as a judge. Neither his pay nor his job should be in jeopardy from the agency whose case he hears. Nor should his office or physical location be with that agency, nor should his formal job assignment be with the agency; for all these things produce loyalties and biases.

Besides absolute independence from the agency whose case he hears, a hearing officer to become a judge should be freed from the status of a recommender to the status of a decider. Presently, it is universal practice for hearing officers to submit their decisions to the agency whose case they are hearing for its approval. The hearing officer merely hears on behalf of the heads of the agency who have the responsibility for deciding. Hearing officers are therefore aptly titled so long as they simply hear. It is true that they make initial decisions which *do* become final whenever the agency adopts (or fails to reject) an initial decision. But this is not final decision-making by hearing officers. Even if 95 per cent of initial decisions ultimately become final, still *all* are potentially not final.

So long as hearing-officer decisions are only recommendations, administrative adjudication will continue to display some terribly questionable practices as a consequence. Many agency heads who now have adjudicatory power are not lawyers: the members of a state board of barber examiners, for example. On the contrary, hearing officers are usually lawyers or are otherwise trained in the handling and packaging of information. The question whether an agency head is or is not a lawyer is significant partly because in administrative adjudication the rules of evidence are relaxed and legal training is useful to handle and assess the great junk yard of evidence that sometimes piles up in an administrative hearing. Hearsay evidence and other evidence which would be incompetent in a court of law is freely admitted into administrative hearings. Courts of law employ rules of evidence partly because of the presence of juries composed of people drawn at random who are more than likely not schooled or experienced in the scientific method or in weighing and handling information. Lawyers are likely to be good judges of information. It is to be hoped that hearing officers, even those who are not members of the bar, are also suitably educated or experienced to weigh information without the help of rules of evidence. But what of agency heads? Are they not likely to fall into the errors of juries? If so, shouldn't they also be protected from hearsay and other incompetent evidence? But they are not.

They receive hearing officer reports which may be strewn with incompetent evidence which a hearing officer could cope with but which laymen on barber boards and the like may not be fit to handle. Why should they be *permitted* to handle it? Why not make the hearing officer decision final? If the board does not like the hearing officer's decision, let them appeal it to a court of law if they think they have legal justification. Let them appeal it just as a private party would have to appeal from an agency decision today. And *if* agency heads are someday forbidden to review the decisions of hearing officers, agency heads should also be forbidden to hear any case sitting *alone* for the same reasons.

A second argument for giving finality to the decisions of hearing officers is that so long as agency heads have power to review or to make adjudicatory decisions, there will exist a morbid union of policy-making and adjudication. Why is that union unhealthy? Because a policy maker has to be (or should be) close to the people for whom policy is being made and he has to be (or should be) in constant touch with them and with their problems. It is difficult for him to suddenly switch hats and sit down as a judge isolated from those he is close to, isolated from influence. He switches from legislator to judge with his head full of ex parte information (information supplied by one party but unknown to the other) and with his feelings oriented in favor of those who have been entertaining him on his legislative tours. One solution to that problem is to separate judicial power completely away from the agency head. Let him be a policy maker, but deny him power to review the decisions of hearing officers, and deny him the power to sit as judge in any case. Make the hearing officer's decision final, appealable only to a court of law.

The most compelling argument for giving finality to hearing officer decisions is that without it agency heads are left with two powers which are offensive to each other and to justice: the power to prosecute and the power to judge those who are prosecuted. The union of prosecutor and judge is the worst sin possible in a system of justice, yet so long as the hearing officer's decision is reviewable by the agency head or so long as the agency head can hear and decide the case himself, that sin is institutionalized. It can be cured by forbidding agency heads to hear and decide cases and forbidding them to review the decisions of hearing officers.

Another objection to permitting agency heads to exercise quasi-judicial power is that it is highly time consuming. Agency heads should work at improving policy and reserve their energy for the study of problem areas within their jurisdiction and for the promulgation of creative policies to deal with those problems. So long as agency heads are mulling over endless cases and controversies, they are not getting down to their fundamental task. If they were not burdened with adjudication they would have time to make better and clearer policies. And if their policies were made clearer, then hearing officers could follow those policies and could make final decisions which more frequently square with agency policy. To keep time-comsuming adjudication away from agency heads hearing officer decisions should be made final. It is argued that the policy makers need to have adjudicatory authority to enforce their policy. They would not need adjudicatory authority, however, if their policies were so carefully sculptured that hearing officers could know with clarity what those policies are. It is the duty of a hearing officer to decide cases in conformity to agency policy. Let that policy be clear and creative, then let the hearing officer's decision be final.

I believe we are moving toward an administrative court, but not toward the kind of administrative court that has been contemplated by any of the bills introduced into Congress. The movement toward the kind of administrative court I see in the future is taking place on an entirely different front. It is evolving as hearing officers evolve toward more independence and as their decisions evolve toward more finality.

The administrative court idea is not altogether new in the world. Administrative courts have long played a central role in the judicial systems of a variety of countries in the world, most notably in France whose administrative court has been a model for those of many other countries. In France most non-criminal cases involving the government are heard by the Council of State which is a large administrative court of 200 or more judges. Many of the cases heard by the Council of State would, in the United States, be formally adjudicated by an administrative agency.

The French Council of State was organized several hundred years ago. In the days of its origin it was considered a grand invention for bringing aristocrats under some semblance of judicial restraint. In those days the executive branch of government, as we would call it, was dominated by the aristocracy. The ordinary courts of law were too powerless and timid to check the administrative excesses of that class. The Council of State was to be (and still is) a court composed largely of the same sort of people who dominate the administration. It is a court staffed largely by persons trained or experienced in admininstration, and therefore it is a court which not only understands the kinds of issues that are litigated in civil disputes involving the government, but it is also a court composed of people who enjoy the same lofty status as administrators. In France and in much of the rest of the world administrators have been and still are persons of unexcelled prestige. By contrast, American courts and judges have always far outstripped administrators as prestige figures. If an administrative court develops in the United States, it will not be because the courts of law are afraid of administrators, nor will our administrative court be staffed with persons educated in schools of public administration. As I see it, our administrative court will evolve out of our system of administrative hearing officers by the process of making hearing officers more independent and their decisions more final.

OMBUDSMAN:

It is currently a fad to advocate importation from Scandinavia of a piece of political machinery called the ombudsman. There might be some value in the idea. It has been argued that modern governments need an officer to whom appeals may be taken by individuals grievously hurt by decisions of the administration which are not illegal but which work an unjustifiable hardship. Scandinavian countries have long had such an officer whom they call the ombudsman. Any level of government might have an official suitably staffed to deal with that kind of problem. Some proponents of the ombudsman idea believe such an officer should be free to range over the whole apparatus of government, making criticisms, general or particular, of the manner in which it is conducted. They believe he should be available to help citizens bewildered by the complexity of government who do not know how to deliver themselves from administrative decisions which are malicious or sense-less or which work a special and unreasonable hardship. It is ar-gued that members of Congress and of other legislative bodies find it increasingly difficult to deal with the problems of individuals and still find time to discharge their other legislative duties.

The ombudsman in America might be called an administrative counsel. Whatever he is called, he should be an individual of high integrity and prestige who, with a small staff of researchers, will consider selected cases, analyze the administrative malpractices which may have created the problem, and report his findings to the public. His greatest influence would be through the public report-ing of his activities by the press and other media. However, he might also draw certain situations to the special attention of the attorney general or to the legislative body or to administrators who can correct the trouble. A federal ombudsman might be appointed by the president with consent of the Senate, or perhaps he could be entirely a creature of the Congress.

Congressman Henry S. Reuss of Wisconsin introduced a bill which, if enacted, would have been known as the Administrative Counsel Act (H.R. 7593, 88th Cong., 1st Sess. [July 16, 1963]). Reuss asserts in his bill that "the increasing complexity of the fed-eral government has created difficulties on the part of private citi-zens in dealing with the government." He goes on to say that the efforts of congressmen to deal with these problems have become "so burdensome as to constitute a serious impediment to the discharge of their other duties." Under the bill the administrative counsel would be appointed by the speaker of the House and president pro tempore of the Senate to serve two years. Cases would be referred to him by individual members of Congress, and he would then re-port his findings back to the member. Under the Reuss bill the ombudsman would be an errand boy for members of Congress. That would be quite different from the Scandinavian ombudsman who picks his own cases and reports to the general public.

Other bills to provide for something comparable to an ombuds-man have been introduced into various state legislatures and even some local governing boards have considered the idea.

Advocates of an American ombudsman are not without their critics. The basic question is whether we actually need an ombudsman of the Scandinavian variety. If his fundamental job is to draw the public's attention to administrative action which is legal but unfair, then we have the press already doing about as much as an ombudsman could do. The only advantage an ombudsman might have is the weight of his prestige. If he were the sort of person whose assertions would carry the force of an unimpeachable reputation for accuracy and honesty, this would add credibility to press reports. But do we have reason to believe that a person of towering credibility would be appointed by the political branches of government? If appointed by a president, would presidents be willing to appoint an ombudsman so honest that he would expose wrongdoing embarrassing even to the president who appointed him? We have seen men of high integrity appointed to the United States Supreme Court by political presidents. Yet an ombudsman might be able to hurt a president more than a Supreme Court Justice.

Critics who say we do not need an ombudsman also point out that in a sense every one of the 535 members of Congress are ombudsmen, and so are all other members of legislative bodies. They spend most of their time helping aggrieved constituents deal with administrative agencies. That is their main job, and if they are overworked they need more staff help. Inasmuch as Congress has lost much of its ability to legislate creatively, one wonders if perhaps the evolving future role of Congress is to be primarily that of a collection of ombudsmen. If so, parliaments are returning to the womb from which they sprang. The mother of parliaments began, after all, as a place where the aggrieved could carry their complaints against the crown.

Critics of the ombudsman idea also claim that besides legislators and the press we also have some rather specific pieces of governmental machinery doing the sort of thing an ombudsman would do. The armed forces have their inspector general. And then there are the grand juries that in many jurisdictions range over the whole official apparatus of government, looking not alone for illegality but for anything that needs improving. And, of course, many state and local governments as well as the federal government have their organization and management offices that keep a lookout for poor administrative practices. In a free and open society there are all sorts of special groups keeping a sharp eye on the operations of various government agencies. This is not a perfect system by any means, but neither would an ombudsman be perfect and while he might do some good, one wonders if he could really hope to add significantly to the checks and safeguards implicit in an open society and in a representative democracy.

SUMMARY:

The administrative process, that is, the process by which administrators exercise a large proportion of legislative and judicial power, is the dominant process in government today and constitutes, for all practical purposes, a new form of government. This new form of government continues to evolve in the United States and in other relatively developed countries in the world. Despite our long tradition of representative government and rule of law, power is slipping irresistibly toward administrators. This is a time of revolution, and the administrative revolution is not the least among them. Administrators are taking legislative and judicial power even in the heartlands of representative democracy and rule of law.

As competitors for power against the executive branch, legislatures are not very successful anymore. Congress is failing because it cannot play a leading role in creative policy making in a society as complicated and technological as ours. Congress does not have the knowledge to do it. On the other hand, executives and administrators do, and are using it. Congress is not powerless, but it is much less powerful than it used to be in its relationships with the president and with the executive branch. Its power is almost exclusively the power to say no. It cannot easily create; it seldom does. For the most part it merely judges policies and proposals made by the executive, and nods yes or no, with modifications. Its power and individuality is demonstrated by being negative, not positive. The mantle of lawmaking has passed largely to the executive who not only has the technical knowledge to do the job, but also the political power owing in part to the mass media used much more effectively by the chief executive than the hundreds of legislators. Congress is too big, its organization is too complex, and its equipment too minimal for successful competition with the president as a policy-maker in this era.

The president has at his command the vast expertise of literally millions of federal employees, many of them very knowledgeable. His ability to influence the public on key issues, the prestige of his office, and his ability to influence most members of Congress is great. Congress frequently accepts his guidance, and in that sense the president is the chief lawmaker. Furthermore, the executive agencies and the president have been given rule-making power (quasi-legislative power) of grand proportions—power to make law directly without going to Congress.

Meanwhile, Congress is about as poor at checking presidential power as it is at initiating broad policy. It can say no to presidential proposals, but in 1965 it said yes to two-thirds of them according to *Congressional Quarterly*'s boxscore, and approved almost all of the president's really main-line proposals.

Congress can defeat obscure presidential proposals much easier than well known ones for which the president has launched a campaign. Important policy proposals introduced into Congress without the armor plate of presidential influence will almost certainly be slaughtered at one of twenty or thirty places on the legislative battlefield.

Congress tries to oversee the executive and tries to exercise surveillance over administrators. It is true that Congress can influence executive officers by threatening (or actually holding) an investigation. But even here Congress is like a bear chasing a flea and there are too many fleas to even think about chasing. It is not very expertly done, and when done it is too often in pursuance of some political vendetta than in pursuit of good government or of any administrative excess. Furthermore, a cozy alliance occasionally develops between the agency and the congressional oversight committee, both of which may also be bedfellows with some client group to which they respond. This can hardly be called surveillance. And, Congress can hardly be very good at giving surveillance to that which it does not understand very well in the first place.

Congressional exercise of its other powers to check the president are also handled clumsily, and often for petty purposes far removed from any concept of the public interest or of any concept of good government, fairness, rule of law, or of anything else very lofty. The legislative veto was discussed as a way of making it easier for Congress to chase fleas by forcing some admininstrative rules to walk naked in single file past the eyes of Congress so that Congress could easily pull any of them aside for the gas chamber. The legislative veto is a step in the right direction because it could place more executive action under the direct routine scrutiny of Congress. Yet, on the other hand, it could simply make it easy for Congress to be a nuisance, increasing its harassment powers without increasing its skill at intelligent useful harassment.

At state and local levels of government the same rising executive power and the same declining legislative power is to be seen in various forms and degrees from place to place.

Courts have survived the twentieth century better than legislative bodies. Courts have not been as overwhelmed as legislatures by the political influence of the chief executive. Courts have been far more effective than legislative bodies as innovators and legislators of large policy changes. Courts have been better able to cope with technological data than Congress. This is partly because the judiciary by comparison with legislative bodies is a compact, small, intellectual group, less beset with political interference.

Nevertheless, courts for various reasons have wanted to or had to surrender a few square miles of adjudicatory power to administrative agencies. Courts suffer several limitations which have led to this transfer of judicial power. First, the hostility of courts to the positive aims of modern government has motivated Congress (especially during New Deal and post-New Deal Democratic administrations) to transfer jurisdiction to hear and settle disputes involving certain service state agencies to those agencies themselves, so disputes will be settled by people friendly to the purposes of the agency. The bar and bench, for various economic and social reasons, have been conservative by almost any definition of the word. The law itself tends to be conservative, which brings us to the matter of judicial lag, a second reason for the rise of quasi-judicial power. The law in the common-law world is conservative partly because it is based very largely on the principle of stare decisis which is the principle or practice of basing today's decision on yesterday's precedent. The law is also conservative because it is so oriented to the preservation of property rights. It takes the common law quite a while to catch up with reality in a rapidly changing world, and we refer to that trailing quality as judicial lag. Third, court procedures have been rather inflexible, and the delay and expense of judicial proceedings have generated pressure for a simplified, speedy, and inexpensive brand of adjudication outside the courts, but which is still fair. Fourth, courts cannot initiate action against wrongdoers. Courts must wait for outsiders to bring an action. On the other hand, an administrative agency armed with adjudicatory power can go looking for trouble, can raise an issue and then settle it. Fifth, courts are inclined to be nearsighted in most of their actions, that is, they tend to have their eyes fixed on the private rights of the immediate parties to a controversy rather than upon the larger question of what is in the public interest. An agency with its eyes fixed primarily on the larger question will more often (in theory) decide cases by reference to some concept of the public interest. Sixth, and very importantly, courts are not technically competent in some areas of litigation. Administrative agencies are supposed to possess expert knowledge concerning matters within the agency's purview, knowledge which, if not in the mind of the agency head, is at least available to him on the agency staff. Seventh, there is so much quasi-adjudication that courts of law would be swamped by it if it were all dumped on their shoulders.

As a consequence of the debilities of courts and legislatures mentioned earlier, there has been a tendency to give legislative and judicial power directly to administrative agencies. However, exercise of these powers by agencies has not been altogether exemplary. Administrative adjudication has drifted into some of the same faults exhibited by courts, although some of the faults of administrative adjudication are unique and have developed as a consequence of the attempt to combine administration with adjudication. Still other faults have to do with a kind of doldrum into which some quasi-judicial and quasi-legislative agencies have fallen.

Some of the shortcomings and difficulties of the administrative process are these: First, for various reasons, adjudication in some agencies has fallen victim to the same procedural inflexibility, the same delays, and the same high-cost characteristic of courts of law. This is not true in all agencies but it is true of many, and the infection threatens all of them. Second, opponents of the service state philosophy of government have sought to attack the agencies which implement that philosophy by doing everything possible to cut their budgets, interfere with their organization and reorganization, and by doing other things which would embarrass the functioning of agencies which try to combine executive, legislative, and judicial power in the service of New Deal type programs. Third, agencies carrying on service state activities do not enjoy much public attention any more. They are not as exciting today as they were in depression days when many of them were founded. While the general public is not looking, groups subject to agency regulation have found it easier to control those same agencies through various kinds of political pressure. The regulated sometimes regulate the regulators. Fourth, as a consequence of public apathy, of the capture of agencies by their client groups, and of the general prosperity of the economy, creative people have not been strongly attracted as they once were to service at the top of agencies. Fifth, it has proven extremely difficult for agency heads endowed with quasi-judicial power to exercise quasi-legislative power at the same time. A judge is not supposed to receive ex parte information, but a legislator is constantly receiving information. How can a person be both a judge and a legislator? Sixth, the idea of making a judge out of the same person who is a prosecutor has been offensive to the idea of fair play. When an agency not only makes the rules but also seeks out offenders of those rules and then sits down and judges them, a serious question of elementary justice to the accused is raised. Seventh (related to the last point), how can there be justice to the parties in administrative adjudication when the agency in its deliberations is motivated by its own policy bias rather than by a desire to dispense justice? Eighth, quasi-judicial power was given to agencies partly because they were expert in certain subject matter, but the persons who exercise that quasi-judicial power often are not really expert and have to rely on the advice of persons on their staff, persons not known to the parties, anonymous judges behind the curtain to whom attorneys have not been able to address their arguments.

This book began by describing a revolution in American government, an administrative revolution. It is against that background that the remainder of the book is presented. The study of administrative law is especially significant against a backdrop of soaring administrative power, and its significance is compounded by the very failures of the administrative process which were also discussed. The more fallible the system the more important become the controls on that system.

After the chapters describing the nature of the administrative revolution, the remainder of the book is a series of discourses on the general subject of administrative law.

The main enthusiasm of most persons interested in administrative law is fair procedure. They are interested in law governing the process by which administrators act in matters which affect private legal rights or legal obligations, and in remedies at law for unfair procedure.

I have categorized administrative law into four varieties for the sake of convenience in my attempt to explain where administrative law is found and what it is: constitutional administrative law, statutory administrative law, common administrative law, and administrative-administrative law. The latter is the law which agencies make to govern themselves. I also take the reader on a rapid tour of how to find administrative law by use of legal dictionaries, treatises, casebooks, legal encyclopedias, court reports, the national reporter system, digests, indexes, citators, codes (statutory and administrative), and other miscellaneous aids to legal research. My aim is to help novices find administrative law in its natural habitat, the law library.

Next, this book deals with the question whether the doctrine of separation of powers is still alive, and whether constitutional law still forbids Congress (or a state legislature) to subdelegate its authority to legislate without getting permission from "we, the people." One is tempted to smile at that question because everyone in his right mind knows that no matter how beloved the doctrine of separation of powers may have been to the Fathers of the Republic (and it was important to them for they saw in separation of powers a key deterrent against executive tyranny), and no matter how firmly the Fathers intended legislatures to make the laws and intended courts to decide cases, both of those functions are being carried on today wholesale by the executive. Also, no matter how ancient and renowned the law of agency may be, and how firmly that law prohibits an agent to subdelegate his authority without the consent of the one who originally delegated it, there is power being subdelegated in measureless quantity by Congress without the legal consent of any principal.

However, the doctrine of separation of powers still exists, and so does the prohibition against subdelegation, and these doctrines are available to the courts to strike down as unconstitutional just about anything quasi-legislative or quasi-judicial although courts seldom do so any more purely on those grounds. There has been some fancy footwork and with the help of slippery words like quasi-judicial and quasi-legislative we have built up a fabric of law to accommodate reality with theory.

In the course of this book I ask and try to answer the question whether quasi-legislation (rule-making) can be made democratic. As we all know, lawmaking by Congress is supposed to be democratic in the sense that the members are elected. But administrators are appointed, except one or two or a handful, and yet they are making more law by rule-making than legislatures are by statute-making. Although it is true that the federal and state chief executives are elected, their ability to control a sprawling bureaucracy is limited. If administrative rule-making is to be democratic beyond the sense that it is democratic through an elected chief executive, we need a very special definition of democracy, and I have supplied one (or, I should say, borrowed one). Democracy in administration means administering in such a way that those who are subject to it feel that they are participating in the formulation of the rules affecting them. That does not mean that they really have to participate; it only means they have to feel that way. It means that the rule-maker has to go through the motions of consulting with the people subject to his rules before he promulgates them. It is to be hoped that the consultation is real, that the rule-maker will truly listen, will genuinely respond, and it is to be hoped that those who are consulted will feel a sense of participation based on reality. But it is the sense of participation that makes administration democratic even without benefit of ballots, elections, candidates, and so on.

Considerable space is allocated in this book to the problem of making administrative adjudication fair. The whole point of giving quasi-judicial power to administrators is to escape the shortcomings of courts and to speed up and simplify the settlement of controversies. But speedy justice may not be fair, and, if one believes that 90 per cent of justice lies in following correct procedure, there is certainly a threat to justice by trying to simplify procedure too much. If we are going to combine quasi-legislators and quasi-adjudicators we have other problems that go to the heart of fairness. If we are going to let adjudicatory decisions be made by people who did not hear the evidence we are going to have more problems. And if we are going to combine prosecutors with judges and let agencies operate on the theory that the purpose of their adjudication is not justice but the enforcement of agency policy, then we have still more problems. Perhaps we are asking for too much when we ask for fair procedure in adjudication but shun the impedimentia and the equipage of fairness built up by courts of law.

In this book there is also a chapter on how courts check ultra vires administrative acts which affect private rights and obligations (that is, a chapter on judicial review). There is no point in having law to keep administrators within their procedural and substantive boundaries unless there is some way to enforce it. That is what courts are for. Courts have their limitations, however, and cannot review everything because they do not always have either the time or the knowledge. Courts try to reserve themselves. Some administrative acts they hesitate to review at all (for example, certain adjudicatory findings of fact, or acts revoking privileges instead of rights). Some courts will not take certain kinds of cases at all, for example, complaints against administrative acts based on the plaintiff's interest as a taxpayer. Courts do not as a general thing like to jump into a case until remedies available within the administration have been exhausted, nor until the agency primarily concerned has been given first opportunity to settle it. Courts try to limit themselves to review of the legal aspects of administrative decisions, leaving the findings of fact untouched so long as they are reasonable and so long as they are distinguishable from legal questions. Courts often welcome opportunities and excuses for keeping out of cases, but they also like to keep a ready supply of excuses for getting into cases when they want to. The fact that courts do often stay out of disputes and do often therefore give finality to administrative decisions is further reason for developing stronger checks within the administration for the purpose of achieving fairness.

This book also discusses the liability of governments and of government officials for the injuries they inflict. Should governments enjoy sovereign immunity from damage suits? Should government officials be liable for all the wrongful injury they inflict in the process of going about their official business? These are important questions because governments can wrongfully hurt people and so can the officials of governments, and it is not enough for a court in those cases where people were tortiously injured to say to the guilty party, "You did wrong. We declare what you did illegal." That is not enough in all cases. Injured parties may want to be paid for the injury they suffered. But, if a state is immune from lawsuit, how can it pay for its wrongs. And on the other hand, if it is not immune, how can it keep from being put out of business by ceaseless lawsuits, for, after all, everything government does hurts someone. The problem is to strike a balance between a legal principle that holds governments completely immune and one which holds them completely liable. As for the liability of officers, it is the same problem: if you make them liable for their mistakes you make them cowardly and uncreative. If you do not make them liable, you encourage insolence of office. The problem that many jurisdictions are struggling with today is how to achieve a balance between liability and immunity from liability of both governments and officers. A middle ground needs to be found, and is being found in some jurisdictions.

Now, finally, I have not tried in this book to analyze all the controls on administrative power that exist in our society, for that would lead us into too many things, into sociology, economics, and, in fact, into analysis of our entire culture and way of life. The discussion has centered around the need for control, and some of the ways that administrative power can be controlled in the interest of fairness and democracy.

Appendix A

Federal Administrative Procedure Act
(5 U.S.C. §§ 551–559, §§ 701–706, § 3105, § 7521,
§ 5362, § 3344, § 1305)

§ 551. Definitions

For the purpose of this subchapter—

(1) "agency" means each authority of the Government of the United States, whether or not it is within or subject to review by another agency, but does not include—

(A) the Congress;

(B) the courts of the United States;

(C) the governments of the territories or possessions of the United States;

(D) the government of the District of Columbia; or except as to the requirements of section 552 of this title—

(E) agencies composed of representatives of the parties or of representatives of organizations of the parties to the disputes determined by them;

(F) courts martial and military commissions;

(G) military authority exercised in the field in time of war or in occupied territory; or

(H) functions conferred by sections 1738, 1739, 1743, and 1744 of title 12; chapter 2 of title 41; or sections 1622, 1884, 1891–1902, and former section 1641 (b) (2), of title 50, appendix;

(2) "person" includes an individual partnership, corporation, association, or public or private organization other than an agency;

(3) "party" includes a person or agency named or admitted as a party, or properly seeking and entitled as of right to be admitted as a party, in an agency proceeding, and a person or agency admitted by an agency as a party for limited purposes;

(4) "rule" means the whole or a part of an agency statement of general or particular applicability and future effect designed to implement, interpret, or prescribe law or policy or describing the organization, procedure, or practice requirements of an agency and includes the approval or prescription for the future of rates, wages, corporate or financial structures or reorganizations thereof, prices, facilities, appliances, services or allowances therefor or of valuations, costs, or accounting, or practices bearing on any of the foregoing;

(5) "rule making" means agency process for formulating, amending, or repealing a rule;

(6) "order" means the whole or a part of a final disposition, whether affirmative, negative, injunctive, or declaratory in form, of an agency in a matter other than rule making but including licensing;

(7) "adjudication" means agency process for the formulation of an order;

(8) "license" includes the whole or a part of an agency permit, certificate, approval, registration, charter, membership, statutory exemption or other form of permission;

(9) "licensing" includes agency process respecting the grant, renewal, denial, revocation, suspension, annulment, withdrawal, limitation, amendment, modification, or conditioning of a license;

(10) "sanction" includes the whole or a part of an agency—

(A) prohibition, requirement, limitation, or other condition affecting the freedom of a person;

(B) withholding of relief;

(C) imposition of penalty or fine;

(D) destruction, taking, seizure, or withholding of property;

(E) assessment of damages, reimbursement, restitution, compensation, costs, charges, or fees;

(F) requirement, revocation, or suspension of a license; or

(G) taking other compulsory or restrictive action;

(11) "relief" includes the whole or a part of an agency—

(A) grant of money, assistance, license, authority, exemption, exception, privilege, or remedy;

(B) recognition of a claim, right, immunity, privilege, exemption, or exception; or

(C) taking of other action on the application or petition of, and beneficial to, a person;

(12) "agency proceeding" means an agency process as defined by paragraphs (5), (7), and (9) of this section; and

(13) "agency action" includes the whole or a part of an agency rule, order license, sanction, relief, or the equivalent or denial thereof, or failure to act.

§552. *Public information: agency rules, opinions, orders, records, and proceedings*

(a) Each agency shall make available to the public information as follows:

(1) Each agency shall separately state and currently publish in the Federal Register for the guidance of the public—

(A) descriptions of its central and field organization and the established places at which, the employees (and in the case of a uniformed service, the members) from whom, and the methods whereby, the public may obtain information, make submittals or requests, or obtain decisions;

(B) statements of the general course and method by which its functions are channeled and determined, including the nature and requirements of all formal and informal procedures available;

(C) rules of procedure, descriptions of forms available or the places at which forms may be obtained, and instructions as to the scope and contents of all papers, reports, or examinations;

(D) substantive rules of general applicability adopted as authorized by law, and statements of general policy or interpretations of general applicability formulated and adopted by the agency; and

(E) each amendment, revision, or repeal of the foregoing.

Except to the extent that a person has actual and timely notice of the terms thereof, a person may not in any manner be required to resort to, or be adversely affected by, a matter required to be published in the Federal Register and not so published. For the purpose of this paragraph, matter reasonably available to the class of persons affected thereby is deemed published in the Federal Register when incorporated by reference therein with the approval of the Director of the Federal Register.

(2) Each agency, in accordance with published rules, shall make available for public inspection and copying—

(A) final opinions, including concurring and dissenting opinions, as well as orders, made in the adjudication of cases.

(B) those statements of policy and interpretations which have been adopted by the agency and are not published in the Federal Register; and

(C) administrative staff manuals and instructions to staff that affect a member of the public;

unless the materials are promptly published and copies offered for sale. To the extent required to prevent a clearly unwarranted invasion of personal privacy, an agency may delete identifying details when it makes available or publishes an opinion, statement of policy, interpretation, or staff manual or instruction. However, in each case the justification for the deletion shall be explained fully in writing. Each agency shall also maintain and make available for public inspection and copying current indexes providing identifying information for the public as to any matter issued, adopted, or promulgated after July 4, 1967, and required by this paragraph to be made available or published. Each agency shall promptly publish, quarterly or more frequently, and distribute (by sale or otherwise) copies of each index or supplements thereto unless it determines by order published in the Federal Register that the publication would be unnecessary and impracticable, in which case the agency shall nonetheless provide copies of such index on request at a cost not to exceed the direct cost of duplication. A final order, opinion, statement of policy, interpretation, or staff manual or instruction that affects a member of the public may be relied on, used, or cited as precedent by an agency against a party other than an agency only if—

(i) it has been indexed and either made available or published as provided by this paragraph; or

(ii) the party has actual and timely notice of the terms thereof.

(3) Except with respect to the records made available under paragraphs (1) and (2) of this subsection, each agency, upon any request for records which (A) reasonably describes such records and (B) is made in accordance with published rules stating the time, place, fees (if any), and procedures to be followed, shall make the records promptly available to any person.

(4)(A) In order to carry out the provisions of this section, each agency shall promulgate regulations, pursuant to notice and receipt of public comment, specifying a uniform schedule of fees applicable to all constituent units of such agency. Such fees shall be limited to reasonable standard charges for document search and duplication and provide for recovery of only the direct costs of such search and duplication. Documents shall be furnished without charge or at a reduced charge where the agency deter-mines that waiver or reduction of the fee is in the public interest because furnishing the information can be considered as primarily benefiting the general public.

(B) On complaint, the district court of the United States in the district in which the complainant resides, or has his principal place of business, or in which the agency records are situated, or in the District of Columbia, has jurisdiction to enjoin the agency from withholding agency records and to order the production of any agency records improperly withheld from the complainant. In such a case the court shall determine the matter de novo, and may examine the contents of such agency records in camera to determine whether such records or any part thereof shall be withheld under any of the exemptions set forth in subsection (b) of this section, and the burden is on the agency to sustain its action.

(C) Notwithstanding any other provision of law, the defendant shall serve an answer or otherwise plead to any complaint made under this subsection within thirty days after service upon the defendant of the pleading in which such complaint is made, unless the court otherwise directs for good cause shown.

(D) Except as to cases the court considers of greater importance, proceedings before the district court, as authorized by this subsection, and appeals therefrom, take precedence on the docket over all cases and shall be assigned for hearing and trial or for argument at the earliest practicable date and expedited in every way

(E) The court may assess against the United States reasonable attorney fees and other litigation costs reasonably incurred in any case under this section in which the complainant has substantially prevailed.

(F) Whenever the court orders the production of any agency records improperly withheld from the complainant and assesses against the United States reasonable attorney fees and other litigation costs, and the court additionally issues a written finding that the circumstances surrounding the withholding raise questions whether agency personnel acted arbitrarily or capriciously with respect to the withholding, the Civil Service Commission shall promptly initiate a proceeding to determine whether disciplinary action is warranted against the officer or employee who was primarily responsible for the withholding. The Commission, after investigation and consideration of the evidence submitted, shall submit its findings and recommendations to the administrative authority of the agency concerned and shall send copies of the findings and recommendations to the officer or employee or his representative. The administrative authority shall take the corrective action that the Commission recommends.

(G) In the event of noncompliance with the order of the court, the district court may punish for contempt the responsible employee, and in the case of a uniformed service, the responsible member.

(5) Each agency having more than one member shall maintain and make available for public inspection a record of the final votes of each member in every agency proceeding.

(6)(A) Each agency, upon any request for records made under paragraph (1), (2), or (3) of this subsection, shall—

(i) determine within ten days (excepting Saturdays, Sundays, and legal public holidays) after the receipt of any such request whether to comply with such request and shall immediately notify the person making such request of such determination and the reasons therefor, and of the right of such person to appeal to the head of the agency any adverse determination; and

(ii) make a determination with respect to any appeal within twenty days (excepting Saturdays, Sundays, and legal public holidays) after the receipt of such appeal. If on appeal the denial of the request for records is in whole or in part upheld, the agency shall notify the person making such request of the provisions for judicial review of that determination under paragraph (4) of this subsection.

(B) In unusual circumstances as specified in this subparagraph, the time limits prescribed in either clause (i) or clause (ii) of subparagraph (A) may be extended by written notice to the person making such request setting forth the reasons for such extension and the date on which a determination is expected to be dispatched. No such notice shall specify a date that would result in an extension for more than ten working days. As used in this subparagraph, "unusual circumstances" means, but only to the extent reasonably necessary to the proper processing of the particular request—

(i) the need to search for and collect the requested records from field facilities or other establishments that are separate from the office processing the request;

(ii) the need to search for, collect, and appropriately examine a voluminous amount of separate and distinct records which are demanded in a single request; or

(iii) the need for consultation, which shall be conducted with all practicable speed, with another agency having a substantial interest in the determination of the request or among two or more components of the agency having substantial subject-matter interest therein.

(C) Any person making a request to any agency for records

under paragraph (1), (2), or (3) of this subsection shall be deemed to have exhausted his administrative remedies with respect to such request if the agency fails to comply with the applicable time limit provisions of this paragraph. If the Government can show exceptional circumstances exist and that the agency is exercising due diligence in responding to the request, the court may retain jurisdiction and allow the agency additional time to complete its review of the records. Upon any determination by an agency to comply with a request for records, the records shall be made promptly available to such person making such request. Any notification of denial of any request for records under this subsection shall set forth the names and titles or positions of each person responsible for the denial of such request.

(b) This section does not apply to matters that are—

(1)(A) specifically authorized under criteria established by an Executive order to be kept secret in the interest of national defense or foreign policy and (B) are in fact properly classified pursuant to such Executive order;

(2) related solely to the internal personnel rules and practices of an agency;

(3) specifically exempted from disclosure by statute (other than section 552b of this title), provided that such statute (A) requires that the matters be withheld from the public in such a manner as to leave no discretion on the issue, or (B) establishes particular criteria for withholding or refers to particular types of matters to be withheld;

(4) trade secrets and commercial or financial information obtained from a person and privileged or confidential;

(5) inter-agency or intra-agency memorandums or letters which would not be available by law to a party other than an agency in litigation with the agency;

(6) personnel and medical files and similar files the disclosure of which would constitute a clearly unwarranted invasion of personal privacy;

(7) investigatory records compiled for law enforcement purposes, but only to the extent that the production of such records would (A) interfere with enforcement proceedings, (B) deprive a person of a right to a fair trial or an impartial adjudication, (C)

constitute an unwarranted invasion of personal privacy, (D) disclose the identity of a confidential source and, in the case of a record compiled by a criminal law enforcement authority in the course of a criminal investigation, or by an agency conducting a lawful national security intelligence investigation, confidential information furnished only by the confidential source, (E) disclose investigative techniques and procedures, or (F) endanger the life or physical safety of law enforcement personnel;

(8) contained in or related to examination, operating, or condition reports prepared by, on behalf of, or for the use of an agency responsible for the regulation or supervision of financial institutions; or

(9) geological and geophysical information and data, including maps, concerning wells.

Any reasonably segregable portion of a record shall be provided to any person requesting such record after deletion of the portions whch are exempt under this subsection.

(c) This section does not authorize withholding of information or limit the availability of records to the public, except as specifically stated in this section. This section is not authority to withhold information from Congress.

(d) On or before March 1 of each calendar year, each agency shall submit a report covering the preceding calendar year to the Speaker of the House of Representatives and President of the Senate for referral to the appropriate committees of the Congress. The report shall include—

(1) the number of determinations made by such agency not to comply with requests for records made to such agency under subsection (a) and the reasons for each such determination;

(2) the number of appeals made by persons under subsection (a)(6), the result of such appeals, and the reason for the action upon each appeal that results in a denial of information;

(3) the names and titles or positions of each person responsible for the denial of records requested under this section, and the number of instances of participation for each;

(4) the results of each proceeding conducted pursuant to subsection (a)(4)(F), including a report of the disciplinary action

taken against the officer or employee who was primarily responsible for improperly withholding records or an explanation of why disciplinary action was not taken;

(5) a copy of every rule made by such agency regarding this section;

(6) a copy of the fee schedule and the total amount of fees collected by the agency for making records available under this section; and

(7) such other information as indicates efforts to administer fully this section.

The Attorney General shall submit an annual report on or before March 1 of each calendar year which shall include for the prior calendar year a listing of the number of cases arising under this section, the exemption involved in each case, the disposition of such case, and the cost, fees, and penalties assessed under subsections (a)(4)(E),(F), and (G). Such report shall also include a description of the efforts undertaken by the Department of Justice to encourage agency compliance with this section.

(e) For purposes of this section, the term "agency" as defined in section 551(1) of this title includes any executive department, military department. Government corporation, Government controlled corporation, or other establishment in the executive branch of the Government (including the Executive Office of the President), or any independent regulatory agency.

§ 553. Rule making

(a) This section applies, according to the provisions thereof, except to the extent that there is involved—

(1) a military or foreign affairs function of the United States; or

(2) a matter relating to agency management or personnel or to public property, loans, grants, benefits, or contracts.

(b) General notice of proposed rule making shall be published in the Federal Register, unless persons subject thereto are named and either personally served or otherwise have actual notice thereof in accordance with law. The notice shall include—

(1) a statement of the time, place, and nature of public rule making proceedings;

(2) reference to the legal authority under which the rule is proposed; and

(3) either the terms or substance of the proposed rule or a description of the subjects and issues involved.

Except when notice or hearing is required by statute, this subsection does not apply—

(A) to interpretative rules, general statements of policy, or rules of agency organization, procedure, or practice; or

(B) when the agency for good cause finds (and incorporates the finding and a brief statement of reasons therefor in the rules issued) that notice and public procedure thereon are impracticable, unnecessary, or contrary to the public interest.

(c) After notice required by this section, the agency shall give interested persons an opportunity to participate in the rule making through submission of written data, views, or arguments with or without opportunity for oral presentation. After consideration of the relevant matter presented, the agency shall incorporate in the rules adopted a concise general statement of their basis and purpose. When rules are required by statute to be made on the record after opportunity for an agency hearing, sections 556 and 557 of this title apply instead of this subsection.

(d) The required publication or service of a substantive rule shall be made not less than 30 days before its effective date, except—

(1) a substantive rule which grants or recognizes an exemption or relieves a restriction;

(2) interpretative rules and statements of policy; or

(3) as otherwise provided by the agency for good cause found and published with the rule.

(e) Each agency shall give an interested person the right to petition for the issuance, amendment, or repeal of a rule.

§ 554. Adjudications

(a) This section applies, according to the provisions thereof, in every case of adjudication required by statute to be determined on the record after opportunity for an agency hearing, except to the extent that there is involved—

(1) a matter subject to a subsequent trial of the law and the facts de novo in a court;

(2) the selection or tenure of an employee, except a hearing examiner appointed under section 3105 of this title;

(3) proceedings in which decisions rest solely on inspections, tests, or elections;

(4) the conduct of military or foreign affairs functions;

(5) cases in which an agency is acting as an agent for a court; or,

(6) the certification of worker representatives.

(b) Persons entitled to notice of an agency hearing shall be timely informed of—

(1) the time, place, and nature of the hearing;

(2) the legal authority and jurisdiction under which the hearing is to be held; and

(3) the matters of fact and law asserted.

When private persons are the moving parties, other parties to the proceeding shall give prompt notice of issues controverted in fact or law; and in other instances agencies may by rule require responsive pleading. In fixing the time and place for hearings, due regard shall be had for the convenience and necessity of the parties or their representatives.

(c) The agency shall give all interested parties opportunity for—

(1) the submission and consideration of facts, arguments, offers of settlement, or proposals of adjustment when time, the nature of the proceeding, and the public interest permit; and

(2) to the extent that the parties are unable so to determine a controversy by consent, hearing and decision on notice and in accordance with sections 556 and 557 of this title.

(d) The employee who presides at the reception of evidence pursuant to section 556 of this title shall make the recommended decision or initial decision required by section 557 of this title, unless he becomes unavailable to the agency. Except to the extent required for the disposition of ex parte matters as authorized by law, such an employee may not—

(1) consult a person or party on a fact in issue, unless on notice and opportunity for all parties to participate; or

(2) be responsible to or subject to the supervision or direction of an employee or agent engaged in the performance of investigative or prosecuting functions for an agency.

An employee or agent engaged in the performance of investigative or prosecuting functions for an agency in a case may not, in that or a factually related case, participate or advise in the decision, recommended decision, or agency review pursuant to section 557 of this title, except as witness or counsel in public proceedings. This subsection does not apply—

(A) in determining applications for initial licenses;

(B) to proceedings involving the validity or application of rates, facilities, or practices of public utilities or carriers; or

(C) to the agency or a member or members of the body comprising the agency.

(e) The agency, with like effect as in the case of other orders, and in its sound discretion, may issue a declaratory order to terminate a controversy or remove uncertainty.

§ 555. Ancillary matters

(a) This section applies, according to the provisions thereof, except as otherwise provided by this subchapter.

(b) A person compelled to appear in person before an agency or representative thereof is entitled to be accompanied, represented, and advised by counsel or, if permitted by the agency, by other qualified representative. A party is entitled to appear in person or by or with counsel or other duly qualified representative in an agency proceeding. So far as the orderly conduct of public business permits, an interested person may appear before an agency or its responsible employees for the presentation, adjustment, or determination of an issue, request, or controversy in a proceeding, whether interlocutory, summary, or otherwise, or in connection with an agency function. With due regard for the convenience and necessity of the parties or their representatives and within a reasonable time, each agency shall proceed to conclude a matter presented to it. This subsection does not grant or deny a person who is not a lawyer the right to appear for or represent others before an agency or in an agency proceeding.

(c) Process, requirement of a report, inspection, or other investigative act or demand may not be issued, made, or enforced except as authorized by law. A person compelled to submit data or evidence is entitled to retain or, on payment of lawfully prescribed costs, procure a copy or transcript thereof, except that in a nonpublic investigatory proceeding the witness may for good cause be limited to inspection of the official transcript of his testimony.

(d) Agency subpenas authorized by law shall be issued to a party on request and, when required by rules of procedure, on a statement or showing of general relevance and reasonable scope of the evidence sought. On contest, the court shall sustain the subpena or similar process or demand to the extent that it is found to be in accordance with law. In a proceeding for enforcement, the court shall issue an order requiring the appearance of the witness or the production of the evidence or data within a reasonable time under penalty of punishment for contempt in case of contumacious failure to comply.

(e) Prompt notice shall be given of the denial in whole or in part of a written application, petition, or other request of an interested person made in connection with any agency proceeding. Except in affirming a prior denial or when the denial is self-explanatory, the notice shall be accompanied by a brief statement of the grounds for denial.

§ 556. *Hearings; presiding employees; powers and duties; burden of proof; evidence; record as basis of decision*

(a) This section applies, according to the provisions thereof, to hearings required by section 553 or 554 of this title to be conducted in accordance with this section.

(b) There shall preside at the taking of evidence—

(1) the agency;

(2) one or more members of the body which comprises the agency; or

(3) one or more hearing examiners appointed under section 3105 of this title.

This subchapter does not supersede the conduct of specified classes of proceedings, in whole or in part, by or before boards or other employees specially provided for by or designated under statute. The functions of presiding employees and of employees participating in decisions in accordance with section 557 of this title shall be conducted in an impartial manner. A presiding or participating employee may at any time disqualify himself. On the filing in good faith of a timely and sufficient affidavit of personal bias or other disqualification of a presiding or participating employee, the agency shall determine the matter as a part of the record and decision in the case.

(c) Subject to published rules of the agency and within its powers, employees presiding at hearings may—

(1) administer oaths and affirmations;

(2) issue subpenas authorized by law;

(3) rule on offers of proof and receive relevant evidence;

(4) take depositions or have depositions taken when the ends of justice would be served;

(5) regulate the course of the hearing;

(6) hold conferences for the settlement or simplication of the issues by consent of the parties;

(7) dispose of procedural requests or similar matters;

(8) make or recommend decisions in accordance with section 557 of this title; and

(9) take other action authorized by agency rule consistent with this subchapter.

(d) Except as otherwise provided by statute, the proponent of a rule or order has the burden of proof. Any oral or documentary evidence may be received, but the agency as a matter of policy shall provide for the exclusion of irrelevant, immaterial, or unduly repetitious evidence. A sanction may not be imposed or rule or order issued except on consideration of the whole record or those parts thereof cited by a party and supported by and in accordance with the reliable, probative, and substantial evidence. The agency may, to the extent consistent with the interests of justice and the policy of the underlying statutes administered by the agency, consider a violation of section 557(d) of this title sufficient grounds for a decision adverse to a party who has knowingly committed such violation or knowingly caused such violation to occur. A party is entitled to present his case or defense by oral or documentary evidence, to submit rebuttal evidence, and to conduct such cross-examination as may be required for a full and true disclosure of the facts. In rule making or determining claims for money or benefits or applications for initial licenses an agency may, when a party will not be prejudiced thereby adopt procedures for the submission of all or part of the evidence in written form.

(e) The transcript of testimony and exhibits, together with all papers and requests filed in the proceeding, constitutes the exclusive record for decision in accordance with section 557 of this title and, on payment of lawfully prescribed costs, shall be made available to the parties. When an agency decision rests on official notice of a material fact not appearing in the evidence in the record, a party is entitled, on timely request, to an opportunity to show the contrary.

§557. *Initial decisions; conclusiveness; review by agency; submissions by parties; contents of decisions; record*

(a) This section applies, according to the provisions thereof, when a hearing is required to be conducted in accordance with section 556 of this title.

(b) When the agency did not preside at the reception of the evidence, the presiding employee or, in cases not subject to section 554 (d) of this title, an employee qualified to preside at hearings pursuant to section 556 of this title, shall initially decide the case unless the agency requires, either in specific cases or by general rule, the entire record to be certified to it for decision. When the presiding employee makes an initial decision, that decision then becomes the decision of the agency without further proceedings unless there is an appeal to, or review on motion of, the agency within time provided by rule. On appeal from or review of the initial decision, the agency has all the powers which it would have in making the initial decision except as it may limit the issues on notice or by rule. When the agency makes the decision without having presided at the reception of the evidence, the presiding employee or an employee qualified to preside at hearings pursuant to section 556 of this title shall first recommend a decision, except that in rule making or determining applications for initial licenses—

(1) instead thereof the agency may issue a tentative decision or one of its responsible employees may recommend a decision; or

(2) this procedure may be omitted in a case in which the agency finds on the record that due and timely execution of its functions imperatively and unavoidably so requires.

(c) Before a recommended, initial, or tentative decision, or a decision on agency review of the decision of subordinate employees, the parties are entitled to a reasonable opportunity to submit for the consideration of the employees participating in the decisions—

(1) proposed findings and conclusions; or

(2) exceptions to the decisions or recommended decisions of subordinate employees or to tentative agency decisions: and

(3) supporting reasons for the exceptions or proposed findings or conclusions.

The record shall show the ruling on each finding, conclusion, or exception presented. All decisions, including initial, recommended, and tentative decisions, are a part of the record and shall include a statement of—

(A) findings and conclusions, and the reasons or basis therefor, on all the material issues of fact, law, or discretion presented on the record; and

(B) the appropriate rule, order, sanction, relief, or denial thereof.

(d)(1) In any agency proceeding which is subject to subsection (a) of this section, except to the extent required for the disposition of ex parte matters as authorized by law—

(A) no interested person outside the agency shall make or knowingly cause to be made to any member of the body comprising the agency, administrative law judge, or other employee who is or may reasonably be expected to be involved in the decisional process of the proceeding, an ex parte communication relevant to the merits of the proceeding;

(B) no member of the body comprising the agency, administrative law judge, or other employee who is or may reasonably be expected to be involved in the decisional process of the proceeding, shall make or knowingly cause to be made to any interested person outside the agency an ex parte communication relevant to the merits of the proceeding;

(C) a member of the body comprising the agency, administrative law judge, or other employee who is or may reasonably be expected to be involved in the decisional process of such proceeding who receives, or who makes or knowingly causes to be made, a communication prohibited by this subsection shall place on the public record of the proceeding:

(i) all such written communications;

(ii) memoranda stating the substance of all such oral communications; and

(iii) all written responses, and memoranda stating the substance of all oral responses, to the materials described in clauses (i) and (ii) of this subparagraph;

(D) upon receipt of a communication knowingly made or knowingly caused to be made by a party in violation of this subsection, the agency, administrative law judge, or other employee presiding at the hearing may, to the extent consistent with the interests of justice and the policy of the underlying statutes, require the party to show cause why his claim or interest in the proceeding should not be dismissed, denied, disregarded, or otherwise adversely affected on account of such violation; and

(E) the prohibitions of this subsection shall apply beginning at such time as the agency may designate, but in no case shall they begin to apply later than the time at which a proceeding is noticed for hearing unless the person responsible for the communication has knowledge that it will be noticed, in which case the prohibitions shall apply beginning at the time of his acquisition of such knowledge.

(2) This subsection does not constitute authority to withhold information from Congress.

§ *558. Imposition of sanctions; determination of applications for licenses; suspension, revocation, and expiration of licenses*

(a) This section applies, according to the provisions thereof, to the exercise of a power or authority.

(b) A sanction may not be imposed or a substantive rule or order issued except within jurisdiction delegated to the agency and as authorized by law.

(c) When application is made for a license required by law, the agency, with due regard for the rights and privileges of all the interested parties or adversely affected persons and within a reasonable time, shall set and complete proceedings required to be conducted in accordance with sections 556 and 557 of this title or other proceedings required by law and shall make its decision. Except in cases of willfulness or those in which public health, interest, or safety requires otherwise, the withdrawal, suspension, revocation, or annulment of a license is lawful only if, before the institution of agency proceedings therefor, the licensee has been given—

(1) notice by the agency in writing of the facts or conduct which may warrant the action; and

(2) opportunity to demonstrate or achieve compliance with all lawful requirements.

When the licensee has made timely and sufficient application for a renewal or a new license in accordance with agency rules, a license with reference to an activity of a continuing nature does not expire until the application has been finally determined by the agency.

559. Effect on other laws; effect of subsequent statute

This subchapter, chapter 7, and sections 1305, 3105, 3344, 4301 (2) (E), 5362, and 7521, and the provisions of section 5335 (a) (B) of this title that relate to hearing examiners, do not limit or repeal additional requirements imposed by statute or otherwise recognized by law. Except as otherwise required by law, requirements or privileges relating to evidence or procedure apply equally to agencies and persons. Each agency is granted the authority necessary to comply with the requirements of this subchapter through the issuance of rules or otherwise. Subsequent statute may not be held to supersede or modify this subchapter, chapter 7, sections 1305, 3105, 3344, 4301 (2) (E), 5362, or 7521, or the provisions of section 5335 (a) (B) of this title that relate to hearing examiners, except to the extent that it does so expressly.

Chapter 7—Judicial Review

§701. Application; definitions

(a) This chapter applies, according to the provisions thereof, except to the extent that—

(1) statutes preclude judicial review; or

(2) agency action is committed to agency discretion by law.

(b) For the purpose of this chapter—

(1) "agency" means each authority of the Government of the United States, whether or not it is within or subject to review by another agency, but does not include—

(A) the Congress;

(B) the courts of the United States;

(C) the governments of the territories or possessions of the United States;

(D) the government of theDistrict of Columbia;

(E) agencies composed of representatives of the parties or of representatives of organizations of the parties to the disputes determined by them;

(F) courts martial and military commissions;

(G) military authority exercised in the field in time of war or in occupied territory; or

(H) functions conferred by sections 1738, 1739, 1743, and 1744 of title 12; chapter 2 of title 41; or sections 1622, 1884, 1891–1902, and former section 1641 (b) (2), of title 50, appendix; and

(2) "person," "rule," order," license," "sanction," "relief,"

and "agency action" have the meanings given them by section 551 of this title.

§702. *Right of review*

A person suffering legal wrong because of agency action, or adversely affected or aggrieved by agency action within the meaning of a relevant statute, is entitled to judicial review thereof. An action in a court of the United States seeking relief other than money damages and stating a claim that an agency or an officer or employee thereof acted or failed to act in an official capacity or under color of legal authority shall not be dismissed nor relief therein be denied on the ground that it is against the United States or that the United States is an indispensable party. The United States may be named as a defendant in any such action, and a judgment or decree may be entered against the United States: *Provided*, That any mandatory or injunctive decree shall specify the Federal officer or officers (by name or by title), and their successors in office, personally responsible for compliance. Nothing herein (1) affects other limitations on judicial review or the power or duty of the court to dismiss any action or deny relief on any other appropriate legal or equitable ground; or (2) confers authority to grant relief if any other statute that grants consent to suit expressly or impliedly forbids the relief which is sought.

§703. *Form and venue of proceeding*

The form of proceeding for judicial review is the special statutory review proceeding relevant to the subject matter in a court specified by statute or, in the absence or inadequacy thereof, any applicable form of legal action, including actions for declaratory judgments or writs of prohibitory or mandatory injunction or habeas corpus, in a court of competent jurisdiction. If no special statutory review proceeding is applicable, the action for judicial review may be brought against the United States, the agency by its official title, or the appropriate officer. Except to the extent that prior, adequate, and exclusive opportunity for judicial review is provided by law, agency action is subject to judicial review in civil or criminal proceedings for judicial enforcement.

§704. Actions reviewable

Agency action made reviewable by statute and final agency action for which there is no other adequate remedy in a court are subject to judicial review. A preliminary, procedural, or intermediate agency action or ruling not directly reviewable is subject to review on the review of the final agency action. Except as otherwise expressly required by statute, agency action otherwise final is final for the purposes of this section whether or not there has been presented or determined an application for a declaratory order, for any form of reconsideration, or, unless the agency otherwise requires by rule and provides that the action meanwhile is inoperative, for an appeal to superior agency authority.

§705. Relief pending review

When an agency finds that justice so requires, it may postpone the effective date of action taken by it, pending judicial review. On such conditions as may be required and to the extent necessary to prevent irreparable injury, the reviewing court, including the court to which a case may be taken on appeal from or on application for certiorari or other writ to a reviewing court, may issue all necessary and appropriate process to postpone the effective date of an agency action or to preserve status or rights pending conclusion of the review proceedings.

§ 706. Scope of review

To the extent necessary to decision and when presented, the reviewing court shall decide all relevant questions of law, interpret constitutional and statutory provisions, and determine the meaning or applicability of the terms of an agency action. The reviewing court shall—

(1) compel agency action unlawfully withheld or unreasonably delayed; and

(2) hold unlawful and set aside agency action, findings, and conclusions found to be—

(A) arbitrary, capricious, an abuse of discretion, or otherwise not in accordance with law;

(B) contrary to constitutional right, power, privilege, or immunity;

(C) in excess of statutory jurisdiction, authority, or limitations, or short of statutory right;

(D) without observance of procedure required by law;

(E) unsupported by substantial evidence in a case subject to sections 556 and 557 of this title or otherwise reviewed on the record of an agency hearing provided by statute; or

(F) unwarranted by the facts to the extent that the facts are subject to trial de novo by the reviewing court.

In making the foregoing determinations, the court shall review the whole record or those parts of it cited by a party, and due account shall be taken of the rule of prejudicial error.

§ 3105. Appointment of hearing examiners

Each agency shall appoint as many hearing examiners as are necessary for proceedings required to be conducted in accordance with sections 556 and 557 of this title. Hearing examiners shall be assigned to cases in rotation so far as practicable, and may not perform duties inconsistent with their duties and responsibilities as hearing examiners.

§ 7521. Removal

A hearing examiner appointed under section 3105 of this title may be removed by the agency in which he is employed only for good cause established and determined by the Civil Service Commission on the record after opportunity for hearing.

§ 5362. Hearing examiners

Hearing examiners appointed under section 3105 of this title are entitled to pay prescribed by the Civil Service Commission independently of agency recommendations or ratings and in accordance with subchapter III of this chapter and chapter 51 of this title.

§ 3344. Details; hearing examiners

An agency as defined by section 551 of this title which occasionally or temporarily is insufficiently staffed with hearing examiners appointed under section 3105 of this title may use hearing examiners selected by the Civil Service Commission from and with the consent of other agencies.

§ 1305. Hearing examiners

For the purpose of sections 3105, 3344, 4301 (2) (E), 5362, and 7521 and the provisions of section 5335 (a) (B) of this title that relate to hearing examiners, the Civil Service Commission may investigate, require reports by agencies, issue reports, including an annual report to Congress, prescribe regulations, appoint advisory committees as necessary, recommend legislation, subpena witnesses and records, and pay witness fees as established for the courts of the United States.

Appendix B

Revised Model State Administrative Procedure Act

The following model act was approved by the National Conference of Commissioners on Uniform State Laws at its annual conference meeting in 1961. The National Conference of Commissioners on Uniform State Laws urges (with the endorsement of the American Bar Association) enactment of its model laws in each jurisdiction. The text of the Uniform Law Commissioners' Revised Model State Administrative Procedure Act follows (brackets enclose words which for various reasons states may wish to omit, change, or adjust):

[Be it enacted . . . .]

Section 1. [Definitions.] As used in this Act:

(1) "agency" means each state [board, commission, department, or officer], other than the legislature or the courts, authorized by law to make rules or to determine contested cases;

(2) "contested case" means a proceeding, including but not restricted to ratemaking [price fixing], and licensing, in which the legal rights, duties, or privileges of a party are required by law to be determined by an agency after an opportunity for hearing;

(3) "license" includes the whole or part of any agency permit, certificate, approval, registration, charter, or similar form of permission required by law, but it does not include a license required solely for revenue purposes;

(4) "licensing" includes the agency process respecting the grant, denial, renewal, revocation, suspension, annulment, withdrawal, or amendment of a license;

(5) "party" means each person or agency named or admitted as a party, or properly seeking and entitled as of right to be admitted as a party;

(6) "person" means any individual, partnership, corporation, association, governmental subdivision, or public or private organization of any character other than an agency;

(7) "rule" means each agency statement of general applicability that implements, interprets, or prescribes law or policy, or describes the organization, procedure, or practice requirements of any agency. The term includes the amendment or repeal of a prior rule, but does not include (A) statements concerning only the internal management of an agency and not affecting private rights or procedures available to the public, or (B) declaratory rulings issued pursuant to Section 8, or (C) intra-agency memoranda.

Section 2. [Public Information; Adoption of Rules; Availability of Rules and Orders.]

(a) In addition to other rule-making requirements imposed by law, each agency shall:

(1) adopt as a rule a description of its organization, stating the general course and method of its operations and the methods whereby the public may obtain information or make submissions or requests;

(2) adopt rules of practice setting forth the nature and requirements of all formal and informal procedures available, in-

cluding a description of all forms and instructions used by the agency;

(3) make available for public inspection all rules and all other written statements of policy or interpretations formulated, adopted, or used by the agency in the discharge of its functions.

(4) make available for public inspection all final orders, decisions, and opinions.

(b) No agency rule, order, or decision is valid or effective against any person or party, nor may it be invoked by the agency for any purpose, until it has been made available for public inspection as herein required. This provision is not applicable in favor of any person or party who has actual knowledge thereof.

Section 3. [Procedure for Adoption of Rules.]

(a) Prior to the adoption, amendment, or repeal of any rule, the agency shall:

(1) give at least 20 days' notice of its intended action. The notice shall include a statement of either the terms or substance of the intended action or a description of the subjects and issues involved, and the time when, the place where, and the manner in which interested persons may present their views thereon. The notice shall be mailed to all persons who have made timely request of the agency for advance notice of its rule-making proceedings and shall be published in [here insert the medium of publication appropriate for the adopting state];

(2) afford all interested persons reasonable opportunity to submit data, views, or arguments, orally or in writing. In case of substantive rules, opportunity for oral hearing must be granted if requested by 25 persons, by a governmental subdivision or agency, or by an association having not less than 25 members. The agency shall consider fully all written and oral submissions respecting the proposed rule. Upon adoption of a rule, the agency, if requested to do so by an interested person either prior to adoption or within 30 days thereafter, shall issue a concise statement of the principal reasons for and against its adoption, incorporating therein its reasons for overruling the considerations urged against its adoption.

(b) If an agency finds that an imminent peril to the public health, safety, or welfare required adoption of a rule upon fewer than 20 days' notice and states in writing its reasons for that finding, it may proceed without prior notice or hearing or upon any abbreviated notice and hearing that it finds practicable, to adopt an emergency rule. The rule may be effective for a period of not longer than 120 days [renewable once for a period not exceeding _____ days], but the adoption of an identical rule under subsections (a) (1) and (a) (2) of this Section is not precluded.

(c) No rule hereafter adopted is valid unless adopted in substantial compliance with this Section. A proceeding to contest any rule on the ground of non-compliance with the procedural requirements of this Section must be commenced within 2 years from the effective date of the rule.

Section 4. [Filing and Taking Effect of Rules.]

(a) Each agency shall file in the office of the [Secretary of State] a certified copy of each rule adopted by it, including all rules existing on the effective date of this Act. The [Secretary of State] shall keep a permanent register of the rules open to public inspection.

(b) Each rule hereafter adopted is effective 20 days after filing, except that:

(1) if a later date is required by statute or specified in the rule, the later date is the effective date;

(2) subject to applicable constitutional or statutory provisions, an emergency rule becomes effective immediately upon filing with the [Secretary of State], or at a stated date less than 20 days thereafter, if the agency finds that this effective date is necessary because of imminent peril to the public health, safety, or welfare. The agency's finding and a brief statement of the reasons therefore shall be filed with the rule. The agency shall take appropriate measures to make emergency rules known to the persons who may be affected by them.

Section 5. [Publication of Rules.]

(a) The [Secretary of State] shall compile, index, and publish all effective rules adopted by each agency. Compilations shall be supplemented or revised as often as necessary [and at least once every 2 years].

(b) The [Secretary of State] shall publish a [monthly] bulletin setting forth the text of all rules filed during the preceding [month] excluding rules in effect upon the adoption of this Act.

(c) The [Secretary of State] may omit from the bulletin or compilation any rule the publication of which would be unduly cumbersome, expensive, or otherwise inexpedient, if the rule in printed or processed form is made available on application to the adopting agency, and if the bulletin or compilation contains a notice stating the general subject matter of the omitted rule and stating how a copy thereof may be obtained.

(d) Bulletins and compilations shall be made available upon request to [agencies and officials of this State] free of charge and to other persons at prices fixed by the [Secretary of State] to cover mailing and publication costs.

Section 6. [*Petition for Adoption of Rules.*]

An interested person may petition an agency requesting the promulgation, amendment, or repeal of a rule. Each agency shall prescribe by rule the form for petitions and the procedure for their submission, consideration, and disposition. Within 30 days after submission of a petition, the agency either shall deny the petition in writing (stating its reasons for the denials) or shall initiate rule-making proceedings in accordance with Section 3.

Section 7. [*Declaratory Judgment on Validity or Applicability of Rules.*]

The validity or applicability of a rule may be determined in an action for declaratory judgment in the [District Court of . . . County], if it is alleged that the rule, or its threatened application, interferes with or impairs, or threatens to interfere with or impair, the legal rights or privileges of the plaintiff. The agency shall be made a party to the action. A declaratory judgment may be rendered whether or not the plaintiff has requested the agency to pass upon the validity or applicability of the rule in question.

Section 8. [*Declaratory Rulings by Agencies.*]

Each agency shall provide by rule for the filing and prompt disposition of petitions for declaratory rulings as to the applicability of any statutory provision or of any rule or order of the agency. Rulings disposing of petitions have the same status as agency decisions or orders in contested cases.

Section 9. [*Contested Cases; Notice; Hearing; Records.*]

(a) In a contested case, all parties shall be afforded an opportunity for hearing after reasonable notice.

(b) The notice shall include:

(1) a statement of the time, place, and nature of the hearing;

(2) a statement of the legal authority and jurisdiction under which the hearing is to be held;

(3) a reference to the particular sections of the statutes and rules involved;

(4) a short and plain statement of the matters asserted. If the agency or other party is unable to state the matters in detail at the time the notice is served, the initial notice may be limited to a statement of the issues involved. Thereafter upon application a more definite and detailed statement shall be furnished.

(c) Opportunity shall be afforded all parties to respond and present evidence and argument on all issues involved.

(d) Unless precluded by law, informal disposition may be made of any contested case by stipulation, agreed settlement, consent order, or default.

(e) The record in a contested case shall include:

(1) all pleadings, motions, intermediate rulings;

(2) evidence received or considered;

(3) a statement of matters officially noticed;

(4) questions and offers of proof, objections, and rulings thereon;

(5) proposed findings and exceptions;

(6) any decision, opinion, or report, by the officer presiding at the hearing;

(7) all staff memoranda or data submitted to the hearing officer or members of the agency in connection with their consideration of the case.

(f) Oral proceedings or any part thereof shall be transcribed on request of any party.

(g) Findings of fact shall be based exclusively on the evidence and on matters officially noticed.

Section 10. [Rules of Evidence; Official Notice.]

In contested cases:

(1) irrelevant, immaterial, or unduly repetitious evidence shall be excluded. The rules of evidence as applied in [non-jury] civil cases in the [District Courts of this State] shall be followed. When necessary to ascertain facts not reasonably susceptible of proof under those rules, evidence not admissible thereunder may be admitted (except where precluded by statute) if it is of a type commonly relied upon by reasonably prudent men in the conduct of their affairs. Agencies shall give effect to the rules of privilege recognized by law. Objections to evidentiary offers may be made and shall be noted in the record. Subject to these requirements, when a hearing will be expedited and the interests of the parties will not be prejudiced substantially, any part of the evidence may be received in written form;

[(2) documentary evidence may be received in the form of copies or excerpts, if the original is not readily available. Upon request, parties shall be given an opportunity to compare the copy with the original;]

(3) a party may conduct cross-examinations required for a full and true disclosure of the facts;

(4) notice may be taken of judicially cognizable facts. In addition, notice may be taken of generally recognized technical or scientific facts within the agency's specialized knowledge. Parties shall be notified either before or during the hearing, or by reference in preliminary reports or otherwise, of the material noticed, including any staff memoranda or data, and they shall be afforded an opportunity to contest the material so noticed. The agency's

experience, technical competence, and specialized knowledge may be utilized in the evaluation of the evidence.

Section 11. [Examination of Evidence by Agency.]

When in a contested case a majority of the officials of the agency who are to render the final decision have not heard the case or read the record, the decision, if adverse to a party to the proceeding other than the agency itself, shall not be made until a proposal for decision is served upon the parties, and an opportunity is afforded to each party adversely affected to file exceptions and present briefs and oral argument to the officials who are to render the decision. The proposal for decision shall contain a statement of the reasons therefor and of each issue of fact or law necessary to the proposed decision, prepared by the person who conducted the hearing or one who has read the record. The parties by written stipulation may waive compliance with this section.

Section 12. [Decisions and Orders.]

A final decision or order adverse to a party in a contested case shall be in writing or stated in the record. A final decision shall include findings of fact and conclusions of law, separately stated. Findings of fact, if set forth in statutory language, shall be accompanied by a concise and explicit statement of the underlying facts supporting the findings. If, in accordance with agency rules, a party submitted proposed findings of fact, the decision shall include a ruling upon each proposed finding. Parties shall be notified either personally or by mail of any decision or order. Upon request a copy of the decision or order shall be delivered or mailed forthwith to each party and to his attorney of record.

Section 13. [Ex Parte Consultations.]

Unless required for the disposition of *ex parte* matters authorized by law, members or employees of an agency assigned to render a decision or to make findings of fact and conclusions of law in a contested case shall not communicate, directly or indirectly, in connection with any issue of fact, with any person or party, nor, in connection with any issue of law, with any party or his representative, except upon notice and opportunity for all parties to participate. An agency member

(1) may communicate with other members of the agency, and

(2) may have the aid and advice of one or more personal assistants.

Section 14. [Licenses.]

(a) When the grant, denial, or renewal of a license is required to be preceded by notice and opportunity for hearing, the provisions of this Act concerning contested cases apply.

(b) When a licensee has made timely and sufficient application for the renewal of a license or a new license with reference to any activity of a continuing nature, the existing license does not expire until the application has been finally determined by the agency, and, in case the application is denied or the terms of the new license limited, until the last day for seeking review of the agency order or a later date fixed by order of the reviewing court.

(c) No revocation, suspension, annulment, or withdrawal of any license is lawful unless, prior to the institution of agency proceedings, the agency gave notice by mail to the licensee of facts or conduct which warrant the intended action, and the licensee was given an opportunity to show compliance with all lawful requirements for the retention of the license. If the agency finds that public health, safety, or welfare imperatively requires emergency action, and incorporates a finding to that effect in its order, summary suspension of a license may be ordered pending proceedings for revocation or other action. These proceedings shall be promptly instituted and determined.

Section 15. [Judicial Review of Contested Cases.]

(a) A person who has exhausted all administrative remedies available within the agency and who is aggrieved by a final decision in a contested case is entitled to judicial review under this Act. This Section does not limit utilization of or the scope of judicial review available under other means of review, redress, relief, or trial *de novo* provided by law. A preliminary, procedural, or intermediate agency action or ruling is immediately reviewable if review of the final agency decision would not provide an adequate remedy.

(b) Proceedings for review are instituted by filing a petition in the [District Court of the _____ County] within [30] days after [mailing notice of] the final decision of the agency or, if a rehearing is requested, within [30] days after the decision thereon. Copies of the petition shall be served upon the agency and all parties of record.

(c) The filing of the petition does not itself stay enforcement of the agency decision. The agency may grant, or the reviewing court may order, a stay upon appropriate terms.

(d) Within [30] days after the service of the petition, or within further time allowed by the court, the agency shall transmit to the reviewing court the original or a certified copy of the entire record of the proceeding under review. By stipulation of all parties to the review proceedings, the record may be shortened. A party unreasonably refusing to stipulate to limit the record may be taxed by the court for the additional costs. The court may require or permit subsequent corrections or additions to the record.

(e) If, before the date set for hearing, application is made to the court for leave to present additional evidence, and it is shown to the satisfaction of the court that the additional evidence is material and that there were good reasons for failure to present it in the proceeding before the agency, the court may order that the additional evidence be taken before the agency upon conditions determined by the court. The agency may modify its findings and decision by reason of the additional evidence and shall file that evidence and any modifications, new findings, or decisions with the reviewing court.

(f) The review shall be conducted by the court without a jury and shall be confined to the record. In cases of alleged irregularities in procedure before the agency, not shown in the record, proof thereon may be taken in the court. The court, upon request, shall hear oral argument and receive written briefs.

(g) The court shall not substitute its judgment for that of the agency as to the weight of the evidence on questions of fact. The court may affirm the decision of the agency or remand the case for further proceedings. The court may reverse or modify the decision if substantial rights of the appellant have been prejudiced because the administrative findings, inferences, conclusions, or decisions are:

(1) in violation of constitutional or statutory provisions;

(2) in excess of the statutory authority of the agency;

(3) made upon unlawful procedure;

(4) affected by other error of law;

(5) clearly erroneous in view of the reliable, probative, and substantial evidence on the whole record; or

(6) arbitrary or capricious or characterized by abuse of discretion or clearly unwarranted exercise of discretion.

[Section 16. [Appeals.]

An aggrieved party may obtain a review of any final judgment of the [District Court] under this Act by appeal to the [Supreme Court]. The appeal shall be taken as in other civil cases.]

[Section 17. [Severability.]

If any provision of this Act or the application thereof to any person or circumstance is held invalid, the invalidity does not affect other provisions or applications of the Act which can be given effect without the invalid provision or application, and for this purpose the provisions of this Act are severable.]

Section 18. [Repeal.]

The following acts and parts of acts are repealed:

(1)   ;

(2)   ;

(3)   .

Section 19. [Time of Taking Effect and Scope of Application.]

This Act takes effect . . . and (except as to proceedings then pending) applies to all agencies and agency proceedings not expressly exempted.

Bibliography

Abrams, Norman. "Administrative Law Judge Systems: The California View," *Administrative Law Review* 29 (1977):487–523.

Albert, Jeffrey. "Application of Rules of Evidence to Administrative Proceedings: The Case of the Occupational Safety and Health Review Commission," *Administrative Law Review* 27 (1975):135–47.

Anderson, Stanley V. "Some Essential Characteristics of an Effective Public Records Law: Sweden and the United States," *Administrative Law Review* 25 (1973):329–33.

Asimow, Michael. "Public Participation in the Adoption of Interpretive Rules and Policy Statements," *Michigan Law Review* 75 (1977):521–84.

Attorney General's Committee on Administrative Procedure. *Final Report* 77th Cong., 1st sess., 1941.

Beytagh, Francis X., Jr. "Judicial Review in Selective Service Cases—Lessons from Vietnam," *Notre Dame Lawyer* 48 (1973):1164–1201.

Black, Henry C. *Black's Law Dictionary.* 5th ed. St. Paul, Minn: West Publishing Co., 1979.

Bonfield, Arthur E. "Military and Foreign Affairs Function Rule-Making under the APA," *Michigan Law Review* 71 (1972):221–358.

Bonfield, Arthur E. "Public Participation in Federal Rulemaking Relating to Public Property, Loans, Grants, Benefits, or Contracts," *University of Pennsylvania Law Review* 118 (1970):540–611.

Boyer, Barry B. "Alternatives to Administrative Trial-type Hearings for Resolving Complex Scientific, Economic, and Social Issues," *Michigan Law Review* 71 (1972):111–70.

Butzel, Albert K. "Intervention and Class Actions Before the Agencies and the Courts," *Administrative Law Review* 25 (1973):135–46.

Cake, Helen McCleave. "The French Conseil d'Etat—An Essay on Administrative Jurisprudence," *Administrative Law Review* 24 (1972):315–34.

Carrow, Milton M. "Mechanisms for the Redress of Grievances Against the Government," *Administrative Law Review* 22 (1969:1–37.

Carrow, Milton H., and Reese, John H. "State Problems of Mass Administrative Justice: The Administrative Adjudication of Traffic Violations—A Case Study," *Administrative Law Review* 28 (1976):223–58.

Cary, William L. *Politics and the Regulatory Agencies.* New York: McGraw-Hill Book Co., 1967.

Clagett, Brice McAdoo. "Informal Action—Adjudication—Rule Making: Some Recent Developments in Federal Administrative Law," *Duke Law Journal* 1971 (1971):51–88.

Cohen, Morris L., ed. *How to Find The Law.* 7th ed. St. Paul: Minn: West Publishing Co., 1976.

Cooper, Frank E. *State Administrative Law.* 2 vols. Indianapolis, Ind.: Bobbs-Merrill Co., 1965.

Cramton, Roger C. "Causes and Cures of Administrative Delay," *American Bar Association Journal* 58 (1972):937–41.

Cramton, Roger C. "A Federal Ombudsman," *Duke Law Journal* 1972 (1972): 1–14.

Cramton, Roger C. "Nonstatutory Review of Federal Administrative Action: The Need for Statutory Reform of Sovereign Immunity, Subject Matter Jurisdiction, and Parties Defendant," *Michigan Law Review* 68 (1970):389–470.

Cramton, Roger C. "A Title Change for Federal Hearing Examiners? 'A Rose By Any Other Name . . . ,' " *George Washington Law Review* 40 (1972):918–31.

Cramton, Roger C. "The Why, Where, and How of Broadened Public Participation in the Administrative Process," *Georgetown Law Journal* 60 (1972): 525–50.

Crowther, Nelson I., Jr., and Davis, Frederick. "The Massachusetts and Federal Efforts to Establish Uniform Procedural Rules for Administrative Agencies," *Administrative Law Review* 24 (1972):213–32.

Currie, David P., and Goodman, Frank I. "Judicial Review of Federal Administrative Action: Quest for the Optimum Forum," *Columbia Law Review* 75 (1975):1–88.

Davis, Kenneth C. *Administrative Law in the Seventies.* Rochester, N.Y.: Lawyers Co-Operative Publishing Co., 1976.

Davis, Kenneth C. *Administrative Law Treatise.* 4 vols. St. Paul, Minn.: West Publishing Co., 1958, Supplement 1970.

Davis, Kenneth C. "An Approach to Problems of Evidence in the Administrative Process," *Harvard Law Review* 55 (1942):364–425.

Bibliography

Davis, Kenneth C. *Discretionary Justice in Europe and America.* Urbana, Ill.: University of Illinois Press, 1976.

Davis, Kenneth C. "Revising the Administrative Procedure Act," *Administrative Law Review* 29 (1977):35–58.

Davis, Kenneth C. "Sovereign Immunity Must Go," *Administrative Law Review* 22 (1970):383–405.

Dolzer, Rudolf. "Welfare Benefits As Property Interests: A Constitutional Right to a Hearing and Judicial Review," *Administrative Law Review* 29 (1977):525–75.

Drachsler, David A. "The Freedom of Information Act and the 'Right' of Non-Disclosure," *Administrative Law Review* 28 (1976):1–11.

Dullea, Charles J. "Development of the Personnel Program for Administrative Law Judges," *Administrative Law Review* 25 (1973):41–47.

Elman, Philip. "A Modest Proposal for Radical Reform," *American Bar Association Journal* 56 (1970):1045–50.

Feller, A. H. "Prospectus for the Further Study of Federal Administrative Law," *Yale Law Journal* 47 (1938):647–74.

Force, Robert. "Administrative Adjudication of Traffic Violations Confronts the Doctrine of Separation of Powers," *Tulane Law Review* 49 (1974):84–138.

Frank, Bernard. "The Ombudsman and Human Rights," *Administrative Law Review* 22 (1970):467–92.

Freedman, James O. *Crisis and Legitimacy: The Administrative Process and American Government.* Cambridge: Cambridge University Press, 1978.

Freedman, James O. "Expertise and the Administrative Process," *Administrative Law Review* 28 (1976):363–78.

Freedman, James O. "Summary Action by Administrative Agencies," *University of Chicago Law Review* 40 (1972):1–65.

Friendly, Henry J. *The Federal Administrative Agencies: The Need for Better Definition of Standards.* Cambridge, Mass.: Harvard University Press, 1962.

Friendly, Henry J. *Federal Jurisdiction: A General View.* New York: Columbia University Press, 1973.

Friendly, Henry J. "Some Kind of Hearing," *University of Pennsylvania Law Review* 123 (1975):1267–1317.

Fritschler, A. Lee. *Smoking and Politics: Policymaking and the Federal Bureaucracy.* 2d ed. Englewood Cliffs, N.J.: Prentice-Hall, Inc., 1975.

Gardner, Warner W. "The Procedures By Which Informal Action is Taken," *Administrative Law Review* 24 (1972):155–66.

Gellhorn, Ernest. *Administrative Law and Process in a Nutshell.* St. Paul, Minn.: West Publishing Co., 1972.

Gellhorn, Ernest, and Bruff, Harold H. "Congressional Control of Administrative Regulation: A Study of Legislative Vetoes," *Harvard Law Review* 90 (1977): 1369–1440.

Gellhorn, Ernest, and Robinson, Glen O. "Perspective on Administrative Law," *Columbia Law Review* 75 (1975):771–99.

Gellhorn, Ernest, and Robinson, William F., Jr. "Summary Judgment in Administrative Adjudication," *Harvard Law Review* 84 (1971):612–32.

Gellhorn, Walter. *Individual Freedom and Governmental Restraints.* Baton Rouge, La.: Louisiana State University Press, 1956.

Gellhorn, Walter. *Ombudsmen and Others: Citizens' Protectors in Nine Countries.* Cambridge, Mass.: Harvard University Press, 1966.

Gellhorn, Walter. *When Americans Complain: Governmental Grievance Procedures.* Cambridge, Mass.: Harvard University Press, 1966.

Gellhorn, Walter, and Byse, Clark. *Administrative Law, Cases and Comments.* 6th ed. Mineola, N.Y.: Foundation Press, 1974.

Giannella, Donald A. "Agency Procedures Implementing the Freedom of Information Act: A Proposal for Uniform Regulations," *Administrative Law Review* 23 (1971):217–70.

Gifford, Daniel J. "The Morgan Cases: A Retrospective View," *Administrative Law Review* 30 (1978):237–88.

Grossman, Harry, and Bechhoefer, Charles. "Public Employment and Free Speech: Can They Be Reconciled?" *Administrative Law Review* 24 (1972):109–19.

Hahn, Gilbert, III. "Procedural Adequacy in Administrative Decisionmaking: A Unified Formulation," Part I. *Administrative Law Review* 30 (1978):467–518; Part II, *Administrative Law Review* 31 (1979):31–66.

Hamilton, Robert W. "Procedures for the Adoption of Rules of General Applicability: The Need For Procedural Innovation in Administrative Rulemaking," *California Law Review* 60 (1972):1276–1337.

Hamson, Charles J. *Executive Discretion and Judicial Control: An Aspect of the French Conseil d'Etat.* London: Stevens and Sons, 1954.

Bibliography

Hantman, Jack H. "For An Administrative Law Court," *American Bar Association Journal* 62 (1976):360–61.

Harris, Joseph P. *Congressional Control of Administration.* Washington, D.C.: Brookings Institution, 1964.

Hector, Louis J. "Problems of the CAB and the Independent Regulatory Commissions," *Yale Law Journal* 69 (1960):931–64.

Jacobs, Leslie W., and Collin, Thomas J. "Summary Enforcement of Federal Trade Commission Orders under the Federal Rules of Civil Procedure," *Administrative Law Review* 30 (1978):331–75.

Jacoby, Sidney B. "Roads to the Demise of the Doctrine of Sovereign Immunity," *Administrative Law Review* 29 (1977):265–89.

Jaffe, Louis L. "The Illusion of the Ideal Administration," *Harvard Law Review* 86 (1973):1183–99.

Jaffe, Louis L. *Judicial Control of Administrative Action.* Boston, Mass.: Little, Brown and Co., 1965.

Jaffe, Louis L. "Judicial Review: Substantial Evidence on the Whole Record," *Harvard Law Review* 64 (1951):1233–61.

Jaffe, Louis L., and Nathanson, Nathaniel L. *Administrative Law: Cases and Materials.* 3d ed. Boston, Mass.: Little, Brown and Co., 1968; 4th ed. 1976.

Johnson, Nicholas, and Dystel, John J. "A Day in the Life: The Federal Communications Commission," *Yale Law Journal* 82 (1973):1575–1634.

Kielbowicz, Richard B. "Discrimination or Discriminating Licensing?: FCC Policy and Newspaper Ownership of TV Stations, 1945–1970," *Administrative Law Review* 30 (1978):423–46.

Klonoff, Robert. "The Problems of Nursing Homes: Connecticut's Non-Response," *Administrative Law Review* 31 (1979):1–30.

Kohlmeier, Louis M., Jr. *The Regulators: Watchdog Agencies and the Public Interest.* New York: Harper & Row, 1969.

Koslow, Stephen. "Standardless Administrative Adjudication," *Administrative Law Review* 22 (1970):407–34.

Krislov, Samuel, and Muslof, Lloyd D., eds. *The Politics of Regulation: A Reader.* Boston, Mass.: Houghton Mifflin Co., 1964.

Landis, James M. *The Administrative Process.* New Haven, Conn.: Yale University Press, 1938.

Landis, James M. *Report on Regulatory Agencies to the President-Elect.* Submitted by the Chairman of the Subcommittee on Administrative Practice and Procedure of the Senate Committee on the Judiciary. 86th Cong., 2d sess., 1960.

Lee, Byron G. "Fraud and Abuse in Medicare and Medicaid," *Administrative Law Review* 30 (1978):1–43.

Loevinger, Lee. "The Administrative Agency as a Paradigm of Government—A Survey of the Administrative Process," *Indiana Law Journal* 40 (1965):287–312.

Lorch, Robert S. "Administrative Court via the Independent Hearing Officer," *Judicature* 51 (1967):114–18.

Lorch, Robert S. "The Federal Administrative Court Idea in America," *American Bar Association Journal* 52 (1966):635–38.

Lorch, Robert S. "German Administrative Courts," *Judicature* 58 (1975): 293–98.

Lorch, Robert S. "Toward Administrative Judges," *Public Administration Review* 30 (1970):50–55.

Miller, Arthur S. "Separation of Powers: An Ancient Doctrine under Modern Challenge," *Administrative Law Review* 28 (1976):299–325.

Miller, John T., Jr. "A Continuing Forum for the Reform of the Administrative Process," *Administrative Law Review* 27 (1975):205–11.

Miller, John T., Jr. "The Education and Development of Administrative Law Judges," *Administrative Law Review* 25 (1973):1–7.

Minnow, Newton H. "Suggestions for Improvement of the Administrative Process," *Administrative Law Review* 15 (1963):146–53.

Morris, Kim Lacy. "Judicial Review of Non-Reviewable Administrative Action: Veterans Administration Benefit Claims." *Administrative Law Review* 29 (1977): 65–86.

Nathanson, Nathaniel L. "The Administrative Court Proposal," *Virginia Law Review* 57 (1971):996–1032.

Nathanson, Nathaniel L. "Report to the Select Committee on Ex Parte Communications in Informal Rulemaking Proceedings," *Administrative Law Review* 30 (1978):377–408.

Nerenberg, Roy. "Regulatory Reform in a Nutshell," *American Bar Association Journal* 62 (1976):121–23.

Nonet, Philippe. *Administrative Justice: Advocacy and Change in a Government Agency.* New York: Russel Sage Foundation, 1969.

Bibliography

O'Brien, David M. "Privacy and the Right of Access: Purposes and Paradoxes of Information Control," *Administrative Law Review* 30 (1978):45–92.

Peck, Cornelius J. "Laird v. Nelms: A Call for Review and Revision of the Federal Tort Claims Act," *Washington Law Review* 48 (1973):391–421.

Pederson, William F. "Formal Records and Informal Rulemaking," *Yale Law Journal* 85 (1975):38–88.

Pfeiffer, Paul N. "Hearing Cases before Several Agencies: Odyssey of an Administrative Law Judge," *Administrative Law Review* 27 (1975):217–31.

Redford, Emmette S. *Democracy in the Administrative State.* New York: Oxford University Press, 1969.

Ribicoff, Abraham. "Congressional Oversight and Regulatory Reform," *Administrative Law Review* 28 (1976):415–45.

Rifkind, Simon. "A Special Court for Patent Litigation? The Danger of a Specialized Judiciary," *American Bar Association Journal* 37 (1951):425–26.

Robinson, Glen O., and Gellhorn, Ernest. *The Administrative Process.* St. Paul, Minn.: West Publishing Co., 1974.

Ruhlen, Merritt. "Virginia's Professional and Occupational Hearing Process," *Administrative Law Review* 29 (1976):207–21.

Schwartz, Bernard. *Administrative Law.* Boston, Mass.: Little, Brown and Co., 1976.

Schwartz, Bernard. "Administrative Law: The Third Century," *Administrative Law Review* 29 (1977):291–319.

Schwartz, Bernard. "Crisis in the Commissions," *The Progressive* 23 (1959):10–13.

Schwartz, Bernard. "Does the Ghost of Crowell v. Benson Still Walk?," *University of Pennsylvania Law Review* 98 (1949):163–82.

Schwartz, Bernard. *The Professor and the Commissions.* New York: Alfred A. Knopf, Inc., 1959.

Schwartz, Bernard, and Wade, H. W. R. *Legal Control of Government: Administrative Law in Britain and the United States.* Oxford University Press, 1972.

Shapiro, David L. "Some Thoughts on Intervention before Courts, Agencies, and Arbitrators," *Harvard Law Review* 81 (1968):721–72.

Sherry, John E. H. "The Myth That the King Can Do No Wrong: A Comparative Study of the Sovereign Immunity Doctrine in the United States and New York

Court of Claims," *Administrative Law Review* 22 (1962):39–58; (1970):591–96.

Shniderman, Harry L. "Securing Adequate Discovery in Administrative Proceedings," *Administrative Law Review* 25 (1973):167–74.

Smith, Jerome. "Social Security Appeals in Disability Cases," *Administrative Law Review* 28 (1976):13–25.

Stigler, George J., and Cohen, Manuel F. *Can Regulatory Agencies Protect the Consumer?* Washington, D.C.: American Enterprise Institute for Public Policy Research, 1971.

Sussman, Jerry R. "SEC Disciplinary Proceedings against Accountants—A Study in Unbridled Discretion," *Administrative Law Review* 27 (1975):255–74.

"Symposium: The Freedom of Information Act and the Agencies," *Administrative Law Review* 23 (1971):129–67.

"Symposium: Review of Administrative Adjudication," *Administrative Law Review* 26 (1974):49–128.

"Symposium: Should Prosecutors Write Agency Opinions? The Role of Agency Counsel in Decision-Making," *Administrative Law Review* 22 (1970):579–96.

Tseng, Henry P., and Pedersen, Donald B. "Acquisition of State Administrative Rules and Regulations," *Administrative Law Review* 28 (1976):277–98.

Verkuil, Paul. R. "Judicial Review of Informal Rulemaking," *Virginia Law Review* 60 (1974):185–249.

Verkuil, Paul R. "A Study of Informal Adjudication Procedures," *University of Chicago Law Review* 43 (1976):739–96.

Wade, H. W. R., Q. C., and Schultz, Franklin M. "The British Ombudsman: A Lawyer's View," *Administrative Law Review* 24 (1972):137–53.

Walker, Timothy B., Blumenthal, Murray, and Reese, John H. "An Empirical Examination of Citizen Representation in Contested Matters before State Administrative Agencies: The Colorado Experience," *Administrative Law Review* 29 (1977):321–66.

Warren, Manning G., III. "The Notice Requirement in Administrative Rulemaking: An Analysis of Legislative and Interpretive Rules," *Administrative Law Review* 29 (1977):367–98.

Welborn, David M. "Assigning Responsibility for Regulatory Decisions to Individual Commissioners," *Administrative Law Review* 18 (1966):13–28.

Williams, Jerre S. "Securing Fairness and Regularity in Administrative Proceedings," *Administrative Law Review* 29 (1977):1–34.

Bibliography

Woll, Peter. *Administrative Law, the Informal Process.* Berkeley, Calif.: University of California Press, 1963.

Woodward, David R., and Levin, Ronald M. "In Defense of Deference: Judicial Review of Agency Action," *Administrative Law Review* 31 (1979):329–44.

Wright, J. Skelly. "Beyond Discretionary Justice," *Yale Law Journal* 81 (1972):575–97.

Wright, J. Skelly. "The Courts and the Rulemaking Process: The Limits of Judicial Review," *Cornell Law Review* 59 (1974):375–97.

Wright J. Skelly. "New Judicial Requisites for Informal Rulemaking: Implications for the Environmental Impact Statement Process," *Administrative Law Review* 29 (1977):59–64.

Zwerdling, Joseph. "Reflections on the Role of an Administrative Law Judge," *Administrative Law Review* 25 (1973):9–40.

Index

273

Robert S. Lorch is professor of political science, University of Colorado at Colorado Springs. He received his B.A. from the State University of Iowa (1949), his M.A. from the University of Nebraska (1950), and his Ph.D. from the University of Wisconsin (1957).

The manuscript was edited by Robert H. Tennenhouse. The book was designed by Peter Nothstein. The type face for the text is Mergenthaler Linotype Baskerville designed by John Baskerville in the Eighteenth Century. The display face is Craw Clarendon, designed by Freeman Craw in 1956 for American Typefounders. The book is printed on paper and bound in cloth over binders board. Manufactured in the United States of America.